A Different Kind of Luxury

A Different Kind of Luxury

Japanese Lessons in Simple Living and Inner Abundance

Andy Couturier

Stone Bridge Press • Berkeley, California

Published by
Stone Bridge Press
P.O. Box 8208
Berkeley, CA 94707
TEL 510-524-8732 • sbp@stonebridge.com • www.stonebridge.com

Write to Andy Couturier directly with your comments and thoughts about this book. Send postal mail to: P.O. Box 881, Santa Cruz, CA 95061. Also visit his website at www.theopening.org.

Photograph on front cover, upper right, by Takanori Mimura. Photograph on page 311 by Junko Motoyama. All other photographs by the author unless noted otherwise.

Map on page 14 by Deirdre Bailey.

Translations by the author unless noted otherwise; in each chapter where appropriate, author and translator credits appear below extracts at the first appearance of a work.

Earlier versions of these chapters have appeared in the *Japan Times, Kyoto Journal, Adbusters,* and the anthology *Progress and Evolution* by MIT Press.

Cover and text design by Linda Ronan.

Printed in the United States of America.

2014 2013 2012 2011 2010   10 9 8 7 6 5 4 3 2 1

LIBRARY OF CONGRESS CATALOGING-IN-PUBLICATION DATA AVAILABLE UPON REQUEST.

Dedicated

to the memory of Jean Jacques Couturier and Akira Ito,

two men who believed in, and succeeded in living, a life that matters

Contents

Introduction

I have always thought it was possible to live a *great* life. Beyond all the nightmares we hear about in the news there is a larger world surrounding us, not just the resplendent world of nature, but also our own potential as people to live well, to connect with each other, to do meaningful work, to make powerful art, and to forge a different kind of future for ourselves and for the next generation.

These ideas were still very unformed for me, however, when, in our mid-twenties, my partner Cynthia and I moved to Japan. Deciding to teach English for a year or two in a country we knew very little about was a bit of a sideways step in pursuit of this goal of crafting this "good life" for ourselves. Before we decided to go to Japan, we had met some vibrant and intelligent people on the West Coast of the U.S. who had created lives in the countryside that were more sustainable and more in touch with nature than the hyper-busy lives of stress and environmental destruction that most people in the U.S. seemed to be living. Japan was supposed to be a way station for us, a means to an end. Our plan was to save money and return to Oregon or California and buy some land where we could build our own house and see how much of our own food we would be able to grow. We wanted to "provide for ourselves" as much as we could.

We'd heard that Japan was even more money oriented and status conscious than the U.S.—though that was hard to believe—and we knew it was a very conservative place. Arriving in Japan, we found much of this to be true, but in the course of doing some environmental activism, we were completely surprised to meet some entirely different types of people from what we had been expecting. One of them, an outspoken woman named Atsuko, invited us to visit her "old farm house in the mountains, where we grow our own food."

I thought, *Here, in Japan?* We accepted the invitation, and that first day when we arrived an utterly different world opened in front of our eyes.

The lushness of the Japanese countryside can hardly be exaggerated. With fertile volcanic soil and plenty of rain, even the insect life is staggering in its variety and beauty. In the mountains the rivers are clear and pure, and waterfalls and hot springs are everywhere. The profusion of plant life in summer crowds every fold and crevice of the steep mountainsides.

On our long drive up into the mountains to Atsuko's farmstead from the provincial city where we were living, we saw old houses among the deep green cedar trees with weathered timbers, old tile roofs, and rice-paper doors. This was the beauty of old Japan. When we emerged from the woods onto the ridgetop and pulled up to Atsuko's house, the steep valley fell away before us, its terraced rice paddies and profuse vegetable gardens just like an old woodblock print. We couldn't believe such a world still existed in modern Japan.

Stepping into the house, we met Atsuko's husband, Gufu, who is not only a potter and a chef but also a veritable encyclopedia of plant lore, the cultural history of India, and esoteric spiritual philosophies of both East and West. As we enjoyed an incredibly delicious meal there, in that old farm house, of elaborately prepared Indian curries, soups, and spicy pickles, we learned that both of them had lived for years on the subcontinent. Then Gufu showed us their ceramics, which were deeply influenced by the arts of Persia, Nepal, and Indian tribal minorities. It was a world we could never have imagined stumbling into when we first boarded the plane to Japan a few months before.

Many meetings followed from that first day. As our friendship with Atsuko and Gufu grew, Atsuko introduced us to some of her friends in different parts of rural Japan who were living lives grounded in similar values. Many of them, intriguingly, had spent years living in India and Nepal, and what they learned there powerfully influenced everything from their emphasis on making things with their own hands all the way to their spiritual and philosophical orientation toward life. Yet I found that the people I was meeting through Atsuko also maintained a connection with "old Japan" that seemed so authentic that I felt as if I might have stepped right into the past. When I said as much, however, I was corrected right away. "I'm not living a life of the past," said Osamu Nakamura, the woodblock carver who lives one valley over from Gufu and Atsuko, "I am alive today, making an experiment, trying to find the best way to live now, in the present day."

I noticed something else. These people I was meeting seemed to have a lot of *time*. All around us in the Japanese city where we worked, people were even more scheduled, even more rushed, and even more overwhelmed by tasks than we had witnessed in the U.S. But out here in the mountains there was time for long conversations . . . and good conversations, too. As my Japanese improved, I came to understand that these people were living out a real philosophy. They had set up their lives—or more specifically, their days—so that they had time to think on the most important questions.

Like people the world over, they had to provide for their needs, but they were doing it with the minimum possible interaction with the huge economic system roaring all around them. In this way they had found a remarkable freedom. And in my estimation they were using that freedom incredibly well. At the same time, they seemed to be solving the many and thorny dilemmas of modernity, yet each of their solutions was unusual and creative, and different from the others.

One of the particularly interesting things I found was that they did not use money to provide themselves with entertainment. They also chose to do many tasks by hand even as the rest of Japan—and the whole industrialized world—were performing these same tasks with labor-saving, push-button devices (which had to be purchased). But—and this amazed me—for all that my new friends did manually they did not seem to be overwhelmed or rushed

at all. And neither did their intellectual life suffer in the least from all this time spent making what they needed or growing and cooking their own food. Quite the contrary. Each person had discovered some deep understanding of what this life is about. Unlike so many people of my acquaintance in the West, whether "mainstream" or "alternative," these people were living profoundly satisfied lives.

As a result of meeting them, Cynthia and I decided to stay in Japan much longer than we originally intended. We have continued to visit over the years, trying, in part, to understand what it is about these people's lives that gives them such fulfillment in their days.

~

This book is not a blueprint for achieving "the good life," nor is it a how-to book. It's a book of stories, the stories of eleven people's journeys, both literal and metaphorical. The stories can be read sequentially, or in any order you choose.

The conditions of their lives are undoubtedly different from ours in the United States. For example, Japan has a national health insurance program, so people need not worry about exorbitant medical costs should they get sick. The old farm houses most of them live in can be rented very, very cheaply because homes have been left vacant by the mass exodus to Japan's cities over the last fifty years. Yet these people who have chosen an individual path in a country where "the group" is revered have also faced challenges in their own society that few of us in the West could even imagine, including staggering pressures to conform. They've tried to find a way to live very free lives, in harmony with their values, given the particular circumstances they find themselves in. I believe, however, that many of the principles they live by, and the insights they have gained, are valid for us in the West as well, as we struggle against the vexing currents of our consumption-and-waste-oriented system. In fact, I have applied these ideas in my own search for a truly "good life."

While these are individuals making individual choices, their choices speak to huge worldwide problems and are small answers to these problems, all the way from global climate change and the unpredictable turbulence of economic systems to the sense of personal alienation and despair that so many people suffer from. The people I've written about in this book have done it not by following any monolithic program, but by finding a different kind of enjoyment in life—not something that we purchase off the shelf, but rather the kind we can create in ourselves, from our very own lives.

Although the answers they provide may seem small in scale, the more each of us moves toward a more fulfilling life, reducing our contribution to the destruction of the earth, and taking care of ourselves and our communities, the better the world we will bequeath to those who come next.

~

A few notes before we start. Almost all the spoken and written words of the people in this book were originally in Japanese and then translated. Over the many years spent studying this language, I never cease to marvel at how very different it is from English. In the translation process I've made my best effort to render what each person said to me as accurately as the distance between the two languages would allow.[*] Also, the stories told here grow from these people's lives as *I've* seen them, with my own filters and limitations, and so these chapters are not necessarily an accurate description of who the people are.

[*] It is generally the custom in Japan to refer to people by their family names. But in some cases they are known by their given names. In this book I have chosen to refer to each person as he or she is most often referred to by the people in their respective communities.

You may notice also that I've avoided the use of the word "lifestyle" throughout, as I think it misrepresents what it is that these people have achieved. What they are doing is not a fashion or a style; it is a deeply considered, and I think, very principled *way of life,* one that can be called truly sustainable, something that people could practice for hundreds of years. None of these people are perfect, but this is not a piece of hard-hitting journalism. It is unapologetically a celebration. I believe in the good.

Each person here has agreed to be in this book, and each of them has generously given dozens of hours of their time, patiently explaining their ways of thinking, bridging the cultural gap, and re-explaining Japanese words or concepts to me when I did not at first understand. They have let me stay in their homes, fixed me meals, provided me with copies of their written work, and have served me innumerable cups of tea, along with hundreds of other small kindnesses. This book is in a large way of their making as well.

I hope you can take your time here, inside of this book. It is a fact that our modern system steals our time. The people you will meet here have forged their good lives, at least in part, by wresting it back. By resisting the urge to hurry through this book you too may start to get a sense of this "slowed down life."

Getting to spend so much time with the people I've profiled in this book has been an authentic joy, and just that would have been enough reason to write it. But I do think this book can have a broader meaning than simply a celebration of these specific individuals.

All over the world people suffer from the unhealthy nature of this system we're in. Some of its distortions of our humanity, however, have become so woven into our way of life that we may not even notice them, like a loud machine in the background that we only become aware of after it is turned off. You might even say our society has a vast scam going on, conning us into looking for satisfaction in ways that simply do not work. This is a book that, I hope, might in some small way show a path out of this formidable morass. But even if it only serves as a window onto a different set of possibilities and lets you meet some very extraordinary people, and perhaps gives you a smile or a laugh, that will have been enough.

Andy Couturier
Santa Cruz, California

MAP OF JAPAN WITH CHAPTER LOCATIONS

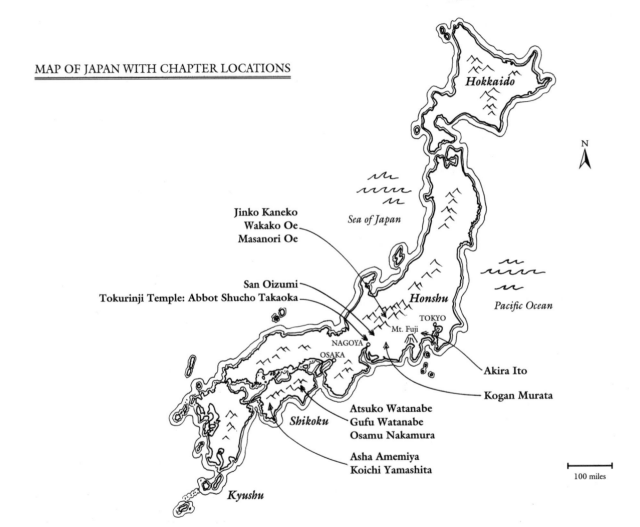

Hokkaido

N

Jinko Kaneko
Wakako Oe
Masanori Oe

Sea of Japan

San Oizumi

Tokurinji Temple: Abbot Shucho Takaoka

Honshu

Pacific Ocean

TOKYO

Mt. Fuji

NAGOYA

OSAKA

Akira Ito

Kogan Murata

Atsuko Watanabe
Gufu Watanabe
Osamu Nakamura

Shikoku

Asha Amemiya
Koichi Yamashita

100 miles

Kyushu

A Different Kind of Luxury

*There is a larger world
surrounding us, not just the
resplendent world of nature,
but also our own potential
as people to live well, . . .*

. . . to connect with each other,
to do meaningful work, and to
forge a different kind of future
for ourselves and for the next
generation.

Sen Oizumi

Potter • Anti-Nuclear Organizer • Anarchist • Community Educator • Father

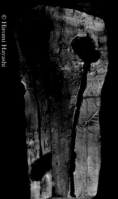

© Junko Motoyama

Osamu Nakamura

Woodblock Carver • Cook • Storyteller • Hand Bookbinder •
Traveler • Craftsman

Atsuko Watanabe

Community Activist • Mother • Homeopath • Seeker •
Anti-Nuclear and Recycling Educator • Self-sufficient Farmer •
Town Council Member

Kogan Murata

Bamboo Flute Player • Storyteller •
Rice Farmer • Student of Zen

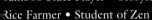

Asha Amemiya

Self-sufficient Farmer • Batik Fabric Artist •
Mother • Author and Illustrator

© Atsuko Matsushita

Akira Ito

Painter • Yoga Practitioner • Student of Theoretical Astrophysics •
Children's Book Writer and Illustrator • Hand Bookbinder •
Woodblock Carver • Prose Poet • Chinese Table Harp Player

Wakako Oe

Organic Farming Mentor • Puppet Carver •
Intuitive Painter • Botanic Sculptor •
Calligrapher

© Takanori Mimura

Gufu Watanabe

Collector • Potter • Amateur Botanist • Indian Cooking
Aficionado • Clay Sculptor • Home Canner • Diarist and
Illustrator

Koichi Yamashita

School Teacher • Rice Farmer • Writer • Professor of Hindu
Philosophy • Father • Anti-Nuclear Community Activist • Tea
Plantation Laborer

Jinko Kaneko

Painter • Chef • Restaurant Proprietor • Hand Dyer • Felt Artist • Flower Gardener

Masanori Oe

Author • Filmmaker • Translator of Sacred
Texts • Community Educator • Philosopher •
Interpreter of Indigenous Traditions • Organic
Farming Mentor

San Oizumi

We get too busy. It's a fact. Part of the reason for our busyness, of course, is the nature of our grasping minds. But some of the blame surely can be attributed to the way society rushes our days. We get carried along with the dominant way of thinking without even meaning to, and get distracted from the things we care most deeply about. After meeting the potter, anarchist, and anti-nuclear activist San Oizumi, I had a palpable idea of an approach to life which was so rooted that the numberless distractions never seemed to sway him from his values and purpose. And he was accomplishing this way of life in Japan, a country where the pressures—whether they be the enticements of money or the fear of social disapproval—are so much greater than they are in the U.S. If he could do so while still being out in the flow of the world, he must have some insight to how we too can resist the big trance that surrounds us, and, perhaps, do so with some flair and panache.

"I was raised in the slums," San Oizumi tells me as we sit in the cozy central room of his large, rambling, mud-walled farmhouse. "There in the tenements was a world that I could never have dreamed of before we had to move there . . . so many people living right on top of each other: sick and broken people, the mentally handicapped, prostitutes. As a fourth-grade boy," he admits, "it was kind of exciting. I even heard

31

about a neighbor woman who killed her husband, crazy with jealousy. It was quite an education for an elementary school student." He smiles slightly and raises one eyebrow. "But," he says, now serious again, "because I grew up as a poor person, surrounded by poor people, I learned a lot about the distortions and sickness that lie at the foundations of our society. I don't have any illusions about what it's really all about."

Such statements are typical of the broad-shouldered potter with the unhurried voice. Although he offers his insights with seeming indifference, when Oizumi looks at me, he's all serious attention. It's not a glare but it's more than a gaze, and it always has a strong element of concern to it. Although Oizumi can at times come off as gruff and brusque—his statements contain none of the polite circumlocutions I am used to hearing when speaking Japanese—I never feel that I am speaking about something trifling with him. This has the effect of making me really consider my words and try to speak from a deeper, more serious place in myself.

I had come to meet him originally because I had heard of his old-style wood-burning pottery kiln of mud and clay, an "inclined kiln" of traditional Korean design that takes three days to fire, and of his organizing against a high-level nuclear waste dump planned for his rural district. After meeting at tonight's gathering of citizens' groups opposed to the dump, we've come back to his house. Sitting around the huge wood-slab table he has made, with pieces of his luminous pottery all around us, we drink tea and talk into the night.

Oizumi tells me of his upbringing and of his father's anarchism and general nonconformism. In Japan in the 1930s and early '40s the militarists were in control of almost every part of society, and I find it hard to imagine that it would have been possible to be either anarchist or nonconformist. "Dad was a poet and woodblock carver," Oizumi says in his thick working-class accent. "But you can't make much money writing poems," he laughs, "so we were very poor. When I was a very young child, before we moved to the slums, we had a house in a small village. The other villagers were very suspicious of my father because he had a record by Beethoven, and they could see by the letters on the album that it was clearly foreign, so they thought he was collaborating with the enemy Americans." This suspicion was corroborated for them because Oizumi's father could speak a little English and refused to go into the army.

"He didn't want to have anything to do with people in the business of killing," says Oizumi in his matter-of-fact way, "and as a result, the village elders shunned him and the other members of our family. But when Japan lost the war and the U.S. Occupation forces arrived in the village, there was no one else but my dad to translate. The same village elders who had ostracized him came begging at his door to ask for his help. But he didn't want to help the Americans either: in his eyes, they were murderers just the same."

A few years later Oizumi's father lost his house in a swindle, and the family was forced to move to a tenement building in Sendai, an industrial city in cold northern Japan. The old man died from tuberculosis when Oizumi was only in sixth grade.

Like his father, Oizumi is willing to make decisions entirely on principle, and he too is perfectly willing to suffer the consequences of his actions. "Growing up in poverty," he tells me now in his calm, slow voice, taking a sip of tea, "I learned that even if I have very little money, that's not the end of my life. I know I can still have an interesting life without it. I don't want to be someone who is completely reliant on money, someone who is *used by* money. That's why I neither borrow nor lend."

The hard-edged world of the slums he grew up in seems such a contrast with the antiqued beauty of this two-hundred-year-old house—with its massive hand-hewn timber rafters, mustard-colored walls, and beautiful *tansu* cabinets—where he lives with his wife and three children today.

I ask him about how he came to be in possession of such a home.

"Well, about twenty-five years ago the house I had been living in was slated to be surrounded on three sides by a golf course, and, as you know, to maintain only one kind of grass on large areas they have to use an incredible amount of herbicides. Also, I hate golf. I was hit in the head with a golf ball when I was a boy. So of course I had to move.

"I got on my motorbike one afternoon and just started driving around looking for a new place. Then I saw an old building far off the road that looked beautiful, and I walked on down to it. Inside there was a very, very old man, and he said to me, 'Ah, you have come. I have been waiting for you.'

"I was quite confused because I had no intention of coming there. In fact, it was just a whim to even go out that particular day. 'I knew you were coming,' said the old man, 'You have come because you are to live in this house.' That old man was a real Japanese shaman."

"Growing up in poverty I learned that even if I have very little money I can still have an interesting life."

I look around the big dining room now where we sit and take in all the intimate clutter of books and papers in stacks alongside pieces of Oizumi's glowing ceramic bowls and cups. On the walls, calligraphy scrolls by Oizumi's daughter hang next to posters for anti-nuclear concerts by Korean rock bands. High up near the ceiling, bookshelves hold volumes of old Chinese classics and reference works covered with yellowing paper.

"Inside the old house there was a very, very old man, and he said, 'Ah, you have come.'"

But before I am able to wax too romantic, Oizumi pulls me right back into a dead serious conversation. "I myself don't expect to live a long life: the world is too dangerous now."

If it were not for this evening's lecture, I might be inclined to think that Oizumi's talk of danger is somewhat overstated. But then I think back to the community hall a few hours ago crowded with over two hundred local residents as a researcher from the U.S. Nuclear Control Institute, Edward Lyman, told the audience story after story of nuclear waste storage canisters corroding and leaking, cancerous substances leaching into the water table, the potential for bomb-capable material being hijacked during transport, cost-cutting by the nuclear industry, and lax regulation by the government agencies that are supposed to be protecting the public.

Oizumi helped to organize this forum because the Japanese government continues to ignore the citizen groups who've been protesting against the proposed high-level radioactive waste dump to be put in an abandoned mine shaft less than ten miles from Oizumi's house.

As Lyman spoke, I spotted Oizumi standing silently, listening in the back with his arms crossed over his ochre corduroy shirt. The information seemed in no way to surprise him. Nuclear accidents and spills are not uncommon in Japan (though they are rarely reported) and there are more than fifty-five nuclear reactors (with more in the pipeline) on an archipelago where regular and often severe earthquakes occur.

After the lecture, Oizumi's wife, Yuriko, and eldest daughter, Nako, a bright-eyed nineteen-year-old, stood behind a table in the foyer handing out information sheets and pamphlets. This job of educating citizens about how they have been lied to is not an easy one in Japan; it is not a culture in which ordinary people, especially rural folks, are used to questioning the directives of the government or the assertions of academicians and experts. Yet now, with the Tokai-mura nuclear accident fresh on people's minds, Oizumi's meetings have been full to capacity.

After walking back from the information table, I found Oizumi speaking with a young local government functionary in a starched white shirt. The contrast was considerable—the large Oizumi in his rough cotton baseball hat, graying long hair, beard, and clay-spotted work clothes talking with the formal and necktied young bureaucrat. Still, Oizumi listened carefully, speaking to the younger man with care and focus.

Now back at the house, thinking about the differences between these two men, I remember the Japanese proverb, "The nail that sticks up will be hammered down."

"Have you ever experienced being 'hammered down'?" I ask Oizumi.

He pauses for a minute, then replies, "No, no. Mostly not . . . Well there was one thing. Years ago, in order to sell my pottery, I was told that I was supposed to go around and meet important people and say polite things to them, and I did that. When I had shows of my ceramic works in important galleries, the gallery owners told me if I made this or that type of piece, it would sell well. They'd point to several of my pieces and say, 'Make ten of these and ten of those, and I'll sell them for you.'

"I did what they said, and sure enough, money came in, hand over fist. I saw that if I were to cleverly accept this kind of advice, I could make a *terrific* amount of money. But for me there was a certain kind of anguish in it. The broker wasn't a bad person. He'd give me all kinds of advice, and it was wonderful advice too sometimes, because he really knew his business. But I started to not want to make those kind of pieces that they were requesting. In fact, I was actually *unable* to make them. There are potters who can, but I stopped doing it. After that, I didn't have someone else looking out for my well-being; I had to go out and sell things by myself. But in that way I was able to do my work in a manner that was actually free."

San Oizumi is not easy to categorize. At times he is mischievous and seems like he might be plotting some kind of trick; at other times he presents orderly, well-woven disquisitions. Yet this is something one doesn't notice at first because everything he says appears to be offered casually. He lets out his short phrases, one after the other, as a fisherman might let out a thick rope slowly into the water over the side of a boat—advancing, waiting, pulling back—but slowly building a logical point or an insight about the world that comes upon you with unforeseen force at the very minute he chuckles to himself at the unexpected conclusion. And the languorous cadence and warm vibrato of his voice make me think about his many years spent working with materials from the earth.

Although he doesn't make much of it, Oizumi is in fact an internationally known potter, and has created a tremendous variety of arresting ceramic objects in his over thirty years of work. His pottery as I look at it now on the table and on the shelves in the main room of his house pulls at my awareness as we talk. The surfaces of the pieces recede back into a place that resists a summary understanding. There are plates and bowls whose burnt earth tones are simultaneously subdued and lustrous—russet browns and tans, beiges and smoky ambers—as well as cups of pumpkin orange and glossy eggshell white. Yet when I ask him about the glaze on a particular tall teacup that fits snugly in my hands, he says to me bluntly, "That piece is not glazed."

"Not glazed? It looks glazed. How did you get this fine shiny surface, then? Is it the type of clay?"

"Aahhh. I don't know. Please ask the kiln."

I wait for a few moments, and eventually he offers, "When you open the kiln after the firing is over, then you know. Even though it's the same clay, the place where you put the piece in the kiln changes the surface. Depending on the flow of the heat, all *kinds* of different colors come out."

After what seems like hours of talking, we notice that everyone else in the house has gone to sleep. We look up at the old wooden clock and decide to turn in. Without any undue ceremony Oizumi shows me to the place where I am to sleep for the evening. We walk through a passageway in back of the main house to an old tile-roofed outbuilding that also serves as his workroom.

Oizumi indicates with a nod of his head the bed I am to sleep in, and takes his leave without a word. I look around at this room filled with all kinds of antique bric-a-brac on high shelves, cabinets, and windowsills. Piled on a desk are catalogs for alternative energy technology and stacks of magazines in French and Korean on politics, music, and ceramics. On the walls, pencil sketches are pinned between announcements for world peace vigils and a poster of Janis Joplin. There's so much to learn about him in this room alone, but as with Oizumi himself, there is clearly no way to "get" it all at once. So I decide to just enjoy the spirit of unknowability and fade off to sleep.

When I awake, I wander outside in the cool, late-October air and look around at the various old buildings and sheds, small workrooms, and animal pens. Then, in a covered passage between two buildings stacked with boxes, tools, and firewood, I come upon Oizumi shoveling some red coals out of a pot-bellied cast-iron stove. His smiling face is lit by the red embers, and I think to myself that fire really is his element.

He invites me in for breakfast.

In the warm dining room with the thick mud walls, Oizumi's two teenage daughters and son are getting ready for school at the large wooden table. Oizumi's wife, Yuriko, brings out a breakfast of white rice, miso soup, vinegared cucumbers, and some greens in a savory broth. In the middle of the table, several long and thin river-caught fish bake over embers of charcoal on a cylindrical clay hibachi.

Yuriko is another powerful person, though not as talkative as Oizumi. She is a classically trained practitioner of the Japanese tea ceremony and teaches one of the most evanescent of arts, *ikebana*, or flower arranging, which I like to think of as a kind of botanical sculpture.

As we enjoy our breakfast with the family, the kids trading repartee with each other, Oizumi gestures at the steaming bowls of soup on the table and tells me how the family makes miso, the fermented soybean paste essential to much of Japanese cooking. "Of course we could buy it in the store," he says, "and it would be far cheaper to do it that way, even if we didn't count our labor time. But during those three days in February in which Yuriko and I and the children all work together, we enjoy each other's company in a different way; there's a kind of nonverbal communication among the members of the family that we cannot get otherwise.

"The process is impossible to do by oneself because it takes a lot of work. And if even one person is just playing around, it can't be done. Making and keeping the fire burning, mixing the miso, splitting the wood. By dividing the work among us, we can make over 130 pounds.

"Long ago, they were compelled to do this, because

"Not glazed? How did you get this surface?" "Aahhh," he says. "Please ask the kiln."

miso wasn't sold in the stores. If you go to the store to buy something nowadays, you'll see that there's an endless amount, and it's usually a cheap kind. But we don't know how they make it, what they put into it. So we go through all the trouble to make it. In doing so a lot of other things are also accomplished. The children, for one, feel for themselves, 'Ah . . . miso. This is how it comes to exist.' So when we eat some soup, even if the parents leave some behind and don't finish it, the kids—as is proper—eat it up." Then he laughs his tenor laugh. "Because they made it themselves, they don't throw it away.

"But it's not a return to the past. The way we live now is a new way of life, even though what is being done—in this case making miso by hand—is old. Walking in the woods has been done by people for centuries, but it was not done for the reasons it is done today; it carries a different meaning. This family hasn't made miso for generations; it was just that at some

point we decided, 'Let's do it.' I don't want to return to the olden days: the very thought of it, there's something not quite right there. And in any case, it's not possible."

As I am thinking about all this he says, "I think you'll agree that this is a much more delicious miso."

I speculate that perhaps the familiarity and comfort I feel in this house is a result of Oizumi's refusal to prioritize getting a job done in the least possible time with the least possible money. Maybe this is the reason why the things he says seem so casual, yet, when I listen to them, they reveal themselves to be so deeply considered. As we speak, the teenagers finish their meals, look at the clock, and head out to school. We clear the table and put on some water for tea. Oizumi then extends his metaphor. "Another example is charcoal," he says, gesturing to the tea water now heating on the clay hibachi in the center of the table. Japanese charcoal, or *sumi*, is both dense and light, and burns clean and hot. I like looking at the jet-black oak branches that maintain their shape as they start to glow a bright orange-red. "Cooking and heating with *sumi* is a way of living from here on out, for the future, I believe," Oizumi says.

"Fifty years ago, they stopped using *sumi* this way, and ten years ago it was completely out of use. But petroleum doesn't come from around here; it has to come by boat from some other country. If you plant a tree, however, right here, the tree grows bigger, and in twenty years, you'll have some *sumi* at your own place. Because we can keep making it every year, you could say it 'rotates' more than petroleum. Thus we can use *sumi* for fuel or heat for a long, long time. People in the past didn't think much about all that; they just had need for something to heat their houses. We use *sumi* like they do, but our attitude about it, that is new."

Oizumi speaks briefly now with Yuriko, and he tells me that she will offer a tea ceremony in honor of my visit later in the afternoon. It will be in the tearoom he constructed, which is, he says, also an underground nuclear fallout shelter. I make a puzzled expression but he tells me there's no time to show it to me before we head out to do some errands in town together.

We then put our shoes on and walk down the stone stairs from the house and climb into his battered old white flatbed truck. Oizumi starts the engine and, with his powerful forearms gripping the black, plastic steering wheel, we head out of the driveway and down the hill into the town and the city beyond.

Oizumi leans forward into the wheel alternately chuckling or somberly detailing the results of some recent contemplation. I am entertained with all manner of tales from his childhood at a Christian boarding school, deep in the snow country of northern Japan, where he would make money by looking after domestic animals, or snowshoe for miles on errands for the school.

"There were only three rules at my high school: be in nature, read the Bible, and work. That was good: a minimum of rules. But I got in trouble for being mouthy. They'd tell me things like 'Jesus will come down from the sky tomorrow,' but I always asked them to prove it. Of course they couldn't, and they just thought I was obnoxious.

"But," and he looks over at me while he's driving, "you can't say it *won't* happen either, can you? There's no proof of that either."

As we drive down through the valley and into a few towns, he tells me of traveling to Korea to learn about wood-burning pottery kilns, of going to France to lecture on the anti-nuclear movement, and of his discovery of a town in Germany that is totally car free. I also find out that after his father died, his mother managed to raise the children by winning a national contest for hand-carved wooden dolls, and thus could make an income (though a meager one) by filling orders for these traditional crafts.

He then tells me a detailed story from the classical Sanskrit epic *The Mahabharata*, and links that to his favorite moviemaker, the Russian director Andrei Tarkovsky. I hear also of Oizumi's own filmmaking, as an art director for a recent movie based on a tale of the Heian period

(A.D. 800), about folk magic and a mountain village's resistance against the government's arbitrary plunderings. The scope of his interests seems boundless.

It occurs to me that his active intelligence is trawling the world for a better way to be, a more *reasonable* and affectionate way to be in this world.

Now we've descended into the real experience of urban Japan, and though I still feel insulated inside our conversation, out the window I see all the familiar gaudily colored flashing neon signs, tangles of overhead wiring, blocky cement buildings next to train trestles rusting in the humidity, electrified vending machines on every corner keeping canned drinks both very hot and very cold in all weather, and steel-panel billboards advertising electrical appliances and gadgetry. And then there are the blaring lights and chrome of the pachinko gambling joints. I never cease to be amazed at how *many* there are. (Pachinko is a type of vertical pinball game in which a cascade of steel balls pours downward with a deafening sound through a maze of metal nails, with a full cacophony of buzzers, bells, and sirens.) The whole thing feels like a binge on electricity, on a culture-wide scale.

Both Oizumi and I know that the proliferation of nuclear power stations is a result not only of Japan's industrial production but of the Japanese public's electricity use run amok. The plants, however, are always sited in ru-

ral areas hungry for jobs, remote from the mass of urban people who use most of the electricity. The predominance of nuclear power, along with the massive use of agricultural chemicals, is linked as well to the rise in cancer rates in this small, crowded country.

But when I mention to Oizumi the cementing of the riverbeds and mountainsides that has been the focus of much environmental concern here, he surprises me by answering, "Oh that? I'm used to it. We all live with contradictions. You have to decide which contradictions you can abide and which you cannot. For me what cannot be tolerated are the things that threaten the *kiseki* of life itself."

I pull out my pocket dictionary to look up the word. The definition, in tiny letters on the small page, reads "miracle." I'm surprised to hear such a word used by someone with the gruff manner of Oizumi.

After a pause, I ask him, "'Miracle,' how do you define that word?"

"A miracle is something that just cannot be explained rationally. It is the impossible thing, which could not be. If you think about it, isn't it really impossibly unlikely that we are alive? What explanation is there? It is completely illogical. That's the definition of miracle to me. And it *is* a miracle that we are all still alive with what Bush people in the U.S. are doing, and the other countries too. The contradiction that I cannot abide is the way they are ruining the gene code of life itself. The genes of my children will be destroyed by radioactive waste dumping and atomic energy. If we destroy the gene code we cannot pass on this miracle to our children.

"That's why, before I go to bed at night—although my kids tell me to pipe down—I say aloud how grateful I am for this unlikely and gorgeous day."

~

Soon we are driving through the city of Toyota, past the massive factories of the automobile company of the same name. On the other side of this industrial conglomeration we stop at a poultry farm run by one of Oizumi's friends to pick up some chicks of a special breed of black chickens known for their particularly healthful eggs.

Then, heading back, we stop by a small bakery where Oizumi drops off a bag of wheat and barley with the baker. As he explains the purpose of this delivery, I realize it's another example of his genius for publicity stunts. The grain is a mix of seed grown near the proposed nuclear waste dump in Oizumi's region of Japan and some harvested in the small village in the far north of Honshu Island at the village of Rokkasho, where Japan's first plutonium reprocessing facility is being built. The plant was hugely

© Hiromi Hayashi

controversial but was rammed through despite massive opposition locally and nationally.

Oizumi's idea is to have local bakers and housewives make cakes and breads from this flour as a way to start discussions about who would want to eat such food once these facilities are in operation. It's brilliant, I think, because it breaks through barriers that middle-class propriety usually erects to political conversations. I imagine the sitting rooms of many stay-at-home house-

I had come to meet Oizumi originally because I had heard of his old-style wood-burning kiln of traditional Korean design.

wives becoming animated with concerned discussions begun by the simple device of these cakes being served. In addition, Oizumi tells me, he and other potters will make plates for these cakes and breads made from two different kinds of clay dug up from nearby the proposed nuclear waste site and near the village of Rokkasho. Who would want to eat off of potentially radioactive plates? Oizumi's stratagem is yet another way to bring his critical ideas into the conversations of the mainstream Japanese public with its love for fine ceramics and regional specialties.

On our way back home, Oizumi decides to take me to a noodle restaurant for lunch. He mentions that after a huge, multilevel parking lot for a pachinko parlor was constructed right next to the restaurant it obscured the view of the small establishment. The owners, also friends of his, had been thinking of shutting down the restaurant as business was off because no one could see it from the street anymore.

As we pull into one of the parking places in front, I comment on the unusual wood and bamboo façade and the cedar timbers used in the signage. It turns out that Oizumi himself had redesigned the whole restaurant, inside and out, to attract more customers. When we walk inside, his aesthetic is evident everywhere, from the huge burl slabs of wood at the counter to the bathroom sink made from a large wok. The small space is packed with people and the proprietors heartily greet Oizumi. He saved their business with his redesign. Listening to Oizumi talk over the counter to the owner, I am reminded of how capable he is at all manner of practical tasks. Oizumi gives him advice on how to maximize barley production by crushing the small plants to increase the number of stalks. Oizumi then explains how to remove the fangs of a poisonous snake from one's skin and how to get the venom out (he learned how to do this when, as a boy, he was bitten by the most lethal snake in Japan, the *mamushi*). Another customer at the counter who knows Oizumi tells me that when the director of the film Oizumi worked on needed some wild boar heads for the movie, it was Oizumi who knew where to get them. And when no one had any idea how to build an igloo, Oizumi offered that he knew how from his boyhood at the countryside school in the far north.

We finish our meal and walk up to the counter to pay, but Oizumi will not let me treat him. He hates any and all forms of indebtedness and obligation. Split it evenly, he seems to be saying: a clean relationship is best.

Soon we are again driving through the sparsely populated valley and up the mountainside to where he lives. Oizumi says he has a few things to take care of before the tea ceremony, and indicates with a wave of his hand in the direction of his wood-fired kiln to go have a look. I feel a bit like a kid going out to explore.

Directly behind the main house, a mossy hillside rises until it runs into the tree-scattered mountain behind, and beyond that at the far corner of the property I find where Oizumi has built his massive "climbing" kiln, looking primitive and imposing and ancient as hell. It is made of a light brown mud that blends into the color of the hillside and consists of six or seven stepped chambers built on a slope, each one a rounded cone shaped like a stack of hay. Each chamber's door is open and though it's dark inside, I can see a few pieces of pottery still on the shelves.

Although the kiln is quiet now, I imagine what it would be like to stand next to this humped tunnel of mud as Oizumi stokes it hotter and hotter, and the heat of burning wood roars through the successive chambers, the earthenware vessels transforming inside. It must require such precision in construction and so much care while firing it for several days of continuous super-high temperatures without anybody, or anything, accidentally getting burnt.

I wonder why Oizumi decided not to use a gas kiln in which one can control the exact temperature so much more carefully. A gas kiln also wouldn't require putting up massive loads of split and dried cordwood and would be eminently safer and much less prone to mistakes in firing that could nullify six months or a year of throwing pots. I believe part of the answer lies in the quality of the surfaces of the ceramics themselves. Perhaps there is something irreplaceable in being part of a river of human experience that has used a technique for thousands of years.

Leaving the kiln area and heading back to the house, I notice how the seemingly random placement of the out-buildings gives a meandering and intimate feeling to this place. I come upon a stone pathway leading down the hill. On the ground floor of the building that I slept in last night I discover a room that seems newly converted to a private library. The door to the small room is finely constructed of both traditional Japanese joinery and gnarled pieces of driftwood, and I enter, take off my shoes, and step up. I take a seat at the low table and look around: I am surrounded by old books: art books, pottery books, history books. On the table I see a book with the author's name in the same characters as Oizumi's. Has Oizumi written a book?

But I look closer and find that the full name is slightly different, and upon opening it and seeing that it is full of striking woodcuts, I figure out that this is a book by Oizumi's father. I gaze into the images looking for clues.

The lines are both rough and bold, and the high-contrast block prints speak of northern winters and country living. One startling, surrealist image is entitled, "Self-portrait with butterflies and a skull." Alongside the pictures, poems have been carved one character at a time. The biography at the end includes the dates of Oizumi's father's life: 1913–60 . . . dead at forty-seven.

Then, looking down on the bottom shelf, behind a sliding glass door, I find a treasure: a complete, thirty-volume character dictionary set of the Japanese language. It lists the thousands upon thousands of meanings, usages, and combinations of the complex characters with all their nuances and implications. It is something that only a family with a love of written language would ever buy or put to use. Oizumi's practicality hasn't foreclosed a rich life of the mind at all.

~

Oizumi's work room.

Although the library holds so many more beckoning volumes, I get up from the table and walk back up the hill.

Behind all the outbuildings, a sloping, yellow-clay cliff bank rises, clothed with fronds of fern. In the face of this cliff I find an arched passageway cut into the earth like the hole of some animal. I look down the dark passage that leads straight back into the clay hillside about ten or fifteen feet, and from here I can see a red glowing light on the ground at the end of the passageway. Then I realize that this might be what Oizumi was talking about this morning when he mentioned a tearoom that is also an underground nuclear fallout shelter.

Then at a distance I hear a soft, high-pitched sound— a kind of smooth shiny whispering. Following the sound away from the cliff, I come to Oizumi's workroom where he is sitting in front of a small perfectly cylindrical grinding stone on a tabletop. The dark and polished surface is a mixture of jade and obsidian in color. When I enter, Oizumi turns toward me, then back to the stone, and smiles. He is turning this exquisite antique with a wooden handle, while a fluorescent green-tea powder shimmers in a circle out of the fine hairline crack between the close-fitting top and bottom part of the stone. With the back of his smallest finger, he ushers a small pile of green tea leaves into a hole in the top.

He says, "This was made in the eighteenth century. Listen to the sound that the stones make." It's a kind of smooth abrasion, similar to far-away wind. "Once all the tea has been ground to a powder," he continues, enjoying sharing his insider knowledge, "the sound changes tone . . . slightly. For centuries, that has been the signal to the guests who have been sitting in the area outside of the teahouse door: when they hear that sound change, they know it is appropriate to enter the teahouse."

As the last leaves disappear into the hole in the top of the stone, indeed the sound shifts just slightly to a higher and less muffled pitch. Oizumi then gathers the tea powder and leads me toward the tearoom. As we walk, I think of several tea ceremonies I have taken part in. It makes me glad to know that this time, whatever happens, I'm sure it won't be another formal but saddeningly empty ritual in which everyone—including the woman leading the ceremony—seems to feel exceedingly uncomfortable.

Oizumi leads me over to the tunnel entrance and, following him, I stoop down and enter into the mountainside. At the end of the tunnel by the ceramic lantern with the red glowing light, there is a sharp turn to the left, and we come to a small wooden door with a rounded top which is paneled roughly—encrusted almost—with mashed pieces of lead or aluminum. The metal armor seems almost like it has been crushed there by a giant hand onto the small hobbit-hole-like door, and then I remember: That's right; it's a fallout shelter.

Oizumi opens the door and we both step inside. The first impression is of quiet, and not just quiet to the ears. The light is low in the small bell-shaped cave room, and the gentle aroma of green tea powder combines with the womblike feeling to create a sense of safety and peace. Yuriko is already here, sitting to the left of the door. We bow to each other as I enter. The chamber is illuminated primarily by four or five large ceramic bell-shaped lanterns of blackened brown—recognizably Oizumi's work—with candlelight flickering out through hundreds of tiny holes. A low earthen shelf wraps around most of the wall, and a small and unusual flower arrangement has been placed on it by Yuriko, a practitioner of the experimental Adachi style. In a sunken pit in the floor, fresh spring water is heating in a large cast-iron kettle. Beside this are the various tea implements, bowls and sweets. The soft reverberation of sound in the circular room heightens the welcoming and soothing feeling of being inside the earth.

After Oizumi and I have taken a seat on the blue cushions, Yuriko begins to prepare the tea for the ceremony. Completely gone is the formality of a traditional Edo-period thatched-roof teahouse, with its preordained dimensions and its protocol for placement of alcove, scroll, and hibachi. Yet the principles of tea, as far as I understand them, have been maintained: an intimate, small space; low lighting; floor seating; and a very small entryway that cues humility as you bow to enter.

Oizumi himself is now almost totally quiet in Yuriko's domain. Although many of the nuances of her preparation escape me, at no point do I feel ignorant or "foreign," as I have in other such settings. It is impossible to be flighty in this kind of space, or to feel attacked. One can only be *here*, with oneself, with the others, present.

As Yuriko uses each implement, pours the hot water, whisks the fresh tea powder, hands us the frothy green bowl, and serves the sweets, she manifests a grace that is utterly lacking in pretension.

The tearoom is difficult to grasp at once; it is small enough that the full feeling of it must be reassembled in the mind. I look closer at the details. The joinery of the floorboards is tight, and perfect. They meet diagonally and are held in place with darker wood pegs. The echo to our voices in the smoothly rounded chamber reminds me of the feelings I have experienced inside of mosques. I know of course that being under a mountainside, this chamber could conceivably collapse on us, but I feel completely safe: Oizumi's solid presence—even more than his demonstrated talents—lets me know that this underground tearoom was built well.

The very small size of the room permits only a single conversation, and this effect is heightened by the sparseness of the decoration. It is as if the room were designed as a support to our intentions to be in authentic dialogue with each other. How different from the world we witnessed this morning in the car with the noise and clutter of the city all around us. I feel that Oizumi and Yuriko have pulled the true essence out of a tradition and have discarded the rest. Tea ceremony in Japan today is an institution, a big business full of encrustations of pomposity. In the building of this space and the offering of this ceremony, my hosts have shown me the heart of this ritual.

~

After we have finished the tea, we lean back against the smooth earthen wall and, in this timeless world, I fall into a true peacefulness. Yet Oizumi's purpose in digging out this "fallout shelter" by hand with a shovel and a wheelbarrow is not to encourage any kind of complacency. He reminds me, "As I said before, I don't expect to live a long life. The world is too dangerous."

It seems to me an odd statement to make here in this quiet grotto deep in the earth. I ask him what he means.

"Well," he asks me in a half-quizzical, half-testing tone, "can you tell the pattern in the wood here?" He points to the floorboards and then to the door, raising his eyebrows and tilting his head. "Can you see the connection to Chernobyl?"

I admit to him that I can't.

"Look at the pegs here," as he points out the wooden nails that he used to fasten the boards together. I notice they are in irregular, but somehow not random groupings. "Four-Two-Six. April twenty-sixth was the day of the meltdown of the reactor core."

He then points out the same 4-2-6 theme in the punched holes of the large clay lanterns that illuminate the room. "You see, it seems beautiful," he continues, "but it's also a warning to all of us not to forget: all of this beauty is sitting right on top of a tremendous amount of danger."

He looks at me, "At any time another Chernobyl could happen."

He's right of course, and I, like most people, prefer not to think about it. Oizumi however doesn't let this forgetting happen to him. Maybe the tearoom is a way for him to remember. Or maybe it is evidence of his refusal to forget.

"A national TV network came to my house once to do a segment on this 'unusual tearoom,' but," he says with a smile half cynical, half knowing, "they left out any reference to it being a fallout shelter, or of nuclear power."

While I suspect I know why the network would have edited that detail out, I can also see how easy it would be for anyone to forget. I too allowed myself to become enraptured with the spirit of the ceremony and the protected feeling in here.

"Nuclear power," Oizumi continues, "is inconsistent with the Way of Tea."

He lets the statement sit there for some time until I ask him what he means.

"The Way of Tea is one of humility and poetic sentiments, not of grandiosity and gorgeousness. The ideal behind nuclear energy is a limitless amount of free electricity lighting up every part of the planet. Also, the Way of Tea requires that one must never bring weapons into the tearoom, or anything that might be used as a weapon. Not only nuclear fuel but even nuclear waste, as you know, can be used to make weapons.

"Although," he says with an absolutely deadpan look on his face, "I've often thought that the cockpit of a tank would probably be just the perfect size for a tea ceremony room. After all, we shouldn't be using them for war, and

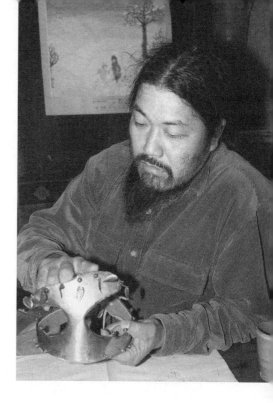

"I designed this crown for a movie about folk magic and a village's resistance to the government."

San Oizumi • 47

we ought to put all these items to good use. And they're even movable!" I laugh out loud.

He continues, "Just think of all the money that is spent on the so-called Japanese Self-Defense Force. With that much dough, we could build a glass tube all the way across the Pacific Ocean, and then next weekend, you and I could jump on our motorcycles and ride across to America!"

I catch just the tiniest glint of mischief in his eye before he turns his head away.

Yuriko smiles at his joke, then stands up to take her leave. I thank her, stumblingly trying to indicate how different this experience has been from my previous encounters with tea ceremony. She bows politely to me, and leaves us to our discussion.

I look back to Oizumi, and I remember something I heard about him. I say, "Your friend Atsuko told me you are an anarchist."

"Yeah. I am," he replies looking at me and tilting his head, as if to say, "What of it?"

"There are so many definitions of that word. What does it mean to be an anarchist in Japan?"

"Of course you don't understand Japanese anarchism! That's because each anarchist, not just in Japan, each one anywhere is different."

And then he takes the conversation, without warning, to France. "A few years ago, I was invited to Europe to speak at a rally. I talked about the nuclear issue here in Japan, and when I finished—there were five thousand people there—everyone started cheering wildly and making noise. It was disturbing. You have to be careful with that kind of thing. I felt like some kind of demagogue with all those people cheering for me."

Like a lot of what Oizumi says, this statement holds the curious power to get one to think about one's own behavior. How would *I* act in a similar situation? Would I bask in the cheering? Would I feel smug that others thought I was right?

He continues, back to Japan. "In this village, during the elections, all kinds of people in the leftist groups came to see me to get my support. But there's always discord in those radical groups—people who are in the Marxist party and those who are not. My father was an anarchist too, and during the war he supported neither side. When the

Japanese militarists came to him, he said, 'I don't know you.' When the Americans came he said, 'I don't know you.'

"So if the Marxist party people come to talk to me, that's OK, and they have the right to exist, but I cannot support them a hundred percent. Likewise, if the ruling conservative party says something good, then I say, 'That's good, isn't it?'—though of course what they say is mostly bad. And if it *is* bad, I say, 'There's something wrong.'

"But I don't read books about anarchism, or any such thing. What I do is simple: I read and write about this current problem, the nuclear waste dump."

For Oizumi, any kind of group has the same problems. "You know, potters often form associations. I don't join those. People in groups get together and do things the same way as everyone else in order to avoid anxiety, even if those things have no meaning at all. For example, wearing a necktie has no meaning. If wearing a necktie would prevent you from getting a cold, I'd wear one!

"If you join some kind of association your own true way of thinking gets shackled. You do things just to give yourself that feeling of ease."

The word in Japanese that Oizumi uses here, *anshin*, literally translated, means "peace-heart," but is used every day in Japan to mean the absence of worry, of relief from fear. As Oizumi uses the term however, it's almost as if *anshin* is a cowardly place people retreat to, and it's definitely something that he doesn't want to control his life.

"In a group, just saying hello and greeting people can become unnatural. Especially if someone in the group has some high rank. You start to speak with them in a way that's completely fake. It's not like he's *actually* that amazing, it's just his position in the company or group. The reason people give high-ranking people respect is because they have a problem with their own self-valuation. It's probably why they joined a group in the first place—that and their own pride. They want to look good as a member of an important group, a group with such important members. This pressure is incredibly strong in Japanese society."

Listening to him, I think to myself, "That's sure true here in Japan, this group-oriented society." But, as if he has read my mind, Oizumi says, "If you state it extremely, it's like the way people are about the Japanese emperor. They think he's a great person. America has this same tendency as well. They don't have an emperor . . . but a lot of people want one."

I have to laugh. He continues, "The problems get worse the bigger the group is. In a small group, if some mistake is happening it's quickly recognized. But if it's a big group, people just say, 'Well, that person is a great person, and he said to do it.' And even if it's a mistake, even if it starts to taste bad . . . they do it!"

It is characteristic of Oizumi's storytelling that he uses different voices for each of the characters, rendering in hilarious ballooning inflections, "that person is a *great* person." He can re-create simply by using the tone of his voice how certain they are (in their error) and how they mock those who disagree with them as idiots.

"Political parties are like this too, even the left-wing parties. That's why I'm an anarchist."

~

Yet another way Oizumi upends the standard hierarchy in Japan is by maintaining a deep connection with Korea, a country against which strong animosities still persist. He has been traveling there since the 1970s to exchange ideas and techniques with Korean potters, many of whom have stayed at his house for extended periods. Last year Oizumi was invited to speak at the Japan-Korea Pottery Symposium. I've noticed that he sprinkles his conversation with Korean words, pieces of Korean history, and details about different types of glazes and the Korean dynastic periods

in which different styles were made. And he regularly attends rock concerts of the wild Korean-Japanese fusion musician, Pak Poe.

In Japan it's easy to forget that Korea is the closest neighboring country, so conspicuously is it ignored in almost every sphere of Japanese life. This gives credence to Oizumi's point that when you get even a little bit of wealth or power, you start to feel superior and you miss things: you perceive less, understand less. Then you start to lose out on so many fascinating things. Oizumi explains, "Most Japanese feel that Korea's culture isn't as advanced as theirs, while European culture is more advanced."

I ask Oizumi why he is so drawn to this country.

"I like to go places where there are people with a real history. In Korea, that same tribe, that same culture has been there for a *very long* time."

"Well," I say, "Europe has a long history too."

"No way! That place is frightening!"

"Frightening?"

"Yes. I went to Italy, Spain, Milan, Florence, and *all* the buildings were made from stone—the churches, the castle walls, and ramparts. Now how did they make that? That would take a *tremendous* amount of energy. In those days there were no bulldozers. Everything was done by hand. A place with that many stone buildings would have needed some kind of slavery system to build them. When I saw that I thought, 'Wow, Asia was still relatively peaceful back in the olden days.' Also, all the big wars of the modern age have come from Europe, haven't they? There's something there that's just frightening."

I smile again. I've never thought about it that way, but once he says it, I can see what he means. He continues, going even further out on a limb, "Of course there's the music from Europe, 'classical,' but I actually really don't much like it. You go into some department store here in Japan and they're playing Vivaldi or something. *Dum dum dum dee tee dum!*" Oizumi puffs out his chest. "Then people start to feel like they are aristocrats." He holds his head high, looking down, conveying the pomposity of the customers. "Then everybody feels like purchasing things. It's got that kind of magic to it. I heard a lot of classical music at my father's house. He loved it and even had his own classical music show on the radio. But I just don't like it."

Although I think to myself that there's much to be said to disagree with such statements, I really honor Oizumi's frankness in making them. And if his presentation is sometimes acerbic, his tone is never unmixed with the feeling of play. It would be a mistake to take the words out of their environment, of his amusement at our human follies. I think that Oizumi's willingness

to go beyond what is commonly encouraged in polite conversation also explains some of the power of his thought.

Indeed, in his next comment, he looks straight at me and says in a manner that could even be interpreted as challenging, "I know you are a writer, so this might seem a little rude, but I believe that words, and especially written words, are the best way for humans to deceive, cheat, and trick one another."

He points out the sounds made by the tea-grinding stones. It's a kind of smooth abrasion, similar to a faraway wind.

San Oizumi • 51

I imagine this kiln with the heat of burning firewood roaring through its chambers.

I raise my eyebrows waiting for the coming explanation.

"Well, if the two of us were to just sit here completely silent, staring into each other's eyes," he says, keeping up his intense but not unfriendly gaze, "do you think I could deceive you?"

There's clearly nothing to hide here for either of us. "No, probably not," I say, returning his gaze.

"But once we turn it into words, and then, further, when those words are written down, it gets easier and easier to trick people. Even if you aren't looking at the person you are communicating with, it's still possible to write things. That's not true with speaking."

Although all the obvious objections do arise—the beauty of well-crafted language, books as ways to communicate with others across centuries or continents, the transcendent process of crafting a poem—wisdom here is not to throw my arguments back at him. And in any case, I'm sure he knows all that (his beautiful library is one testament) and he is in no way making a belligerent assertion. He is simply adding to the conversation.

Oizumi then smiles, "And then, when you add computers, there's even *more* possibility for cheating."

And, for Oizumi, it is the the reality of chicanery and deception in politics that is the central problem he is up against. I remember last night's lecture and the very real plans the government has to put the most toxic form of nuclear waste into a mine shaft not far from his house. To Oizumi, it is critical to find a way to unmask the government's marketing campaign that aims to convince the local population that the waste dump is absolutely safe.

Last night at the meeting, Oizumi showed me a slick booklet that the government hands out to citizens entitled "Geoscience." Inside were charts, graphs, and diagrams with smart-looking arrows and labels explaining how carefully everything will be done. In a resort to a higher authority, there are a number of photos of Caucasian researchers in glasses and lab coats listening to Japanese nuclear scientists with rapt attention. The presentation is all so neat and sharp that it is hard to remember that the booklet's purpose is to get a group of villagers to consent to a plan that could poison them and their descendents for the next ten thousand years.

Then, while I am thinking of all this, Oizumi suddenly changes directions, laughing now at himself, "Of course making a movie like I did, a fantasy movie, well, the *whole thing* was a deception!"

∽

By now hours have gone by talking and relaxing inside this cave sanctuary in the earth. I realize that the quiet restfulness of this place has helped me really hear and take in what he has been saying.

At this point, Yuriko pokes her head back in the low door and invites us in for dinner. As Oizumi and I walk out into the evening air I ask him, "Remember you said that you don't think you'll live that long?"

He nods his head. "It's true, I don't."

"Why is that?"

"Well, I'm having too much enjoyment in my life. Everyone is."

I find myself even more confused than before.

"We're all doing the same thing, trying to have 'fun,' and most of the time using electricity and gasoline to do it. And if we keep it up, we'll just keep making the world more and more dangerous. We have cars, nuclear power, nuclear weapons; it's part of the 'fun' that we are having. It's the exact same dynamic. Every country has a preposterous amount of weapons so people in that country can do whatever they want—Japan too. There's no guarantee at all that a war won't happen, no guarantee at all. But what I want for my children is a world that is safe to live in."

We walk through the door of the main house, remove our shoes, step up into the big dining room and sit down at the table. While we wait for the children to arrive, I ask him about how busy everyone here in Japan is all the time.

Oizumi again answers with a story, "You know, one of the local potters came by here the other day—an older man—and he said to me that when he isn't busy, he gets ill at ease, frightened. Part of the reason is that when he doesn't have a lot of work, he won't be making money.

"A lot of the potters around here use molds and machines; they make thousands of the same item: twenty thousand cups or bowls in a day, just so that they can feel *anshin*. Then they add up how many yen they will make, and that stops their worrying. They do that just to feel at peace for a bit.

"But for me, it's just the opposite: I get scared when I *am* busy. For one thing, I might get in a rush and forget something and have an accident working with my kiln. But even more importantly, if I'm too busy, I might overlook something magnificent and splendid like a rare mushroom in the forest . . . and who knows when I might see such an amazing thing again?" He looks at me, as if waiting for an answer.

"But," I ask, "surely you need money too, don't you?"

"Of course there's some need for money, but when you use money to solve problems the necessity to think for yourself disappears. You can resolve all your difficulties by using money, or buying a product to fix it for you. Just like being a member of a large group or organization: you can let the group do a lot of the thinking for you. But for me, the opportunity to think for yourself is too valuable to be wasted that way. And who knows how long we will be here? We've got to treasure the time we have."

~

After dinner, I gather my things together, put them in my old car, and prepare to head out to meet my next interviewee. Oizumi brings out a couple of boxes of *sumi* he's made to give me, and I put them in the back seat.

Just before I leave his homestead on the mountainside, we say to each other, "Let's meet again some day soon," even though we both know we have no idea what will happen in our futures. I am thankful to him, though, for reminding me of the uncertainties of life.

As I drive down the road out of the mountains, I hope I can always remember his words, "If I'm busy, I might overlook something magnificent and splendid like a rare mushroom in the forest . . . and who knows when I might see such an amazing thing again?"

Osamu Nakamura

It's easy to see the benefits of modern production techniques: convenience, access to an incredible range of "goods and services," getting a lot done in a very small amount of time. Machines do give us an incredible leverage. What is more difficult to see is what we have lost. Although I had read in many places about the alienation that often accompanies "progress," it wasn't until I met the craftsman Osamu Nakamura that I could experience exactly how his "simple" life and his palpable contact with the physical world is actually so much richer than the hamster-wheel lives of overwork, busyness, and rush that so many of us have become accustomed to. By using his hands to provide for his needs, he has found a richness of heart and a sensitivity of perception that so many of us long for.

Far into the interior of the sharply cleft mountains of Shikoku, if you follow a steep dirt path past terraced rice paddies, past rough stone retaining walls that wrap themselves along the contour of the valley and through the shade of dark green stands of bamboo and cedar, you will eventually come upon the small wooden cottage of Osamu Nakamura, the artisan. Standing in front of his house, now out in the clear, you can look across the narrow valley and pick out, on the opposite side, a few other tile-roofed farmhouses set amongst the tapestry of blue-green trees that cover the mountain.

Several hundred feet below, the rushing, boulder-filled creek cuts along the valley floor.

Nakamura is someone who is almost always at home—except when he's studying in the tiny Sherpa village in the mountains of Nepal where he learns woodblock printmaking from his teacher, a Tibetan Buddhist monk. So when I stop by late one winter's morning eager for another lively conversation with my friend, I find it odd that he's not around. He has no telephone, so one just has to climb the winding path and see if he's in.

I leave a note in the mailbox made from weathered slats and traipse back down the path to where it meets the road. Walking along, I watch the creek spill over the rocks into deep, turquoise-colored pools, and, when it joins the larger Katsura River, I cross a bridge and make my way to the local public hot spring. Entering the bathing area, I am surprised to find the shaven-headed gentleman himself soaping up in the adjacent stall.

We exchange greetings, and I mention that it was unusual to not find him at home. "Yes," Nakamura says, "during the winter, I only go out about three times, and that's usually to the hot spring. With the snowfall last night, the pipes to my bathtub are frozen, so I decided to come down here."

We talk a little as we soak in the mineral-rich waters, and later, as we are drying off, he invites me back up the mountain for some locally produced tea—*Awa bancha*. As we walk up the road, our breath forms little puffs of vapor in the cold mountain air and Nakamura tells me that this special fermented tea is now only made in two remote regions of Japan and, interestingly, rural Burma.

When we arrive back at his house, he slides back the glass doors and we step into a dirt-floored entry room typical of many old farmhouses in Japan. Less typical, however, is the Nepali-style clay cookstove on which Nakamura prepares all his food. We take off our shoes, step up into the living area and sit down on rough straw mats around the sunken fire pit in the middle of the floor. As he prepares to make a fire, I look around at the few old hand tools hanging on the mud-and-straw walls and, in the corner, two large circular grinding stones for making flour from wheat berries.

Nakamura builds a fire well. He places several logs in a cross pattern in the ashes, between which he arranges crisp, dry cedar needles that he takes from a woven straw basket with a tight-fitting lid he keeps near the wall. He then puts a few pieces of split bamboo—which burn quickly and hot—on top of the cedar, and finally some short, one-inch-diameter branches. Each of these items has, over the preceding year, been gathered, cut to length, dried, and stacked neatly by size and type under the eaves in front of his house.

As always, the fire lights on the very first match.

Being with Nakamura inevitably provokes questions: Why grind wheat by hand when the efficiencies of mass production and distribution can deliver ten different varieties of flour to the nearest commercial outpost for pennies? Why collect wood from the forest, dry it, store it, and then deal with the inconsistencies and demands of a fire (not to mention the smoke) when propane gas or electricity can provide for all one's cooking or heating needs? And why ignore all the achievements of science and technology—brought as a result of great toil by generations of engineers, researchers, and laborers—in order to live a way of life that millions of people were glad to leave behind once the technical means were available?

The full answers to such questions, as with most things with Nakamura, come slowly, in time.

Nakamura has lived in this house for almost sixteen years now, since returning from Nepal at age forty-two. When I first visited him here, I imagined that his apparently austere way of life was based on some moral or ethical philosophy.

"No," Nakamura says, "everything I do is because I completely enjoy doing it this way."

He places an elegantly shaped cast-iron kettle on the hook that hangs over the fire pit and when the water starts steaming, he takes a small handful of dried, olive-

© Junko Motoyama

colored tea leaves from a tin canister and places them in a mottled, russet-colored clay teapot. He pours the boiling water slowly over the tea leaves in a circular motion with as much care as one might take when transplanting a seedling. He then reaches over to the wooden shelves behind him for a second canister containing another specialty, this time of Nepali origin: hard, twisted biscuitlike snacks made according to a recipe he learned from the Sherpa villagers. He tilts the canister and five or six slide out onto

Nakamura says, "Everything I do is because I completely enjoy doing it this way."

Osamu Nakamura • 57

© Junko Motoyama

a small earthenware plate. Each one is coated with unrefined sugar, is delightfully crunchy, and makes an excellent complement to the fragrant yellowish-green tea.

As we warm ourselves by the fire, the smoke billows and gathers around the blackened roof timbers above our heads. We look out between the open sliding doors on the snow-dusted mountains, and he begins to tell me of the travels that eventually brought him to this life he now leads.

"Ever since I was a child," he says, "I always looked at the hills behind where we lived and wanted to know what was on the other side. Many people are satisfied with where they are and with what they have. I don't judge that at all, but for me, as soon as I was able, maybe seven years old, I got on a bus by myself to see what was in the next town. As I got older I would go farther and farther away. Eventually I had seen a lot of Japan, but I still wanted to know what was beyond. By that time I was working and had a steady income, but I had that same yearning. I wanted to know what was on the other side of the ocean."

Nakamura's way of speaking, like the minute geometric designs he chisels into wooden blocks, is both precise and evocative, but never overly serious. When Nakamura tells his travel stories his thoughtful face often breaks up in animated laughter, and he can easily spend four or five hours just relaxing on the straw mats, drinking tea, and talking of life.

"The decision to actually leave," he continues, "happened in an instant. I looked at my life, and I knew that I didn't want to wake up one day and find myself an old man filled with regret that I hadn't seen the things of this world.

"Of course," he continues, "there are two kinds of regret I could have faced: I knew it was quite possible that I might end up stranded in some foreign country, miserable, without any money, and knowing that I had given up my job. But when I compared that possible regret against retiring at sixty-five years old, having known nothing except working at my job—that was when I knew. The decision, as I said, came in an instant."

In Japan in the mid-1970s it was extremely uncommon for someone, especially a man with a salaried job, to leave that security and its whole universe of expectations simply to travel abroad, especially with no particular goal or end point in mind. His father and mother, he tells me, did not approve.

In the world system of increasingly discrete labor, in which each person contributes an ever smaller part to an ever vaster manufacturing of so-called "goods," the act of disentangling oneself from the whole might, in hindsight, appear quite radical. But for the person concerned, in that moment, exiting the system feels like the only available path. "Long, long ago," Nakamura says, "there were very few choices for most people in the world. The majority couldn't even think of choosing what kind of life they would live. Then over the past two hundred years, more and more people had one, or two, or three options open up to them." Nakamura makes a branching movement with his hands, like a tree. "But now, there are thousands and thousands of choices; it's like there are so many branches that people have a hard time deciding on anything."

~

When Nakamura quit his job, he was twenty-eight. He left Japan and boarded the Trans-Siberian Railroad, and changing trains in Moscow, came down into Europe. He spent the next two years on the road. He rode a bicycle from northern Europe through France, across the Alps, and down the entire length of the Italian peninsula, and then all the way back up and through Germany, through most of Eastern Europe, down through Yugoslavia, and then into Greece—all on his own. When I inquire about the length of his bicycle journey, he calculates for a moment and says that it must have been around fourteen thousand miles.

"At one point," he tells me, "I ran out of money and began to look for work. I was in Sweden, and my money was going fast. Every day I went to *fifty* different shops asking for work. And each place just told me 'No.' Every night my stomach hurt from hunger and especially from stress—I was so worried about what I would do. In the back of my mind I even started to think about stealing food, just to get something to eat. If a person is starving, it's quite natural to think about doing bad things."

"Why didn't you just write to your parents," I interrupt, "and ask them for money?"

"No," he answers simply. "I did not consult my parents before I left, so I would not ask them for any kind of assistance."

I can only nod my head silently.

He continues, "Just before I completely ran out of money, someone gave me a job as a dishwasher. I decided then that living a life focused on money was *definitely* not for me. Thinking about money all the time just twisted my personality too much."

It occurs to me that most people after such an experience would probably decide exactly the opposite. Beyond everything else that is different about Nakamura, the way he tries to detach himself from money shows how decisive a break he has made from the common way of living a life.

While this experience in Sweden was pivotal, it was not until he visited the high mountain villages of the Himalayas that he first encountered people existing almost totally outside the cash economy. He went there originally to study woodblock print carving, but then, living amongst the villagers, he gradually began to adapt to their way of life. In the end, he spent most of the 1980s living in a Sherpa village in a small mountain hut.

"Sometimes when you reminisce," Nakamura muses now, looking up from the fire, "and reflect upon a particular turn your life has taken—say, if you had not realized as you were walking out of your guesthouse in New Delhi that you had forgotten something and gone back to get it, you would not have met that man in the lobby who suggested that you talk to that Buddhist priest in Kathmandu about traditional crafts who, when you met him, told you about a woodblock print teacher living in the mountains. And if you hadn't gone to study woodblocks, you wouldn't have learned the attitude toward living that has allowed you to lead the life you now do. It all seemed quite ordinary at the time, but looking back you see that your life would have been completely different if you had not forgotten something in your room."

∼

Now it's getting on toward evening, and Nakamura asks if I would like to spend the night. Having nothing to do the next day, I happily accept. We then move back to the dirt-floored entry room with the large clay cookstove and he selects the ingredients for tonight's dinner. I know from my previous visits that I am in for a treat. Nakamura is one of the most accomplished—though understated—cooks I have ever met. Cooking and eating are not things he does because he has to; they are central to his life.

"I am reading *Walden Pond* now," he says, "and though it's interesting, I was hoping that there'd be more about growing and cooking food. A life in and with nature should be fifty percent about food.

"Also, it's strange—Thoreau only lived there for a little more than two years. It's more like he moved there in order to write the book. But someone needs about ten years, I think, to understand a particular way of living. Thoreau seems like he was more of a tourist."

I laugh. I've never heard such an unorthodox opinion about the man who, to most people's thinking, pioneered the idea of an urban person intentionally choosing a rural life. But Thoreau did discover an important truth early on: urbanization and mechanization, under the guise of progress, have a tendency to create alienation. People keep finding themselves in an unforgiving matrix of overwork, stress, and unwilling complicity in the destruction of the earth. Underneath, however, we sometimes sense that we might be here for a reason other than to just get by from day to day.

Nakamura now goes into the back room and brings out a book, *Rhythms of a Himalayan Village*. "This book was written about the village where I lived," he says, pointing to a black-and-white photograph of a misty, barren mountainside with several mud-and-tile houses scattered along the ridgeline and distant snowy peaks towering in back. "This is the monastery where I studied woodblock carving, and," he turns the page, "this man is

my teacher, Tapkhay Gendun." He points to a photo of a monk sitting by a window, his face lined by years of cold-weather living and meager conditions.

Paging through the book, I lose myself in its beautiful photographs juxtaposed with quotes from the Sherpa villagers and passages from Tibetan Buddhist scriptures. As I read, I begin to sense how the villagers' way of living, in its utter simplicity, could give Nakamura a physical, bodily understanding of how to live a life of reduced desires and reduced consumption when he returned to Japan. The villagers, living five days' walk from the nearest roads or electric lines on a windy ridgetop covered in stunted grasses and rock, show both a physical strength and, in their words, humility, steadiness, and a remarkable self-possession.

"It was because I saw the Sherpa's way of living, and had lived it myself," says Nakamura, "that when I came to this valley here in Japan and first saw this house, I knew

"I learned to adjust my imagination and plans to what was actually possible."

Osamu Nakamura • 61

© Junko Motoyama

He offers me snacks made from a recipe he learned from Sherpa villagers in Nepal.

I could live in the same way right here."

Now he switches on one of the three lightbulbs in his house and starts to grind together cumin, ginger, salt, garlic, and red pepper in a rough-hewn stone bowl. Then, starting a wood fire in the low, clay cookstove, he places a blackened frying pan on top, cuts up some onions into tiny cubes with a well-sharpened knife, and slides them into the oil in the pan. He puts a great deal of intention into each action: adjusting the fire, carefully eyeing (but not measuring) the quantities of each item. It's a pleasure to watch. He then adds some cut potatoes and some cabbage, and then the spice paste from the heavy stone bowl.

As I watch I think how funny and wonderful it is to be this far back in the mountains on a cold winter's evening about to eat an Indian potato curry when in the closest city (a provincial Shikoku town two hours away by bus) it is impossible to find real Indian food at all.

Though he lives in a remote area, Nakamura is far from uninformed. During dinner, our discussion meanders through topics such as the transition of the Japanese economy from manufacturing to information-processing; his theories about representational versus abstract art; and even the symbolic issues of identity and self in the phenomenon of young Japanese people who blacken their faces and dress as though they were urban African Americans. He gets a lot of his information from the excellent national radio broadcast network, on which one can often hear essays and literary forums at a level of a sophistication and nuance surprising to somebody familiar with radio in the U.S. When I ask him what he usually reads, he says, "I like this literary and arts quarterly, *Ginka*," and picks up a thick, illustrated magazine sitting beside his table. The date is 1973.

"The tone has not been as elegant in recent years as it was in the '70s. That's why I tend to re-read the issues from that era rather than buy any new ones."

I smile to myself. Nakamura isn't someone who is hypnotized by some vaguely defined idea of "cutting edge." So many people believe—perhaps without thinking about it too much—that the newest must be the best. Yet even for those of us who question this ideology, when we hear traditional peoples speak of "following the ways of the elders," what does that mean for us living in industrialized nations? What does "cultural survival" mean in practice? How do we take from the past to build a future that makes sense for us today?

Because we live in the flow of time, we will necessarily get alienated from what happened last year, and even more so from what happened last century. So for us to feel what previous generations understood, we have to make a conscious effort to touch and experience what was present in their lives, as Nakamura seems to, whether that is their stories and books, or the techniques and tools that they used.

If we only apply the blunt instrument of "progress" to the making of choices about our lives, we sever our connection to the intelligence of the past that had been tempered over so many hundred generations. We disinherit ourselves from these ancient and intricate understandings.

Yet if we want to keep old culture alive, we cannot preserve it as an artifact in a glass display case, defending it against decay with temperature and humidity controls. If we label it and date it and put it under a halogen bulb and call it "the past," it becomes static: it is no longer alive.

It seems to me that Nakamura's answer to this dilemma is one that preserves the essence and sensibility of a traditional way, and continues the vital cross-fertilization with the realities of our own time. When I first met Naka-

mura, I had an idea of "the traditional life" as something that does not change. But tradition was never something that was permanently nailed down. It existed in flux, part of an entire way of living. Each aspect of our heritage is not a "thing" but part of an integrated and connected life that shifts and moves with time.

When Nakamura chooses to cook on a mud stove with firewood or to grind his own wheat to make flour, he tries to understand these techniques on a physical, experiential level, to feel what they meant in the past by doing them himself today. Meanwhile he keeps their vitality alive in his own daily practice, enjoying the pleasure of meeting his needs with his own hands, which is fundamentally different from studying something in a library.

And now, as I sit at Nakamura's table and compare his absolutely simple, almost bare, existence to the sophisticated level of his thought, I admire his decisions about what to prioritize in life. For all the time he spends cutting and gathering firewood, growing food, carving woodblocks, cooking, or just gazing into the fire, it doesn't seem that his intellectual life has suffered in the least. It is as though the mastery he has achieved as a craftsperson suffuses all the other spheres of his life.

~

After dinner, we go to the far back room where Nakamura carves his woodblocks. He reaches inside the handsome antique *tansu* chest, pulls out his most recent work, and puts it on a low wooden table. It is a collection of prints that he has mounted on traditional Japanese mulberry paper and then hand-bound with a dark, indigo-dyed cloth cover.

It opens accordion style, the way many books once did in Japan. Each set of pages reveals, on one side, a rectangular sample of rough-woven Nepali cloth printed with a red and black geometric design, and, on the other, a rendition of that same pattern by Nakamura as a woodblock print on handmade paper. Nakamura's reproductions use the same color scheme as in the Nepali cloth, but the flawlessly matching chevrons, diamonds, waves, and zigzags fit so perfectly that they merge and shift and my eyes start to play tricks on me, as if I were looking at an optical illusion.

As I page through the fine book, I see that Nakamura has both preserved the originals and found, by his extreme precision, something inside of them that I had not noticed at first. In the Nepali cloth samples, the lines of the black and red patterns don't fit exactly with each other, but the cloth nonetheless exhibits the beguiling beauty of folk items that are made to be used. In Nakamura's paper reproductions, I see in the exact fit of the lines the shifting, pulsing forms that play with my perception.

"When I first arrived in Nepal," says Nakamura, "more than ninety percent of the people wore clothing that had been hand printed using small woodblocks. On my most recent trip, it was less than ten percent. Silk screens can print much more cloth in a much shorter time."

He now reaches again into the *tansu* chest and selects several of the heavy rectangular wooden blocks that he used to make these prints. Each one has rows of intricate, identical patterns, and each pattern is cut deep into the thick, solid block. A single slip of the chisel, I realize, would ruin the pattern, and he would have to start over from scratch.

I ask him if this repetitive, unforgiving work sometimes gets on his nerves.

"Well, it's true that making something of minute detail takes a lot of focused concentration; and at first you do feel some tension because you are worrying about making mistakes. In my experience such feelings can continue for a half hour or more. However if you keep working, all of a sudden you slip into a timeless space, where the work and you cease to be separate. There's only the work itself. When you come out, you don't know whether several minutes or several hours have passed. I think it's a particular feature of this kind of work.

"A craftsperson's job is half meditation, half creation.

It takes creativity to design whatever you are working on, but it takes meditation to do it right. Making things with one's own hands cultivates a certain generosity and openness of the heart. It nourishes that state of mind in the craftsperson themselves, which is intimately connected with an entire way of life."

Hearing this I am reminded, with sadness, of the epidemic levels of depression in my own country, and wonder whether it might have something to do with the aversion we have to working with our hands. For people in industrialized societies, perhaps the problem is not that manual labor is intrinsically unpleasant, but that we get frustrated because our attitude is one of resentment toward something demeaning. Viewed differently, however, such work presents us with an opportunity to know ourselves and the physical and natural worlds better by exploring this essential aspect of being human: our relationship with our hands. How funny it is that one of the fundamental definitions of being "modern" is the ability to avoid physical labor, when it might be that very thing that could provide us with such depth of connection to ourselves and to the world.

Nakamura shows me a diagram that is used for practice by the beginning student of Tibetan wood carving. Instead of images or patterns, it's a chart of Tibetan lettering, with arrows indicating the correct angle and pressure that the chisel should take. The Tibetan script is tremendously attractive. It has the flow and sweep of Arabic, but also an angular, bladelike assertiveness. It moves from right to left, and drops down like curved icicles from a ledge that runs along the top.

"Learning how to accurately carve all the letters of the Tibetan script," says Nakamura, "gives the learner all the skills with the eyes, fingers, and hands that he needs to be a proficient wood carver."

Nakamura then shows me a number of other books that he has bound by hand, and explains the Japanese method of sewing together the cloth-and-paper covers. I look at each of them and shake my head imagining how much time and care went into making them. Given how much labor they take, I realize that it is only possible to make a few copies of each, and that only a few people will ever see them. It seems a lot of effort for very little reward. But then I think that in contrast to a book published by

"Making things with one's own hands cultivates a generosity and openness of heart."

machines in a factory, the simple potency and beauty of a hand-sewn book gives the reader pleasure of an entirely different order.

One of the books Nakamura has bound comprises a few photocopied pages on how to weave sandals from rice straw. Paging through it, I see how much my way of thinking about "craft" has changed over the period I have known him. Instead of craft being a "nice" pursuit with which to fill some unoccupied hours around the house, I have come to understand it as one of the most fundamental and ancient ways that humans have to meet their needs: baskets for winnowing grain, woven cloth to cover the body, forged and hammered iron tools with which to cultivate the soil, and woodblocks to print books and communicate with others. Craft is something every person *needed* before machines made everything we use. Spending time with Nakamura, I see that the process of making something like straw sandals or a handmade book cultivates humility while connecting us with something

fundamental about our humanity: the interaction between the remarkable capacity of our own human hands and the ingenuity of our minds.

And yet as he starts to explain to me the painstaking process of sewing the cover on a book—how the cloth has to be tucked in at a certain angle under the paper, how the cover should extend just one millimeter beyond the stack of pages—I still wonder whether it's really necessary to be *that* careful.

Nakamura's answer is simple, and clear: "If you make it this way, every time you look at it later, it's an enjoyable experience." It is almost as if the energy he puts into making something remains stored in the object and feeds his spirit every time he looks at it or touches it.

Now, picking up the book on how to make sandals from straw, its pages only photocopies, I understand that through his binding them in a cover of black and red Nepali cloth, they have become something of beauty where something functional would easily have done. I think of my own piles of papers in stacks and in boxes all over the place, and compare them less than favorably to the grace of Nakamura's way of keeping information he deems important.

When I share this thought with him, and how I feel that what he is doing is so beautiful, he replies by walking over to his bookshelf and pulling down a tiny book covered in yellowed kraft paper. "If I were to leave this house and this way of living behind tomorrow, this is one of the two or three books I would take with me." It's entitled *The Culture of Handicrafts* and was written in the 1920s by Soetsu (Muneyoshi) Yanagi.

Nakamura says, "Yanagi asked himself the question: 'What is beautiful?' And the answer, for him, was: 'Everyday things; things that are used in daily life by ordinary people.'"

Yanagi, I learn, was one of the pioneers of the Japanese folk handicrafts movement, which rejected ostentatious ideals of beauty held by many Japanese of the time. He traveled throughout the Japanese islands and Korea as well, living with peasants and farmers, looking for rough earthenware rice bowls, handmade wooden buckets, bamboo and straw baskets, all of which, to him, expressed a more subtle type of beauty.

Here I find the foundation of Nakamura's approach to his life: in Yanagi's words, "The Beauty of Usefulness."

As I look again around the three rooms that make up Nakamura's house, I'm able to take in its aesthetic in a new way, and appreciate this house seemingly empty of everything except the smoke from the fire. Next to the *irori* fire pit, where we have now returned to rekindle the fire for another cup of *bancha*, I look more carefully at the simple fire implements, the several woven, wheat-colored kindling baskets, and a blowing-tube of bamboo for bringing embers to life. Each object, I see, he has chosen with deliberation.

In the adjacent cooking area, back in the shadows, stands a heavy ceramic, nutmeg-colored urn almost three feet high in which Nakamura stores his water. To the right of the sink, there is an ochre earthenware pot with a fitted lid containing ash from the fire, which, along with a stiff, natural-bristle brush, is all that he uses for washing dishes. Amber-colored wooden shelves hold glass jars of spices, powders, chili peppers, and several types of flour, all lined up and classified by size. A well-proportioned cast-iron spatula with a long tapering handle and a blade shaped like a ginkgo leaf hangs on a post in the center of the shelves. Behind the shelves, his cereals and grains are stored in glass jars in large hanging straw baskets suspended from the ceiling.

Nakamura keeps his small collection of books (each of which has been covered in yellow paper and labeled in his distinctive hand) in the back storage room instead of having them on display in the living room where they might distract from the sparse sense of emptiness one has sitting by the fire.

Perhaps most enigmatic of all the things to look at in Nakamura's house, however, is the texture and coloration of the walls and the sliding paper doors. Though much of the rich patina is simply the result of years of smoke from the fire and the aging of natural materials—wood, paper, mud, and straw—the effect is that of a fine piece of art, a kind of supplication to the senses. One can gaze at it for a very long time. Starting from the dun-colored mats on the floor, the mud walls and rice paper *shoji* panels change hues in a subtle gradation from a parchment yellow moving through amber to dark tan and then to a thick caramel brown, where they meet the blackened timbers that run along the ceiling. The tannins and oils from the burning of firewood have left a speckled pattern on the walls, accumulating gradually like fine siltation on the shore of a lake.

The water is again boiling, and Nakamura takes out more tea. Smelling the fragrance from the teapot, I think back to the previous summer when I came up to the mountains to learn the process of making fermented *bancha* with Nakamura and some of the people in the village. In the heat of July, we picked the large, rough leaves from bushes on the mountain slopes and then transferred them from the straw baskets we wore on our chests into boiling cauldrons of water. After crushing the leaves with a long-handled wooden press, we packed them into large wooden barrels and covered them with stones so they could cure for a month. Many of the older village residents have been making this tea in exactly this manner

since they were small children, when almost everything was, of necessity, done by hand.

It surprised me when I learned that in Japan, even up through the 1950s, most rural people made do with little more than what they could grow or make, hardly using cash at all. The mountains themselves, Nakamura tells me, used to be the central resource for people all over Japan, providing them with wild vegetables, medicinal herbs, materials for tools, fuel for their fires, and thatch for their roofs.

But now, with cars and the almost universal use of cash to meet people's needs, the mountains are simply the location of the houses of people who—as it is thought—are unfortunate enough to have to stay, for one reason or another, in such an "inconvenient" place. Over the half-century of Nakamura's life, millions of Japanese have left the rural areas to live in the vast cement conurbation that stretches for hundreds of miles from Hiroshima to Tokyo. Up here, with Nakamura, it's easy to forget that world—which is the reality for most Japanese people—of dams, factories, power lines, containerized shipping ports, cemented-in rivers, robotized factories, and fleets of beeping and groaning earth-moving equipment.

And yet, though the values that Nakamura lives by seem to be antithetical to the majority of Japan, he tells me that his ability to live where and how he does is the direct result of these changes. He says now, "It is only because of the shift in values and ways of life in rural areas that I am able to live here at all. A hundred years ago, it would have been impossible for an outsider like me to have come here: this house, for one thing, would not have been empty, and it would have been impossible for me to use the community water or the community roads because I had not been part of helping to maintain them for all of the previous years. My life here is only possible because I am a small minority. If everyone today lived like this, I would have to run out early in the morning to gather wood; otherwise someone else would get it first, and it would all be gone."

Though Nakamura is one of the most self-reliant people I know, he does use cash. For the four thousand dollars or so a year that he needs, he leaves his village in October and for about forty or fifty days works at a reconstructed nineteenth-century crafts village baking *mochi*, a traditional sticky white rice cake, over a charcoal fire for urban visitors eager for a taste of old Japan.

For his woodblock prints, however, he will accept no money. "If I did," he says, "it might spoil the enjoyment I get from the process of carving." And losing the pleasure he gets from his way of life, I've learned, is the last thing he is willing to do.

"Gathering firewood," he says, "or when I spend time making this *bancha* with the older villagers, it's 'work,' but it's not *labor*. Making tea is something I do once a year because I want to do it, and afterward, I have enough to last me a whole year. Wage labor, like I do at the crafts village, is when I hand over my time for money, and I will do whatever is asked of me, whether I enjoy it or not."

As the fire burns down and we stare into the coals, I think about how little he uses, yet how satisfied he is with his life. Even things that Nakamura has in abundance, such as water or garden space, he uses extremely sparingly. He keeps only a few books. As he says, "I can re-read the most important ones every two or three years and, as I grow older and change, I receive different things from the same words." It is as if he is training his spirit by refraining from any form of psychological or material gluttony.

Yet he is not deprived in any way. His attentiveness to the materiality of the world connects him to a different kind of richness. And the lack of clutter in his house and

Nakamura is in no way deprived. His attention to the materiality of the world connects him to a different kind of richness.

The road to Naka-mura's house.

in his mind gives a feeling of peacefulness to his presence that his visitors can immediately sense.

When I first met Nakamura and saw all the firewood stacked and drying under the overhanging eaves of his roof and the bamboo trellises in the neatly weeded garden and the wooden washboard with which he cleans all his clothes, I thought to myself, "Although it's beautiful, what a burden it must be to do *everything* by hand, and with this level of care." But when I said that to him, he replied in his typical manner, cutting through layers of misperceptions with a single statement, "If you have *time*, a lot of things are enjoyable. Making this kind of woodblock, or collecting the wood for the fire, or even cleaning things—it's all enjoyable and satisfying if you give yourself time.

"Humans have a tendency to create a visual image in their minds of what they think they can accomplish in a particular period of time—say in a day or a week or a year. But one thing I noticed when I first came here was that there was a gap between that image and the amount I can actually accomplish. I felt ill at ease and irritable all the time. I eventually learned, however, to adjust my imagination, and plans, to what was *actually* possible."

Perhaps this is another way that Nakamura keeps his presence so calm: by reducing the number of plans he makes so that they fit easily into the time he has available, instead of trying to accelerate his life to accomplish a long list of projects. And, I speculate, maybe he has come to this understanding of how to live a satisfied life precisely because he has set a pace slow enough to observe the processes of the mind.

One of the first times I met Nakamura he said, "I choose this kind of existence as an experiment, as a way to discover the best way for me to live my life." Now, after many conversations, I understand that he is not living according to a set of abstract ideals. As he says, "Everything I do is because I enjoy doing it this way. I could start cooking on a gas stove, but then I would lose the pleasure I get from gathering and splitting firewood. Or if I didn't grow my own food, I would lose the enjoyment of working the soil."

I can see he has found in his palpable contact with the reality of the world the very thing so many of us are searching for as we go deeper and deeper into our ever more virtual worlds.

~

Outside, the snow has turned to rain, and with its gentle sounds on the roof, Nakamura lays out some old futons for me to sleep on. As my body begins to warm up the bedclothes, the familiar tranquillity of the Japanese countryside settles over me again, and, with the sounds of the river below and the rain falling on the roof, I drift off to sleep.

In the morning, when I awake, Nakamura is already up and making breakfast. Out the windows, mists are gathering and drifting on the dark green cedar forest across the rainy valley, looking like nothing so much as an old Chinese ink painting.

On the cookstove, Nakamura is making some sticky bread muffins in a set of stacked bamboo steamers over a wok full of boiling water. The crackle of kindling reminds me again of Nakamura's wood-centered life. At the table he is cutting up dates and other dried fruits to add to our *tsampa*, the Tibetan staple food made from toasted barley flour, dried fruit, a chunk of butter and (in Nakamura's case) *Awa bancha* tea, all of which is then mixed into a paste. It's not what I usually have for breakfast, but it's warm and tasty, and the dried fruit makes the meal particularly delicious.

I look outside, and it seems like it might just keep raining all day. I ask Nakamura what he usually does on days like today.

"Sometimes I carve woodblocks, or read, but mostly, when I have nothing to do, I just stare into the fire," he says, his face showing an expression of a person lost in the movement of flames flickering their mesmerizing dance.

I raise my eyebrows, and then he says with a smile, "Doing nothing all day—it's difficult at first. Being busy is a habit, and a hard one to break."

But then I think that perhaps such a life—very little production, very little consumption—might be an important part of the solution to the world ecological crisis.

As we look out on the clouds on the far mountains, I ask Nakamura, "Do you feel that you are living a life of luxury?"

"Luxury? No, not luxury. It's an ordinary life. But I do feel an abundance, a sense of plenty. A hundred years ago, I would not have been able to choose what kind of life to live. I feel very lucky to be living in this age."

Atsuko Watanabe

Everyone is in a hurry. There may be many reasons for this, but one result is certain: we don't get much time to think. If we want to be more fully human, one of the places we could start is to consider what exactly "a human being" is. What are we here for? The first time I met the outspoken activist Atsuko Watanabe, I had little idea how profoundly she would shake up the way I think. As a mother and an environmentalist she is motivated by principles quite unusual in our times. Meeting her gave me insights into such a variety of things: what it means to educate a child, or why a modern person would choose to pursue a spiritual life, or in what direction this whole world, our earth, might be moving. She has deeply examined the question: Given our small share of days here, what priorities should we make?

We are sitting up late sipping homemade plum wine from small glasses at Atsuko Watanabe's dinner table next to the woodstove in an old farmhouse deep in the mountains of Shikoku Island. You can almost *feel* the quiet up here as the warble of night insects fades in and out on the other side of the sliding glass door. We've just enjoyed a sumptuous seven-course Indian vegetarian meal cooked by her husband Gufu and served on the Watanabes' pottery. A single lightbulb covered by a green glass lampshade hangs over the wooden table where we speak, and upstairs Atsuko's two daughters are engrossed in their drawing as usual. We can hear Gufu doing the dishes in the kitchen down the hall.

"The office worker in Japan is always being used by somebody," Atsuko says in a plain, stating-a-fact tone of voice. "They have no freedom at all."

Atsuko is always making these kind of statements. But there's strangely no anger or churning to her voice. She's simply stating something she feels is obvious to anyone who wants to see. She continues, "and if you are being used by someone, you have very little freedom of heart. That's the saddest thing for the office worker; being told what to do. And because he's always in a hurry, there's no energy left to think. In Japan, they just don't grant you time." She strokes the orange and white cat sitting in her lap, and says, "And if you are selling your time, no matter how much money you get you can't ever buy back that time. I knew from when I was eleven or twelve years old that I didn't want to live that kind of life."

When I was first invited up to Atsuko's house I thought the unadorned rural life that she lived was a return to the past. It was an almost magical feeling when I arrived, as if I had gone through a time machine and could step into a Japan of long ago. Atsuko and Gufu cook their meals on a wood-fired stove made of mud and brick; they grow almost all of their family's food in the terraced vegetable gardens that descend from their house on the ridgetop, and in the late fall, freshly harvested rice plants hang upside down from bamboo poles to dry. For their modest income, Gufu throws the pots and Atsuko hand-paints flowers, birds, fruits, and animals onto them. In their house there is no television, very few electronic appliances, and almost no items made of plastic. At night they bathe in a handmade wooden bathtub. So I understandably thought I was seeing a way of life long gone from modern Japan.

But when I told Atsuko that I respected her traditional way of living, she corrected me immediately. "I am not a traditional person. I am a just a woman living a simple life in the mountains. That's all."

In fact, she adds, the way she lives is in some ways a reaction against the kind of traditional life her father was forced to live. "Really," she says, "his life was quite sad. He was never able to be a full human being."

"What do you mean by that?" I ask.

"His parents raised him with an extremely old way of thinking. In Japan eighty years ago, it was only the eldest son who was valued at all. He was forced to study every second of his boyhood, and he was never allowed to play or develop as a human being. In a sense," she says, "he was never really completed as a person; it's actually somewhat tragic."

It is I who was being romantic about tradition.

"So," I ask, "you aren't trying to return to the ways of the past?"

"No, of course not!" she says. She then explains that each choice about how to live her life was an individual one with a particular purpose in mind, often environmental or spiritual. "I gave up using a gas stove to cook on because here in the village there are a lot of lumber mills that throw away their scrap wood; I didn't like seeing it all go to waste. It's also quite interesting to cook with wood.

"And planting rice by hand," she continues, "makes me feel happy and at peace. When I cut the stalks for the harvest, I feel a connection to my ancestors, to their lives and their world. Also, I like knowing where my food comes from. As for television, we don't want it here because I don't think it's healthy for the development of the children's minds."

Atsuko's life, however, was not always thus. She was born in a medium-sized city and is the youngest of four children. Her brother is now a lawyer, one of her sisters is an office worker, and the other is a homemaker married to a well-off doctor. But somehow her life took a different course. It started, she says, with flowers and plants.

"When I was a child I played in the rivers and fields near our rural relatives. I would lie in the fields and sketch weeds for hours at a time. My mother would tell me all about different kinds of grasses and plants, and explain the medicinal uses of certain leaves, or sometimes tell me folk tales about a particular flower."

As she speaks, her words transport me to the Japanese countryside in summer with its intense profusion of weeds, moths, wild flowers, dragonflies, beetles, and fragrances. The thickness of these summers seems to me to be part of the music of her voice. "I also loved to spend hours looking at the moon, musing about philosophical questions. Even when I was a child, I felt that I would have to have a life with enough time to contemplate, to let my mind range freely. And I also knew then I wanted to live in the midst of nature. I began to think that the ordinary way of living life would be boring and tedious in the extreme."

I think I know what Atsuko means by "ordinary way of living life" in Japan. The city she was born in is about an hour and a half by car from her house and is where I teach English. The overwhelming majority of women there stay at home to care for the children and keep the house spotless while their husbands work extremely long hours. A very small percentage of them have careers—the word "housewife" is very common here—and not many of the husbands, some of whom I teach, seem to much enjoy their jobs. Traffic, pollution, advertising, plastic, fluorescent lighting and noise surround me everywhere I go.

~

Yet for all of Atsuko's strong opinions and her willingness to confront people when she thinks they are wrong, her personality is almost always buoyant and full of enthusiasm. She really *listens* to people, leaning in toward them when they talk. Her high soprano voice is melodic and she is laughing and smiling so much of the time. It's a pleasure to be in her presence.

As Atsuko pours another glass of sweet plum wine for me now, I ask her how her vague sense of not wanting an "ordinary life" led her to the life she now lives.

She laughs, "It started out more or less an accident . . . when I went to Afghanistan."

"That seems like an odd place to end up without really intending to," I say.

"Yes. I was part of a women's 'adventure' club in college. There were four women going to Afghanistan, and at the last minute one of them couldn't go. And they thought, if we had one more person, it would be more . . . how shall we say . . . convenient."

"Convenient?"

"Yes, you know, riding in rickshaws, two at a time, or going to the toilet; one person could watch the bags, and things like that. It's not easy to have an uneven number when you are women traveling."

"But you had never been overseas?"

"No, but I had wanted to, and this seemed like a good chance."

"And did you have some special interest in Afghanistan?"

"I am not a traditional person. I am just a woman living a simple life in the mountains. That's all."

*For their modest in-
come, her husband
Gufu throws the pots
and Atsuko hand-
paints flowers, birds,
fruits, and animals
onto them.*

"No, not really," she says in an almost offhand way.
"Going to Afghanistan didn't have much to do with me.
I was invited, so I went."

I try to imagine the kind of person who would just
up and go to Afghanistan in 1976 simply because the party needed a fourth member, and I smile to myself. Despite
her protean determination in some situations, some other
part of her seems ready to float along with whatever ap-

pears in front of her. I remember that she once told me
she wanted to be like plants are, producing an uncount-
able number of seeds, or like wildflowers in a meadow,
not thinking of herself as so unique and special. "I admire
how they simply sacrifice themselves, hundreds of thousands of seeds, and only a few grow into plants. I'd like to
be more like that myself."

What a release of self-importance, I think to myself.

I ask, "You didn't have any other reason to go? You
were just invited, and you went?"

"We were also stopping in India and Pakistan along
the way and I had wanted to see Hindu and Buddhist art
there as well."

"Why was that?"

"I had studied it in art school, and I was really interested in it. And in my university, some of the professors were Buddhist priests. One I liked particularly taught
Buddhist art. I really respected this teacher and he got me
interested in seeing the Hindu stone sculptures. I had seen
photos of those Hindu sculptures in books, and I thought,
wow, that's really good, I'd like to see the real thing, particularly the dancing Shiva: the way the sculptor had him
moving his arms and legs was incredibly well done."

"But behind that, was there anything else?"

Atsuko pauses, either thinking, or deciding how
much to say.

"Well . . . when I first went to college I had no religion at all. And as for God, or any of that, I didn't believe in it. Then I became close friends with a woman named Jinko who eventually became my roommate. Her father was a Buddhist priest. And you know how Buddhist priests chant sutras? I thought that was completely meaningless. But Jinko said that when her father did that chanting it gave him some powers—depending on the prayer—some extraordinary powers to change things in the world. I started to think, 'Hmmm . . . *does* Buddhism have some powers to it?' And this question extended to religion in general. Basically I had a lot of doubt, and kept wondering, 'Is all that stuff really true?'

"Also my teacher in art school, the Buddhist priest: he was not only a good and gentle teacher, and incredibly learned and knowledgeable about art, but he also chanted sutras regularly at the temple where he was an abbot, and practiced his religion with a full heart. Until I met him, I was sure that religion was a big fraud."

"So," I ask her, "was it in India that your life started to diverge from the lives of other Japanese?"

"It was even before that, in 1976, before I went traveling. That was the period when all the other students were starting to talk about getting jobs. It occurred to me that once I *did* find a job, and took it, and began working and having money . . . most likely it would be hard to change back to a life without money later on."

Then she pauses, thinking, and says, "Also there was likely '*something else*' I wanted. . . . I had wanted it since when I was small."

"What kind of 'something'?" I ask.

"I didn't know exactly what then, but it was not working a job and living an ordinary life."

"What kind of feeling was it? When you think back can you recall anything specific?"

A little perturbed at my not getting it, she answers, "It's a feeling that everybody has as a young person. There are songs about it too, with lyrics like 'I want to travel far away . . .' or 'On the other side of that mountain, there's probably something.' *The Wizard of Oz* is like that too, isn't it? It's a feeling like that."

"Yes, Atsuko," I say, "but if everyone has it, then why did *you* listen to that small voice?"

"Probably because I saw the people living around me: every day they just gobbled up their food and then fell asleep. That was it." There's a disheartened tone to her voice, a tone so different from her usual enthusiasm. We both let a silence sit there between us, thinking.

"But," I press on, "there are so, so many people who become reconciled with that kind of life and say, 'Well, I guess it's okay,' or 'I have no choice.'"

"Yes, there are," she says agreeing plainly. "But I didn't think that."

Then she adds, "Also, from the very beginning I liked the mountains. I wanted to live there. There's such quiet around here. And of course there's the wind, the air, the water. Especially the wind . . . " she adds in a dreamy voice. As she says this the insects outside the window, as if on cue, lift their voices in both pitch and volume.

"When I first had that thought, that there's 'something' up there in the mountains, I thought that I would just leave school and go and live in the mountains in Japan. But then by coincidence there was the chance to go to Afghanistan. And when I went there I realized, maybe that 'something' could be overseas."

"What kind of 'something' did you think it was, then?"

"Meeting all kinds of people from other countries, of course." Then she adds, laughing, "Especially interesting was meeting those scruffy Europeans. Really, some of them were pretty dirty—a different kind from the ones we saw on television in Japan!"

In a quieter tone she says, "Also, seeing the customs and ways of desert peoples: their costumes, their habits, buildings, food, all of it's different, right?"

"So do you think the trip really changed you that much?"

"Absolutely. If I hadn't gone to Afghanistan, I most likely would have just fluttered about, restlessly wandering from place to place in the mountains of Japan. I probably would have kept working at these mountain lodges, making food and doing cleaning at this one and that one."

Something else happened to her overseas, she says. When the other women from the explorer's club returned to Japan, she kept on traveling for several years. For them, perhaps, the club was a college-age adventure, but for her, she says, "In India, traveling alone, I had a lot of time to just sit and think, and to wonder about the reasons that I am here on this earth.

"At the same time, I saw that the Indians spent a lot of time in the temples, working to improve their souls, to move up when they go on to the next life. It was clear to me that spirituality was absolutely central to their lives in a way that it isn't for us here in Japan. I started to give a lot of thought to what the purpose of being alive actually is.

"Many Japanese don't have the opportunity," she pauses, "don't *make* an opportunity, to think deeply about things for an extended period of time. Maybe that's why many of them aren't satisfied with their lives.

"I saw the people's way of life there—their lives were very poor—and inside of their houses there wasn't much of anything, almost nothing. And if they went shopping, they didn't even put things in bags sometimes, they just held on to the vegetables with their hands, or in a basket. So whatever it is that a person has in India or Nepal or Pakistan, it's plain for you to see when you travel there. It's not hidden like in Japan. If it's vegetables, it's just vegetables, it's not shrink-wrapped vegetable side dishes. It's very simple, and it seemed incredibly beautiful to me. I realized that humans could live a completely fulfilling life in simple houses without much money or even electricity. This was an entirely new concept for me. And I started to believe that I might be able to live such a life myself."

On her first journey, Atsuko also found out about a small lodging house in Kathmandu run by a young Japanese Zen priest who was documenting traditional Nepali Buddhist woodblock printing.

"The first time I met Takaoka, I was kind of surprised because I heard he was doing research, and I expected him to be scholarly. But he wasn't at all," she laughs, remembering. "I thought it was so funny to meet this strange-looking Japanese guy, dressed in Nepali clothing in the middle of Kathmandu.

"But," she says more soberly, "later when I met him after my first trip and he was back in Kyoto—this was an important experience for me—I made dinner for him, but he told me that he couldn't eat what I made because it had meat and he was vegetarian. This was the first time I

had ever met a Buddhist priest in Japan who actually kept to the Buddha's precept that practitioners were not to eat meat." Then Atsuko looks at me, "Of course everyone in Japan knows that these are supposed to be the rules, but also everyone understands that almost no actual priests keep to this."

I imagine the young Atsuko stopping to consider the meaning of Takaoka's choice to keep to a principle, even though he didn't "have to."

On her second trip to Nepal, Atsuko decided to travel with her roommate from college, Jinko. "We met up in Nepal in November of '78. This time at Takaoka's lodge there were a *lot* of people. That was where I first met Ito-san, Amemiya-san, and lots of other people. The whole atmosphere was fabulous and it seemed like everyone was having a lot of fun."

The lodge, Shanti-kuti ("House of Peace"), had become a meeting place for Japanese travelers who would spend long hours sitting around drinking tea, discussing the culture and teachings they had come across, and trying out the new dishes of Indian and Nepali food that they had discovered in street stalls and from vendors in marketplaces along the way.

Many of them were studying Nepali market life more formally, and going to festivals to document Nepali customs and religion. Also a cultural anthropology project was being carried out by the scholars Ito and Takaoka to document the 108 manifestations of the Nepali goddess of compassion (known in the West by her Chinese manifestation Quan Yin), which would then be preserved on woodblock prints in a handmade book.

By helping Takaoka with his studies of Nepali arts and ceremonies, Atsuko and Jinko were able to absorb the perspectives of a Buddhism quite different than the more bureaucratized, money-oriented one they were familiar with in Japan. In a sense, these young Japanese people were all trying to discover or to create a new way of living for themselves that didn't involve them in the striving for social status or in the constant rush that was their inheritance from the Japanese society where they had been raised. The gentle, peaceful, and quiet culture of Nepal in the 1970s proved to be the perfect antidote.

"So," I ask her, "did you have a sense of Ito-san and Takaoka-san being your elders?"

"*Very* much so! Especially Ito-san. His hair was long and he had it in a topknot, he wore a long vest and a kurta, and was incredibly good looking. He had such a soft, easy voice. I thought, 'Wow! What a person!'" As we talk, Atsuko quickly sketches out his garb on a scrap piece of paper.

"Was he much older than you?"

"Oh yes, almost twenty years. But lots of young people really liked him. I wanted to become a part of that group."

During this time, she tells me, she also started to think about what she felt was the central question of human existence: the fact of death. "The best way to discover how it is we are supposed to live this life is to think about what it means to die, and about where we go after we die." And this, she says, is what led her to first start reading books about Buddhist philosophy that they had at Shanti-kuti. "There was that *something* I felt in there for me; something . . . indefinable. And I allowed Buddhism in."

～

I am visiting the Watanabes again at their lovely farmstead. It's afternoon, in the summer, and I'm again having a long, leisurely conversation at the dining room table. When we were making lunch earlier, Atsuko told me that she doesn't want to travel much anymore, saying "I already comprehend what that's about." I now ask her what she meant by that.

"Well I realized at some point that if you just keep traveling, you eventually get unsettled, you aren't able to calm down. You're on a train at night, and it's *daaark* out and you can see little dottings of lights here and there. And you think, 'I'll be in the train station soon, and then I'll have to go out and find a place to spend the night.' So when you're thinking about this and seeing the little lights, you get envious: all those people have a proper place to sleep, and dinner on the table.

"Even now I can remember one time in Nepal, sitting on the roof of the Shanti-kuti lodge, looking down in the evening onto the tree-lined street in front, and people were coming and going in the evening. The sky had just a little bit of light, and the crows were crying *Kaaa, kaaa!* Cows were coming down the street in both directions and people were carrying—what was it?—cauliflower: it was that season. There was a man selling it, weighing it out on his little brass balance scales, and there was some other man buying it who might have been working perhaps as a clerk somewhere, putting some cauliflower in his net bag. And I thought, 'Ahh . . . now people are finishing their workday, going back to their houses.' It very much had the atmosphere of a single day's ending, and now it's time for people to go home and be with their family and begin to make food."

And, laughing she says, "I understood that wherever you go, every single person, in order to eat, they have to work. They need a place to sleep, and no matter what, in the future, I won't be able to escape that. But look-

ing at this scene, I thought that even though there was no way to run away from working to provide for yourself, it can also be a really *wonderful* thing, a beautiful thing. I really felt that."

"So you hadn't felt that before?" I ask.

"Before I went traveling, my feeling that there must be 'something else' out there besides ordinary life was much more of a frivolous feeling, you know, like a ditzy young girl going *'Hee hee!'*"

She seems somewhat embarrassed remembering her younger self. "It's like when you don't really have your feet on the ground, like in a dream. And I realized I had to change that in myself."

"So did you decide that there *wasn't* 'something' there?"

"No, I just realized that it wasn't what I thought, and that I couldn't escape having to take care of myself. It is like what Rousseau said, *Il faut cultiver son jardin:* You must cultivate your own garden. They say that 'A

"They say that 'A rolling stone gathers no moss,' and I wanted to have some moss."

Atsuko Watanabe • 81

"Planting rice by hand makes me feel happy and at peace. Also I feel a connection to my ancestors, to their lives and their world."

we wanted to live in the countryside, and that we could make a living with pottery. That was about it." Then she adds, "At that time, a lot of people were talking about the Nostradamus prophecy, that the world would be destroyed in the year 1999; so we decided," she says laughing, "well, we might not be able to stay with each other forever, but at least until then, we'd try making a life together."

~

The very first time I visited Atsuko and Gufu's house house, many years ago now, their daughters were two and four years old. They were both extremely chattery and would squeal in mock fear when their mother warned them that "Grandmother Rat" would get them if they didn't behave; or would laugh repeatedly about the animal they had just read about in a picture book—the sloth—shouting in unison: "Three fingers . . . and *lazy!*" collapsing into gales of hilarity. On subsequent visits, I would see their older daughter Junko spending hours cutting and coloring pieces of paper to make them into different kinds of "food," making bento boxes, and serving them up to everyone present. Once Gufu told me that Junko even made a fake vending machine that would

rolling stone gathers no moss,' and I wanted to have some moss."

So Atsuko decided to return to Japan. It would be different from "ordinary life," but perhaps not in the way she imagined when she was a girl.

It was also at Shanti-kuti that Atsuko met a man, a Japanese potter named Gufu (meaning "crazy or foolish wind") who also dreamed of living a simple life in the mountains. "We didn't talk about it too much, just that serve drinks. "Without a TV, they make up all kinds of games for themselves," he said.

The extent to which Atsuko puts faith in a child's innate wisdom was also evident in her decision to allow Junko to quit going to school for a few years and do homeschooling. "If my child doesn't want to go to school, I am not going to force her." Homeschooling was so unique, and so against the grain in this part of Japan, that the local television station did a half-hour program on the Watanabes' life, focusing on Junko's studying at home. The reporter asked Atsuko why she thought Junko didn't want to go to school. With the plainest, most unaffected expression on her face she looked at the camera and said, "Well it's probably because the classes are boring." Then she nodded her head, looking at the reporter, naming the elephant in the room, so matter-of-factly, as she often does. "They make them do the same thing again and again."

When Junko was at home all day, Atsuko simply encouraged her to pursue her own interests. "Sometimes we studied things together, she and I." Then she adds, laughing, "It was difficult to keep up with her! And when she decided she wanted to return to school a few years later, she was actually ahead of all the kids in her class."

This I do not doubt. The two girls often initiate dinner-table conversation about topics such as seventh-century Chinese geomancy and its relation to court intrigues in Kyoto, or engage in linguistic punning that makes use of knowledge of complex ideographs not taught to most students until the later years of high school. The lack of a television in the house probably has also contributed to the depth and range of the children's abilities.

But then, with a look of concern on her face Atsuko says, "Thinking back, studying at home may or may not have been the best for Junko, but if school wasn't working for her, I told her that studying here would be okay too. We need to stop thinking 'You *must* go to school; I order you to go to school.' We have to find a better place for children who don't fit in the system, and give that to them. It must be a place that is comforting and nurturing and free. I mean, their future is important; after all, they are human beings."

It would be hard to exaggerate the restrictive nature of Japanese schools. One mother of a child who didn't fit in with the school system, a woman who also lives in Atsuko's village, said to me once, "In Japan, they think if you don't go to school, you aren't even a *person*. That's how important it is for most people."

I have heard many a horror story about situations in the schools. Once, a high-school exchange student from the U.S. told me she saw a PE teacher (also a karate black belt) kick a boy in the chest without warning when he discovered the student had altered his school uniform—something forbidden—by tapering the pants cuff, which was a fashion at the time. In another incident, which became national news, an eighth-grade girl was crushed to death in a mechanical metal gate because she tried to get through it after 8 A.M. as the teacher was closing the gate. The teacher was not fired, and the principal made a statement that if the girl hadn't been late, it wouldn't have happened. Half the students in my English class of businessmen agreed with me that the teacher's behavior was reprehensible, but the other half said they could understand the teacher's position: children should learn to get to school on time.

While this is an extreme example, it is not uncommon for children during entrance exam preparations to spend almost all of their waking hours studying. A common expression is "four pass, five fail," meaning if you let your child sleep five hours a night during exam preparation periods, he or she will fail to get into university.

"You can see," Atsuko says, "how powerful a force education is in Japan when you look at our history, and Japanese militarism in World War Two. All those boys were willing to die because they were told that the emperor was above them, a god, and that their death would have meaning. I don't think the basic philosophy of ranking, of 'above' and 'below,' has changed that much even today."

After a few years of homeschooling, Junko decided to return to public elementary school. When she graduated from the sixth grade, the parents' group was asked by the administration to choose someone to give the traditional "Thank You to the Teachers" address. No one in the parents' group wanted to, and several asked Atsuko to do it. She wasn't particularly eager, but in the end she agreed. Hearing this, I imagine how the school administrators might have felt upon hearing that it was Ms. Watanabe—known for her outspoken views—who was going to be given a platform at a public function.

"What did you say?" I ask.

"I told the teachers I couldn't thank them. At least not yet, because their relationship with the children has just begun."

"I don't understand," I tell her, "what you mean by 'begun.' The children are just graduating, saying goodbye to those teachers."

"Children at that age are just starting to have a real interaction with what they have encountered so far in life. Up until this point, they have just been receiving all that has been told to them, all that the teachers have said and taught. Now they are entering the age at which they can reflect and criticize. So their interaction with the teachers is actually just beginning. That's why I told the teachers that it's too soon to thank them. Once my child has a chance to really relate to their teaching, I'll be able to know whether to thank them or not."

"But," I ask her, "don't you think it might be perceived as a little rude to not thank the teachers? After all, they did work all those years."

She raises her eyebrows, "They received their salary, didn't they? I personally don't think they did anything beyond the minimum that might be expected. They just were saying, 'Yes sir, yes sir!' to directives from the Ministry of Education in order to protect their own position. They got paid really well, but they weren't doing any research of their own into ways of teaching. And anyway, I don't like such formulaic ceremonies in which school officials pressure parents into saying 'Thank you' when the parents might not feel it. In our case, a lot of the parents felt just like I did: those teachers did at best an average job. But none of the other parents would even consider saying such a thing. I, however, have no problem in that regard, so the fact that I was chosen to say so was perfect."

It occurs to me that her ability to break with the ritual practice of saying what's expected exhibits the kind of inner fortitude that has allowed her to create the kind of richly satisfying life that she has, despite all the societal pressures to just do as expected.

~

Atsuko and I are in her garden, pulling weeds, something she says she really loves to do.

"When," I ask her, "did you first start getting active in politics?"

"It was the incident at Chernobyl. After that I realized I couldn't just live a humble and plain life in the mountains. I had to get together with other people and

As we talk, the lyrical bird calls and the crescendoing insects outside are always reminding me of the place Atsuko has chosen to live.'

Power Detective and Investigation Group"). She's also fought the construction of an acid-rain-producing, coal-fired electrical power station upwind from her home by filing a suit with other citizens against government fraud. For ten years she was part of a campaign against a massive dam construction project that would have destroyed the ecosystem of Shikoku's largest river. She also engages in the quiet activism of Amnesty International, writing letters to dictatorial governments protesting human rights violations.

In all of these I can feel her emotional connection to people and the earth, and what's happening to them. She does not boast of her activities, yet neither does she hesitate to bring up these issues in conversations with mainstream people, where the standard Japanese middle-class preference would be for avoiding any kind of topic that might disturb the harmony of the group.

Opposition to authority (especially outside of the biggest cities) is widely frowned upon in Japan. Companies pressure employees to sign political petitions at work against progressive initiatives and make vague threats that bad things will happen to them if they don't, and shame or even ostracism is often spread to the family members and associates of those that step out of the accepted framework. One doctor I met had trouble renting an apartment for more than two decades after participating in a stu-

try to make changes. Actually, I think it would be much more ideal to have a world where it wouldn't be necessary for mothers to go out into the society just to protect their children, but since other people weren't doing it, I felt I had no choice."

In fact it was at a meeting for an Earth Day event that I first met Atsuko. Over the years that I've known her, she has protested the building of nuclear power stations and edited a monthly newsletter with a few other women, (titling it, somewhat humorously, "The Moms' Nuclear dent antiwar protest on the other side of the country. His name, it seemed, was on some sort of blacklist. I thought to myself when I heard this, "and this guy is a *doctor*."

I know that activists in Japan must resign themselves to the reality that their chance of success is low—citizens rarely win any kind of battle against the government or large corporations here, even when the law is on their side. But none of the difficulties seem to prevent Atsuko from carrying on with her organizing, weeding her vegetable gardens, talking and telling stories, laughing and enjoying her life, and spending time with her wide network of friends.

Atsuko's firmness and stark decisiveness can take me unawares; she's fiercely sure of herself sometimes.

I remember an incident a few years ago soon after *yet another* nuclear accident in Japan. I attended a protest that her anti-nuclear group organized at the electricity company office downtown, a brown, boxy bureaucratic building. As is often true in conformist Japan, only a small number of people turned out to the protest. When a few older male officials came down in their blue suits to make a show of "listening," I was surprised to see Atsuko Watanabe step out of the group to confront them, looking them in the eyes. She became furious when they started lying to her.

"Don't you have children? Don't you give a damn about your own child?" She almost shouted at them. "How can you expose your children, and my children, to atomic radiation leaking from the plant? Why won't you take any responsibility for what has happened?"

I was almost as startled as the bureaucrat seemed. It's not culturally smiled upon to show anger, especially in public, especially for women. But she was dead serious. I then remembered the photo exhibition of victims of the Chernobyl disaster that Atsuko had invited me to. I could almost feel the grief in her voice when she talked about the children deformed, or dying of cancer, the land blighted.

~

From a letter:

Dear Andy,

I promised you as a present for your birthday some of the contemplations I have had recently. One of them is that if someone is using their talents and their smart brain or skills solely to pursue their excessive enjoyment in life, they're abusing them. This seems very obvious, but still not many people are using their talents in a proper way. So if we think about that, we already know lots of good things, and the problem is just that we are not putting them into practice. We act against our good will. So we have to strengthen our will. How? By knowing yourself. And this is one of the oldest and most well-known pieces of wisdom. "Practice the known wisdom, and know the wisdom anew." That's it.

Best wishes to you,
Atsuko

The main focus of her activism over all these years is one of the most direct manifestations of human disrespect for our own place: garbage. I admit that when I first heard her talk about how important an issue it was in Japan, I didn't quite get why. But it didn't take long to notice the smell of garbage burning in rusty oil drums in every neighborhood, freely dispersing dioxin and other carcinogens into the air, to wake me up to the severity of the issue here. The amount of plastic garbage that even a careful consumer produces in everyday life in Japan has to be seen to be believed. Even a simple product like sugar is wrapped in layer after layer of pretty packaging.

Over fifteen years, however, I've seen how much Atsuko's slow, steady attention to the problem has changed things in her rural village. She's organized slide shows and lectures, research trips and articles, and spoken with regional and national leaders. With some other women in the area, she's worked with the village administration to set up a recycling station at the old dump site that has grown into a national nonprofit organization, "The Zero Waste Academy," with a funded staff and education programs and which has received extensive coverage by nationwide news programs. Even in remote parts of rural Japan, her small town of Kamikatsu is known by many.

I recently attended a lecture that Atsuko gave there. With a headset microphone attached to a speaker she wore on a belt, she spoke to a group of thirty-five people from all over Japan, including people from similar villages in far-off places, looking to find solutions to being overrun by their own garbage. She spoke rapidly and authoritatively, leading the group from the composting sector to the used-goods reuse section and to the recycling bins (over forty different types of garbage, including aerosol cans, plastic bags, watch batteries, film canisters, and spray paint cans, are separated by village residents themselves). She then brought the group to the meeting room where she answered various questions about toxicity of different materials, ways to overcome initial resistance by rural people used to burning or dumping, as well as the comparative economics of incineration, transport, and materials recovery. I was amazed that she could speak authoritatively, chapter and verse, on all of these issues.

And then, just recently, she was elected to the local town council, where she helps to direct the future development of this small village that now holds national art festivals and symposiums and has representatives sent to foreign countries to make presentations on the Zero Waste Academy. In the past few years young people in their twenties have started to move to Kamikatsu from the large cities to start their own lives of self-sufficiency and living on less.

～

As the long luxuriant hours of one of our interviews progresses, tea time often comes around, and the discussions between Atsuko and Gufu veer into dialectics about this or that kind of tea, the grade of the tea, the size of the cut, and the proper kind of tea cup to use when drinking this particular variety, or how the glaze on the cup does or doesn't fit this kind of tea.

"Let's at least drink the first cup in the proper fashion," says Atsuko.

"Huh? What's wrong here?" Gufu says. "It's jammed up in the pot! . . . Oh, it's *powdered* tea! It's a good quality, but it's cheaper because it's powdered!"

I admit to loving this minutiae of connoisseurship, even as I know they are both half-parodying it, laughing at the rarefied world of "Tea in Japan" that they, simultaneously, just happen to know a hell of a lot about.

Now Gufu is wincing as he drinks the tea. "Yaaa! It's too bitter!" Atsuko lets out another gale of laughter, then looks at me, "Hey, that's like when you made the mulled apple cider for everyone and put too many spices in it! I remember, you just suffered and drank it down like it was supposed to have that much spice in it!"

As we talk, the lyrical bird calls and the crescendoing insects, which then fade back into the silence of the afternoon, are always reminding me of the place Atsuko and Gufu have chosen to live. I can also feel the thickness of the air coming in from outside and the scents of the plants that live on the wealth of the fertile soil, which make me aware too of the permeability of the house itself—Japanese architecture not walling off the outside world. Each of these things is speaking, subliminally, of what is valuable to Atsuko and Gufu, and, I recognize, to me.

～

"Perhaps the most important thing that happened to me," Atsuko says as we continue our interview, "maybe in my whole life, was learning about Rudolf Steiner. I was concerned about what was happening to the girls in school, and was reading a book on pedagogy by a Japanese woman who was living in Germany, Munich I think it was. She had a daughter who she sent to school there. She didn't even know it was a Rudolf Steiner school, a Waldorf school; it was simply closest to where she lived. And she wrote a book about Steiner's methods. It was *incredibly* interesting to me, and I responded with a very powerful emotion."

Rudolf Steiner, a philosopher and Christian mystic born in late-nineteenth-century Austria, was one of those extraordinary humans who could speak, write, and make new discoveries in a bewildering variety of fields. Trained in mathematics, he became a Goethe scholar and a pioneer in organic agriculture and educational theory and practice, designed highly original buildings, and was a sculptor and an innovator in medicine, the theater, and care of the developmentally disabled.

One incident that Atsuko tells me about—"this is just *one* incident, mind you," she says—happened when he was giving a lecture on philosophy. He invited questions of any kind from the audience. Two skeptical doctoral students of botany thought they would trip him up by asking an extremely technical question that was current in their research. "He answered that question with incredible detail, and very rapidly," Atsuko says. "Those two researchers were astonished. Both of them became followers of Steiner after that.

"He wrote such amazing things about the problem of education. I kept saying to myself, 'That's true, that's right, yes, yes,' as I was reading. And I started to read more and more about Steiner, and who he was. He had answers for so many things I had been wondering about—not just education—and I just kept saying to myself, 'Oh, OK now I understand, now I get it.' I started to really regret that I hadn't encountered Steiner earlier. He explained myths and old folk tales, and things about science and history, and not only explained it in easy language, but he connected them together. Reading him, I feel as if I were able to look backstage at a theater to all the ropes and stage tricks behind the changing scenery of all of life.

"He's written piles and piles of extremely complicated things, on all kinds of topics. Not only is it exceedingly complex, it's very specific, so much that your head starts to spin. But there is not even one single contradiction to it. I thought that it would be impossible to write all this if he had just made it up. And because of that, I felt that

I could really, really trust him, I could rely on what he has said.

"But for humans today, there are so many things that Steiner has written about that seem quite unbelievable, that could seem suspicious or untrue. You have to develop enough trust in him first, reading about something like education, before you can read other things. The need to develop that trust reminds me of something that I read when I was in Nepal. I found a book at the Shanti-kuti lodge by a man named Shinran, the person who originated the Jodo Shinshu sect of Buddhism in the thirteenth century. An amazing person. You could say that he was like a modern person—he didn't believe the more metaphysical things his teacher said. But Hounen, his teacher, said that if you prayed to the Amida Buddha he would help you. Shinran wrote that because his teacher believed it, and he knew and trusted him, he believed in it too." She stops, then says, "This way of believing is an extremely important thing."

"Important to you?"

"Me, of course, but to all modern people, actually, it's a very important thing."

"Why is that?" I ask.

"Because for us today, we no longer understand the spiritual world. Even if someone tells us about it, we think it's probably a lie. That's how we think. We cannot sense

© Junko Motoyama

and feel that world directly. But there are people alive who do. So it's a question for each of us: if I absolutely trust and have faith in *this* person, and if *this* person is saying it, then it's not a mistake."

"So modern people don't do that?"

"No. For example, when they read the things that Gautama Siddhartha Buddha said that are rational, and are explained with a lot of reasoning, everybody is able to believe them. But those more spiritual, fantastical things

"I finally understood that I couldn't avoid working to provide for myself, but that can also be a wonderful thing, a beautiful thing."

Atsuko Watanabe • 91

much better than I. We modern people always think that we are more clever and more intelligent than others.

"But I don't recommend Steiner to anybody because many people can read his books and not get the importance at all."

"Why is that," I ask, "if he is so amazing?"

"The reason I personally believe something is 'correct' is because that is what is necessary for me now, to grow. . . . Something may be truth for me, but to someone else it's not truth."

"But how can that be, if it's truth?" I ask.

"The kinds of thoughts that are close to where you are will seem true to you." She pauses, then adds, "I think there's a *width* to truth, and it's very wide. *This* is truth, and this also is truth, and this too is truth. This is because we are evolving, and also at the same time God is evolving, along with us."

One of Steiner's main influences on Atsuko was his idea about what it means to succeed in this life. "Getting famous or rich by painting pictures or winning prizes—," she explains, "these things have no value at all. It's not important to focus on what people think of me. That is not what this life is for."

Hearing her say this brings to mind my recent interview with Atsuko's mother, Michi, now almost ninety. I've met her many times. She's a compact, earthy

"Painting flowers was to help me evolve, maybe, though I was not aware of it. The actions each of us needs to take for our development are different."

he says he experienced, the ones written in the sutras, modern people ignore that part. They just ignore it!" There's even a tinge of frustration in Atsuko's voice, as if she might be exasperated at our arrogance. "But to those parts too, I feel I should give my faith. It's totally rude to say that because you cannot understand it, you will ignore it.

"I really believe," she says now, laughing at having to say such an obvious thing, "that Gautama Siddhartha is much more intelligent, and much more spiritual, and woman with short gray hair—muscular and tough—who in her eighties still spends sweltering days in midsummer pulling weeds and digging in the garden. Over the years I had seen her at different occasions, and since she always greeted me with such a warm smile and told all kinds of stories about plants and their uses, I thought she was in total agreement with the way Atsuko had chosen to live her life. Thinking to find out more about Atsuko's childhood, and to get her opinions, I asked Michi if I could interview her. But almost as soon as the interview began, Michi told me, "I really hate the way she lives."

"Really?!" I said, pulling my head back. "You do?"

"They don't have any money at all. They should live a normal life. Normal is best, I think." And then she adds, shaking her head, "It all started when she went off to Afghanistan. That was the beginning of her living that strange kind of life."

I find out later in the interview that she has the same opinion about Atsuko's brother, who is a well-off lawyer and lives in Osaka, and that makes me speculate that Michi's opinions may perhaps have more to do with a mother's usual disappointments about how her children have turned out, or perhaps just a normal cultural hesitation about speaking too well of one's own children.

Later, I ask Atsuko about her mother's opinion.

"It's natural for a mother to worry about her children's economic situation," Atsuko says, almost as though she were scolding me for being so dense. "But she's a very normal person, and very innocent. She completely accepts society's way of thinking as it is given to her. She listens to what everyone around her is saying without logically thinking about what is the better choice, and she adopts the normal world's definition of success. She's very typical for her era."

"Is this what you meant about not wanting a 'normal way of living'?"

"That is part of it; most people spend their time relating entirely to things that are made solely for the purpose of keeping the economy spinning, of making money for someone, such as television shows, and eating food that's not good for them. And to get that money, everyone throws away their own time that was free before, even if the work they do is not useful. Everyone around them thinks it's natural and normal. Even though they're incredibly busy on the physical, body level, moving around all the time, they are empty on the level of the spirit."

"So why do they do it, do you think?"

"Because they don't stop to consider, 'Why is it that I as a human am alive?'"

~

After encountering Steiner, Atsuko converted to Christianity, though as she has told me, her way of belief is quite different from much official doctrine. "I don't believe, for example, that we have only one life and either go to heaven or hell. I believe that we pass through different incarnations and gather up abilities, passing from one life to the next. 'Hell' is what happens to you after you die, and all the things you have done to hurt other people are played back, except that they are being done to you. A concept such as 'sin' just means those things that get in your way of moving to another level."

I remember being surprised when first meeting her to find that in this land of very few Christians, this extremely progressive woman had chosen not only Christianity, but Catholicism, perhaps one of its most traditional forms. "I became a Catholic because I was interested in those teachings and practices that might have remained intact, passed down century by century all the way through from Jesus Christ himself. I wanted to understand what, specifically, are the essential elements of Christianity and what has been mixed in later by ordinary people. Also, I figure that there's a reason it's the biggest, most widely practiced form."

"So then are you satisfied with the Catholic Church?"

"Absolutely not!" she retorts, as if I've said something absurd. "But I don't *expect* much from Catholicism. Probably higher up in the hierarchy there are people who understand the mystical parts, otherwise Catholicism couldn't have continued all these centuries. It would have died out. But these days religion for most people is more like a kind of ethics. They don't really think about miracles much, although I'm sure some people are looking into it somewhere in the church."

Atsuko reads widely about all faiths, and is always eager to enter into discussion with people with other beliefs. She once hosted an American monk in the Thai Buddhist tradition at her house for several days. She would ask him why he chose Thai Buddhism, and how he maintained his strict observances such as total celibacy, never touching cash, only eating what was offered to him, not laboring or earning money, and how he kept to his tenets for years at a time.

"I was very inspired by his piety," she says, "and his earnestness about his spirituality. There was a kind of . . ." she pauses, searching for a word, "a purity about him, I felt. He followed the rules of his Buddhist order strictly, even though he may or may not have agreed with all of those rules, or understood their purpose. I think this is extremely important—spirituality cannot always be about analysis and comprehension."

When I ask her if she plans to travel again to India, she tells me that the most important journey for her would be to do the Christian pilgrimage of *Santiago De Compostela* in northern Spain. "There is a devotion and faith in those pilgrims that we lack here in Japan. I want to understand the root of their faith. Doubt is an easy thing in the modern world—the culture today encourages you to question everything—but belief is so much more difficult to achieve."

One of the things that she says has been most useful to her about reading Steiner is that he explained specific empirical methods to develop perception of the spiritual world, which he says is as concrete and real as our own. "It's very similar to us having eyes such that we can see things, or having ears to hear. So if you want to perceive that other world, there's a necessity for something like an ear or an eye. But in this era we don't have that kind of perceptual organ. So it's necessary to create such a thing. And to do that you need to do practices or training."

"You said that five hundred years ago, people were able to see that world, and now they can't."

"That's right."

"So then humans are *not* evolving?"

"No, they are. Steiner wrote that in order to evolve or progress, it was necessary for people to first become unable to see that world, because long ago they could

not see material things as clearly as we can. It was like they were in the middle of a fog. But they could really see the immaterial world, the world of spirits. Since it was necessary for humans to be able to sharply see the world of the material, to get rid of the fog, we had to lose half of our ability to see the world of spirits. And now," she taps the table, "that we alive today can correctly see material things, we have to learn again how to see that mystic world. We can't go any further in the materialistic direction: we are in a crisis period. We have to be able to see *both* worlds. That is the path that we must walk."

"That's interesting."

"It *is* interesting! Doesn't that make sense?" There's such a sureness to her.

"But why did we have to see material things so clearly in the first place?"

"We came to this world of the material, so there is something we have to achieve here."

"What is that?"

She pauses a long time. "Probably something . . . *artistic.*"

"What do you mean?"

"We have to bring things from the spiritual world and cause them to permeate, to saturate the world of the material. There's some necessity for humans to do this."

Atsuko Watanabe • 95

"So they're not already there?"

"Not yet."

"And it's possible for humans to put them in?"

"That is one way of saying it . . . " she says. "And that's why we have to make effort, expend our energy doing it. And we can do this consciously, or perhaps even without knowing it."

"So do you think we humans are here to move 'up'?"

After a long, long hesitation, she answers, "*Probably* we are coming and going. You see, that other world is incredibly complicated as well. Even this plane is unbelievably complex; therefore the plane just above us certainly is not simple either. Most people think it's monotone. But that's like someone who looks at the ocean and sees the surface and thinks it's just water. But we know the ocean is just as complex as here above ground."

While I am taking this in, she continues, "What Theravada Buddhists believe is that you are sacrificing now in order to have an easier life in the next incarnation, but I think the sacrifice is not individual, but for the evolution of everything and everybody. But there's no consciousness of giving up or sacrificing. Everyone is joined in the evolution of the universe; conscious of this or not, they have their role. It's like a grain of sand: if you look at it,

you think it is not an interesting thing, but a sandy beach, that's wonderful. If each grain of sand thought, 'I'm going to get myself off this boring beach and do my own thing,' there'd be no beach at all."

"Is that what you meant when you said you wanted to be more like a plant yourself?"

"Yes, some seeds sacrifice themselves so that other seeds survive. There are different ways of sacrificing for the progression of all others. Some people stay in the human realm for the time being. Some are faster, and they pull us along. You could say they are the leaders for us. Their lives, and their way of living their lives, is a sacrifice, just like it is necessary to have tens of thousands of painters with talent to have a Picasso. All the ones who sell pictures on the street, they all have their roles, and without them, no Picasso. There are many saints in India, and almost all of them are anonymous. On some occasions there's a necessity for them to make themselves known. They are preparing the next world; they are bringing the 'form' to a higher level—if there even is a form. Or you could say that they are evolving the form of what it is to be a human."

"So are we supposed to *do* something special, do you think?"

"As long as we live naturally and don't just work for our own profit, we are progressing. That's why I am always concerned for people who are relating only to money, or work in stocks. But . . . " she adds after a long pause, "perhaps I look at this only from the near distance, and perhaps narrowly. Maybe they do this so someone else can accomplish something else. I don't really know."

"So how does this relate to your life?" I ask.

"When I was in college I was drawing plants. I didn't have a spiritual life. I was trying to achieve something, but I was half conscious. What I was doing was actualized as painting. It gelled as painting. Maybe in your case, Andy, it is writing. There was some wish, some desire, some idea, or impulse to do better. Everyone has it. Painting was to help me evolve, maybe, though I was not aware of it. The actions each of us needs to take for our development are different.

"If you give all your energy to something, that action is evolving you, whatever you are doing. Just like in Hinduism, there are many yogas: shakti yoga, karma yoga, hatha yoga. If you use up all of what you were given, and give your best in your normal, daily life, then naturally and automatically you will come closer; some spirituality will appear. The interesting thing is that people, all with different levels of development and with different needs, are all humans alive at the same time on the same earth."

© Junko Motoyama

~

As I've been thinking about Atsuko's life, I imagine that she's saved herself a lot of regrets, the kind of regrets many people have later when they don't do what they know will be best for their lives. But when I ask her, it turns out I'm wrong again.

"My life is strewn with regrets!"

"Really?"

"People of our modern era are focused on 'having fun.' Before, humans did what they needed to do, and if pleasure came their way, they welcomed it."

absolute conviction. It's almost frightening, her intensity. "I can at the very least say that even if it isn't much, I've made some progress." And then, finally she adds, in a very sweet voice, "And that's good. Because I have regrets, I have done well."

As the old wooden clock strikes its resonant brass tones and we finish the last of the tea, I say to her that maybe more people would live this way if only they knew how much fun it could be.

Never hesitant to correct a misconception, she replies that she didn't make her choices based on ideas of enjoyment.

"People of our era are focused on 'having fun.' I think that's a totally modern concept. Before, humans did what they needed to do, and if pleasure came their way they welcomed it. But enjoyment was not the purpose of life then. Now we need everything to be entertaining. When it ceases to be entertaining, then we stop doing it."

"So do you think people today have gotten more greedy?"

"It's not that the greed has changed since long ago, but that the chance to actually get these things, to satisfy our greed has increased, so that so many, many people are able to do so. And as a result, people have begun to pursue their greed avidly, and to chase after it. A long

"Absolutely!" (Her tone is, 'What the hell did you think?') "I'm *always* thinking, 'I should have done it this way, or that other way.'"

"Really? I'm so sad to hear that."

"You are?" She looks at me almost as if I were some kind of fool. "Because I've made progress since when I was young, that is why I have regrets. People who have made no progress," she says with something close to derision in her voice, "look back and say, 'I'm so satisfied with that! My life was wonderful!'" She's speaking rapidly, with

Stone, vase with a branch of red berries, notebook, paint brushes, telephone.

time ago most people didn't have a chance to own cars, or to win prizes for their art; that was only for a few. Now everyone wants that. But there's no *need* for that kind of desire. These days, as Japan has gotten rich, even people like us, who are poor, can have a car. And for me, I don't need any more than that. When I think about the people I saw when traveling, or the people I hear about on the news, the people who really are living in poverty, I say to myself, 'I have *more* than enough.' I have a feeling of 'I'm sorry' toward them, living the way I do. If I were to live in too much excess, it would just feel bitter in my heart."

After a moment of consideration, Atsuko says, "What I really want is more *time*."

I look up at the clock. We've been talking now for almost four hours. I compare this with how hard it is for my English students to make time for even a one hour lesson, once a week. People are insanely busy here.

Then Atsuko adds, "Long ago people probably didn't have time either." I imagine rural life of two centuries ago, peasants struggling all day long, every day, just to provide enough to survive. "They were really busy; they couldn't realistically expect or seek having more things *or* time. Now, as long as you don't desire too many things, you can have some time."

I recall now what Atsuko said years ago when I first met her, that her priority has been to have the time to muse and reflect and really think about things. She's been making this her priority for years. The results, I speculate, are the subtlety of her thinking, and the deeply considered nature of her choices. Perhaps it is simply about making sure that you have time for yourself. "Most people have directed their attention toward having *things* more than time, and that's why they are always running."

"But you have a lot to do as well," I say, thinking of her time weeding, or hand-peeling chestnuts, or cooking, or doing her environmental work.

"I do, but while I'm doing them, my spirit is free. No one is telling me, 'Work!' That's the most important thing. And in any case, I didn't choose this life for the pleasure of it, but because it seemed to be the right way to spend the life that I was given."

I consider that Atsuko is one of the most buoyant and lively people I know. Her life is full of laughter. Yet this happens, it seems, without her trying to pursue it, without it being her goal.

"It's the same way with comfort," she continues. "As I told you before, in Nepal and India, I could see that millions of people were living without a lot of material things that we have in Japan. And living alongside such people, I knew that the purpose of my life was not to live in the maximum amount of comfort."

Again the seeming contradiction causes me to

smile. Her life, it seems to me, is suffused in the tranquillity that can be found only in nature—breathing crisp mountain air early in the morning, listening to the gentle calls of the night insects on a warm summer's evening, or resting her eyes on the colors and textures of an old wooden farmhouse instead of the harsh geometry and neon of a city. It is as though through her practice of not grasping for either pleasure or comfort, she has both in abundance. Sometimes, like this evening, the pleasure is just that of sitting and talking deep into the night.

It is, now that I think of it, a kind of comfort that we humans could practice in perpetuity for thousands of years.

Kogan Murata

With the flurry of stimuli that is this world, sometimes it's hard to know what's important. The ten thousand distractions hold out their promises and we forget what we really need. How can we avoid getting lost in the supermarket of diluted ideas? For many years I had been nibbling birdlike around the edges of a lot of Buddhist thought—a book here, a meditation retreat there. Many of the ideas seemed deeply persuasive, yet the discourse of Buddhism sometimes seemed unnecessarily ponderous. The more time I spent with the exuberant Kogan Murata, the more I knew I could bring the insights about nonattachment into a life that was decidedly not monastic, and not sacrifice one iota of enthusiasm for being alive.

"You could say that I'm an addict," laughs Kogan Murata with his big-energy grin, infectious and slightly wild. "If I play, I feel good. The more I play, the more I feel good. So I just keep playing. I'd rather be doing this than anything else. That's why I don't have a job. It's just better to play the flute."

We are sitting together on the tatami mat floor of this almost empty, sunlight-drenched house. The present seems especially luminous here, high in the jagged mountains of central Japan. As we talk Murata holds his bamboo flute against his body, leaning the long piece of amber-colored wood on his shoulder and rubbing camellia oil into it with boundless affection. He has been playing this instrument, more meditation than music, for over ten years, sometimes up to eight hours a day. "They're more sutras than songs," he says.

"This next piece is one of the very oldest ones," he tells me. "It's over twelve hundred years old."

Twelve hundred years. I try to imagine what that means. When he begins to play, I feel some of that ancientness echoing through me. It is a sound that makes you really experience the silence. Long, low drones slip up into higher octaves without any forewarning. Both rough and pure, falling in and out of refinement, the notes are at times cavernous and awesome, and at others clear like a bell. There's a faint tremolo, and the overtone of a whisper. The music is powerful and transporting, and yet just hollow breath through a tube of bamboo. If anything can hint at that ineffable term "emptiness," this sound would be it.

The instrument itself is stunning. The long bore of the flute is flaxen brown, and at the thick base, where the bamboo plant used to join the roots, rough knots gleam through the weathered finish. Over the years, Murata tells me, the color will continue to deepen, as will the richness of the tone.

Murata's flute is not technically a *shakuhachi* flute, but a *kyotaku*, which is almost twice again as long as a *shakuhachi*, and less smooth inside. Not really a "musical instrument" at all, it is considered a tool for both practicing meditation and transmitting its insights. To get a tone from it one more breathes over the opening than blows. Being so long, it's very hard to get the *kyotaku* to sound at all.

Although the harmonics and intonation of Murata's playing are sometimes otherworldly, his personality is enthusiastic in the extreme. With his big toothy smile and wide protruding ears, his dramatic Kabuki-like gestures, his rambunctious "Ay-ya Baba!" when he greets me, I can see why he once thought he would be a street performer when he grew up.

Yet it would be a mistake to think that Murata is not serious. In some ways, he's one of the most serious people I've ever met. He's serious about growing rice, pouring his whole life energy into the care of his rice paddies, working for hours in the broiling sun of midsummer Japan. And he is obsessed with his playing of the flute, giving over some days to it entirely, especially in the winter when work outdoors takes up less of his time. "You have to go mad when you are playing the flute," he proclaims. "You have to do it all the time. Otherwise it's meaningless!"

By making his own charcoal for heating, gathering all

the firewood for the cold winters in the mountains without a chainsaw (carrying the wood from the forest to his house on his back) and, with his partner, Sayaka, growing not only vegetables but beans, squashes, potatoes, peanuts, and all their grains (and then grinding the wheat and making the bread), they with their young son, Kohei, manage to survive on an almost unbelievable $3,500 a year. The family has taken self-sufficiency to a level I had not thought possible in our modern age.

This is the third home I have visited Murata and Sayaka at in the fifteen years since I first met them. They've been living here since they left an old farmhouse amidst the tea plantations of the southern island of Kyushu, where Murata studied for seven years with the renowned bamboo flute master Koku Nishimura. Before that, when I first met them, the young couple was living at the top of an impossibly steep valley in an almost inaccessible corner of Shikoku Island, looking from their front veranda down thousands of feet into a rain-drenched canyon of grayish blue trees and hazy shifting mists.

Now they are here in yet another forgotten corner of Japan, in the widest part of the main island of Honshu, the high mountainous backbone of the archipelago—a place where, looking out over the long vistas at granite-peaked mountaintops in all directions, it is almost impossible to believe you are on an island at all.

Sayaka is certainly less vociferous than Murata. She looks on amusedly at our conversations, and when she occasionally does feel talkative, contributes hilarious imaginary scenarios to help me understand something Murata is telling me, especially when he is being particularly feisty or opaque.

She is definitely on board with this life in the mountains, spending perhaps even less money than he does, if that can be imagined. It's almost like a game for them, trying to see how little they can spend. Sayaka is an ac-

"It is a wonder to grow rice!" Murata exclaims. "Exciting!"

It's not impossible to find a sturdy old house in the countryside to rent surrounded by fertile soil and abundant water.

complished fiction author; she won a local prize and had her novella published a few years ago, with the prefectural governor himself writing a recommendation.

She likes to cook, and loves the garden. She enjoys time with her son, and spends almost as much time as Murata out in the rice fields. Perhaps even more than any of the other people in this book, she really does live *simply*.

But when I ask several times if I might be able to write about her, she smiles her broad smile and says,

"Here. Wouldn't you like to have a bit of tea?" Even I am not so insensitive to Japanese cultural practice that I don't understand what she means.

∼

One of the reasons Murata is so vital—although unhurried in every single way—is, I think, that he has always been in such direct contact with the physical world. He has worked jobs on oil tankers and in construction, and as a boy he played shortstop (I can still see that in him now—fast reflexes, sinewy muscles, and his ability to pivot on a dime). He spent more than a decade of winters doing ski rescue for the Red Cross, and has ridden thousands of miles by motorbike from the far north to the far south of Japan. He loved camping as a boy, and still sleeps outside in a tent many nights with his son, Kohei.

When he was small, he'd run home after school and instantly go out again playing Tarzan or war in the vacant fields around his house. With his crowd of ten or twenty friends, he would run off to the mountains outside of the city. "We'd play tag or 'explorer' or run through the woods looking for acorns or crawl under the shrines and temples—it's so cool and quiet and dark there in the summer."

But school was harder for him. "I loved books. I had lots of books. I just hated studying. Besides gym class, I got a lot of bad marks. That was difficult for me. But as for playing . . . no problem at all," he says, followed with his usual laugh.

But, Murata says, there was one thing he read all the time: the encyclopedia. Even now he has that same set of volumes, from 1961, out on a shelf right next to where we are talking. "I still read it a lot."

He pulls one out to show me as we sit on the tatami mat floor. "*Soooo* many interesting things! Napoleon . . . and snakes, and Queen Elizabeth, and the life of ants, and what the ancients' view of the universe was . . . " He's paging through, pointing at all these photos. Kohei, who has been circling the edge of our conversation looking every part the rascal, starts to let his curiosity overcome his hesitancy, acting more and more intrigued as his father gets more enthusiastic. "Here's stuff on the samurai period. Porcupines. Here's mummies, from Egypt. Mummies! This really widens your imagination. It's why I wanted to travel. I said to myself, 'I want to go here! I want to go here too!' It's limitless."

Now Kohei has his own volume down from the shelf, and he's poring over it quietly as we talk. Watching this child I'm struck by how natural boyhood is, and amazed to see a child in the twenty-first century so connected to the physical world. There's no computer, no TV, no video games. (I have to remind myself that this is *Japan*.) He plays outside, and makes toys out of bamboo (he nailed me with his bamboo-plunger squirt gun when I arrived). He goes fishing all summer long, and tells me about different kinds of fish. It seems like the way things should be. In the middle of our conversation, suddenly he almost shouts, "Hey Dad! What's this?!" pointing at a picture in the big book.

"Volcano!!" Murata shouts back. "It goes *doh-Kaaan!*" as he throws his hands dramatically up in the air, and Kohei looks up with a gleam of fire in his eyes. I think, could a video of a volcano or a TV special possibly do any better than this?

Murata now tells me that ever since he was little he's always been interested in sound. "My uncle bought me a trumpet when I was a kid. It was really just a toy, but it started there." Growing up in the late fifties, he got interested in records, 45s: the Ventures, Paul Anka, and the Beatles. Then he tilts his head back, remembering, "And . . . ahhh Presley! "Jailhouse Rock." It was a completely fresh feeling for me in the fourth grade."

I smile, thinking about his journey from listening to *Your Hit Parade* to what he does now, following one of the most ancient musical traditions in the world, imbued with a deeply Asian Buddhist philosophy, playing tunes from seven to thirteen centuries old, and looking like a shaven-headed monk.

In high school, he spent a lot of time in used bookstores, picking up copies of the old Chinese classics, about which he still has strong feelings. "Confucius: not interesting. But Lao Tsu and Chuang Tsu, really unusual. They turned Confucius' morality completely upside down and backward."

"So was it those writers that made you choose such a nonconformist life?"

"No. It started with a misunderstanding. My mother told me again and again that to be the same as others was not a good thing," he laughs. "What she meant was that I should try to exceed them, get good marks in school, and get to the top. But I thought that she meant I should do my damnedest to not do anything other people did."

He tried to get into university, wanting to study philosophy, and took one of Japan's high-pressure entrance exams, twice.

"I failed the test," he exclaims cheerily. "I didn't study at all!"

Also, he says, he already knew he wanted to go overseas.

"Were your parents opposed to that?"

"They were. My father was even more against it than my mother. He asked me, 'What possible meaning could there be in you doing this?' But I told them, 'It's not your problem. It's my own behind, and I can wipe it myself.'"

～

He eventually got a job painting on a Japanese oil tanker. Large ships must be protected from the salt air, and that requires someone to repaint them all the time, covering over rust spots, chipping off peeling paint. It's grueling work. Wherever there are ships, there is someone continuously painting them.

"Why did you choose that kind of job?"

"It was totally a calculation. I could make the most amount of money in the shortest amount of time doing it."

When he saved up enough, he headed for Europe on the Trans-Siberian Railroad. It was 1974 and Murata was twenty-one years old, about to start his long career of living on almost nothing. He was gone for almost four years. Between three-month stints working at a youth hostel in Heidelberg, he'd shoot off somewhere else, one time to Scandinavia, another time to Greece, sleeping outside in the parks at night.

"Why did you sleep outside?"

"I like it! That's why. I don't know." He says with an almost 'What-kind-of-answer-were-you-expecting?' attitude.

In one sense this is the answer he has to almost everything. Why does he do it? Because he likes it. I find the approach completely refreshing.

"Sleeping outside is great in Turkey and Greece and Israel. There are lots of old ruins; you can sleep out among them."

"The police didn't come?"

"No. But once there was a dog." He makes barking sounds, baring his teeth.

Then it was on to Syria and Iran. He went everywhere and had infinite time because he didn't need anything, and didn't have anything he was trying to accomplish, or live up to, or to prove, or to be. He was already completely free. Even today he is thoroughly comfortable inside his skin, something not all that common (in my experience) in achievement-oriented Japan.

In 1977 Murata made his way back to Japan. He'd work any job, doing construction, or working at a ski resort, just to make some money. "I would be skiing every day, all day. I didn't really do any 'work' at all."

The next year, he headed back overseas, and this time it was to India first. He had planned to go onward from there, but, as he says, "I looked around and decided that a country more interesting than this could not possibly exist."

For the next ten years, it was back and forth to India. He could get a six-month visa, and when that ran out, he would return to Japan and work the winter in the ski resort. When the season was over, he'd head off around Japan by motorcycle, living light. Whatever he did, he did it, he says, *isshokenmei,* a word that translates loosely as "with all your heart," but a more literal translation would be "hanging your whole life on it."

And then as soon as he could, he'd get on a plane and go back to India.

"But what did you do all day when you were in India?" I ask him.

"Eating," he says plainly, in English. "Eating delicious food."

"So what about going to see temples or Buddhist ruins, or things like that?"

"Nah, you get tired after a month or so of looking at temples. That's just an outside thing. My interior didn't change at all. Even if I saw it, I asked myself, 'What do I *do* with this?'

"So what did you do?"

"Mostly talk to the Indians. It's great. Just *talking* to them. Indians are really interesting. And I started to learn some Hindi."

"You studied Hindi?"

"I didn't study!" He laughs at every third thing I ask him. "I just picked it up, talking."

"So you talked to people, walked around, and . . . ?"

"You can look at people for hours in India. Watching human beings is the most interesting thing."

"So you would wake up, eat breakfast, and then do what until lunch?"

"Slowly." He answers. As if "slowly" itself was an action. "Then I'd walk around town, drink tea."

"Then after lunch?"

"I'd take a nap." He says, and I laugh.

"So all those years you lived that kind of life?"

He pauses for a second, as if just thinking it over for himself. "Yeah, I did, that's true," giggling as if slightly embarrassed. "To another person's eyes . . . perhaps they might have wondered whether all that added up to anything. But to me, it was a really good feeling. And India is so hot, you really don't feel like getting very active, right? I just gazed out into space, drinking tea . . . "

"But you didn't feel like you should be accomplishing something, studying or . . . "

"Nope," he shakes his head, considers a little bit more, and then adds, "Nahh . . . "

". . . you didn't go to concerts?"

Brightening up, as if remembering, "Concerts, yeah, I did do that. That was exciting!"

Listening to Murata, I think about how snookered a lot of us get by the trance of "accomplishment," with new books published on time-management every year and the squadrons of consultants we hire to help us get even more productivity out of each day. As if that's what we are alive for.

"So did living in India change your personality?"

"Hmm," he thinks out loud. "I really got a lot more patient," he says, using a word in Japanese that encompasses both restraint and tolerance. "I was able to endure a lot more."

"What did you have to endure?"

"Ha!" he begins. "At first I would get angry so quickly. It's hot there, right?" He's looking straight at me across the table. I know what he's talking about now: the constant battles with taxi drivers or shopkeepers, each attempting to get more money than was initially agreed.

"Oooh," he says, using one of my favorite Japanese idioms, "my stomach stood up!" Murata growls, "I got so like *this*"; demonstrating, he crunches up his face, all the muscles red and tight, squinting with one eye, the other one wide open with the eyebrow up over it, and his hands in fists above his head.

"And I started to think, 'This is pointless.' And I got tired. Incredibly tired. Probably it was the same for you in

India, right, Andy? I must have lost twenty pounds in my first month there. So then I decided, 'This is a total loss.' After all, the argument was usually over five or ten rupees, I figured, ten or twenty yen [about 10–20 cents]. So I decided, 'Forget it. If they overcharge me, I just pay it.'"

"Really?!" I say, leaning back in disbelief.

"Yeah, they'd raise the price, and I'd give it to them, and buy them a cup of chai too. We'd talk for a couple of hours. And then," he says, with a satisfied grin on his face, switching to English, "Everything is getting peaceful! I was relaxed, all the time. Can you imagine letting your head and heart get like that? 'You bastard, you lied to me!' and all that. So I'd give him the money, and then go and get tea for him. 'Drink some chai. Take some time. Drink, drink!' Really, it's an incredible coincidence to meet this rickshaw driver. And then he would say 'Thank you' to me. That's better, isn't it? I just thought back to my old way, fighting with them all the time, and I thought I was just such an *idiot!* Ten or twenty yen!"

"But if the motor rickshaw driver charged you twice the price, you just gave it to him?!"

"Sure! I'd say, ' You want it? OK, here it is. No problem.'" Murata's voice is now utterly sunny and happy. "Over something small like that, getting all . . . " he makes his face of mock fury again, eyes bulging out . . . "like that, it's just a bad bargain. So I changed. My way

of thinking turned *all* the way around."

Then suddenly, completely calm Murata says, "I developed a solemn principle: 'If you go to India, getting into fights is completely prohibited.' And that's why even today, I feel that *whatever* is fine. I have no credo now, no principle to insist on."

"What do you mean?"

"You know, there are all these 'isms,' right? That-ism and this-ism, all these beliefs. For me, however you want to do it is OK. People say, 'It must be this way, or that way.' But it's just a matter of taste, right?"

I think now about how well he gets along with the people living around him in this small community, or when he goes down to the city, seeing all the hurried businesspeople or fashion-conscious teenagers: their way of living doesn't bother his head a bit. Nor does what they may think of him alter his continual proclamations on the benefits of laziness.

He dons a wooden donation box that reads, "Without Existence, Without Extinction."

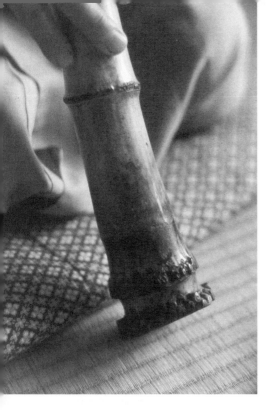

Murata's flute is both a tool for practicing meditation and transmitting its insights.

"Do you think," I ask him, "that your attitude is different than most Japanese people's?"

"Well, maybe. I stopped getting concerned about what other people were doing and saying. Before, I used think, 'Hey, that guy, why did he earn so much money?' Or, 'He went to that great place in India, or climbed Mt. Everest,' and so on. But after India, I thought, 'That's pretty meaningless.'" And then he adds, "At least for me. That's easier, and much more relaxing, isn't it? Because if you compare yourself to another person," he hangs his head and slumps his shoulders, demonstrating physically, "your energy goes down . . . You think, 'I'm defeated!' and the disappointment starts coming. But then I remember, I'm not studying for some entrance exam!"

Murata then tells me that after more than a decade of going back and forth to India, things began to change for him inside.

"At first, I thought I would just keep traveling, all the way till the end. But then," he says, laughing at himself, "I got tired of it. I just got tired. It was fun, of course, trekking in the Himalayas, absolutely so. But during the last two years in India I started to think, 'If I continue doing this, what is there for me?' You know what I mean? Repeating the exact same thing, again and again. And I began to suspect," he adds with a contemplative tone, "that maybe there wasn't anything." And that's the point where it all changed for me. Also, at about the same time, I started asking myself, 'What is the *most* important thing?' And I came to the answer, 'Eating.'"

Then, as many of us do, Murata started to read about all the chemicals used growing our food. "I thought, 'Shouldn't I grow it myself?'"

He had also always dreamed of living in the mountains. "It's actually an ancient Japanese ideal. In school we all read about these famous people in the Chinese and Japanese classics: go off to the mountains and live by yourself in a hut like a hermit; spend your day singing and reading poems. All Japanese people have this longing. It comes originally from Lao Tsu." Then he adds with his typical flair, "Hiding! Everyone yearns for this."

"So," I ask him, "You wanted to be one of the literati?"

"There's all kinds of forms: you can be a farmer, or do pottery, or be a woodcutter, or a painter."

I picture Murata as a little boy, wearing his regulation uniform, sitting at his schoolboy desk in conservative, economically aspiring, early 1960s Japan reading about such poet hermits in some digest-version textbook approved by the Ministry of Education intended to give children a few basic facts about their nation's cultural history. But Murata stops on one particular sentence, written by someone eight hundred years ago, "escaping the dust of the world," and looks up at the ceiling, dreaming. I consider the magic of words coming off a page from another century and inspiring an actual life right now. And then I think, in contrast, of times when I've found myself on a crowded train in Tokyo or Osaka on my way to interview one of the people in this book. I remember looking at the businessmen all around me, their suits and ties perfect, but exhaustion hanging over their faces, pallid and overdrawn like a bank account, and I wonder if, like Murata says, they also dream this dream.

This ideal Murata speaks about, I mention to him now, is very similar to that of ancient India, where the texts talk about retreating into contemplation as the fourth and last stage of life.

"Yes," Murata says, "for after you finish your working life, in your fifties or sixties . . . "

"But you wanted to do it sooner?" I ask.

Laughing he says, "Yes!" And then he adds, solemn as if he's quoting something, "Whatever you *can* do, it's best to do it soon."

And he's right: any one of us could die tomorrow.

And then Murata adds, "Living in 'the world' is a pain. You have to work a job. You have to do this, that and the other thing. So if you want to be free of all that, it's best to head into the mountains."

"When did you finally leave India?"

"In 1988. I graduated!"

I smile. While all of Japan is racking up credentials and certificates, Murata has graduated from drinking tea all day in India. Although one could view Murata's years in India as a complete waste of time, for him that kind of a life was a foundation for how he lives now. When he needs to spend hours out in the rice paddies in the blazing sun on a humid day, he's got that patience. When he collects firewood in the fall for the coming mountain winters, and has to cut a big log with a handsaw and walk it all the way home, he's not cursing the time it takes, or wishing he had a chainsaw to speed up the process. And he can spend up to eight hours a day practicing the flute. He's enjoying himself thoroughly. For myself, without his background, I know it would be hard. How did he entertain himself in India? By walking, by talking, by not even "entertaining" himself at all. And whenever I visit, Murata always has time to talk. There's no rush inside of him, no conflict in his soul between talking all day and some other thing he might have to do.

As I listen to him, espousing the gospel of taking it easy, the absolute belief in doing only what he loves, and doing it slowly, I all of a sudden notice the muscles in his forearms. No rush, no push, yet he is *full* of life and energy. Fifty-five years old and as strong as a twenty-year-old. Stronger, perhaps.

~

Finding a house in rural Japan to rent for almost nothing is not as easy as I first heard it was when I came here. True, the depopulation of the countryside as people moved to the cities had left thousands of finely built old residences standing empty and in need of care. One mountain village I know of experienced a population drop from nine thousand to three thousand people over the last fifty years. So great is the preference for the city these days, many rural people even feel ashamed of being from the countryside.

Some of those houses have fallen too far into disrepair to live in, but the main reason that many recently urbanized families are not willing to rent their houses to strangers has to do with their graves. The homes are ancestral, and it has been the custom for many generations to inter family members' ashes next to the old house. So in some respects, traditionally raised rural people may feel that they are letting strangers move in with their ancestors, who they believe to still be there.

Yet it is not impossible to find a sturdy old structure, surrounded by fertile soil and abundant water, and some families are glad to have someone who will live in the house and take care of it. This was what Sayaka and Murata—who had met in India—began looking for when they returned. At first they stayed with some friends, Atsuko and Gufu Watanabe, who lived more than an hour and a half from the closest city. A third friend found an empty house on his first day looking, but Murata and Sayaka couldn't find an appropriate one for almost a year. "I went around looking every day. Nobody would rent to us," Murata says with a note of frustration. "It's difficult."

When they did find one, it was even further back into the mountains. Although the island of Shikoku is the smallest of the four main islands of Japan, and although it appears as little more than a tiny brush stroke on a map of the world, I was flabbergasted the first time I was taken to their place how far one can drive into the backcountry. I remember driving with Atsuko, who first introduced me to Murata, winding through the steeply forested slopes, cresting over narrow pass after narrow pass, going by smaller and smaller villages, eventually crawling up a one-laned strip of pavement just wide enough to be called a road, passing the last few farmsteads before we reached their fine old house at the top of the valley and caught sight of the glowing smiles of Murata and Sayaka.

That first visit was in 1993. I had not yet even conceived of the idea of writing a book; I was just filled with the new joy of meeting such people, and with the beauty of their way of living. It was early fall and bright red flowers on tall stalks were in bloom along the rice terraces. The house itself was low with black-painted boards on the outside, and an old-styled mud floor room for cooking. Murata, I remember, was talking excitedly about how many cabbages he had been able to grow that season, and the potato crop was bounteous as well. I spent just one night there, joining Murata for one of Sayaka's savory meals of miso eggplant and roasted green peppers which we ate sitting on the weathered tatami mat floors, the valley gaping behind us through the open, *shoji*-screen doors. After dinner I was treated to a bath in an old-style tub, which I can only describe as resembling an upturned cast-iron bell under which Murata stoked a fire of sticks to heat the water.

By then Murata had already begun to make and play the bamboo flute, although years later he referred to the flutes he made in that era as "toys."

"It was a complete coincidence," he tells me when I ask him now about coming to the path of playing the bamboo flute. "I had been totally inside the 'do-re-mi' world of Western music all through my twenties. But in that house you first visited me in, one day by chance I heard the real sound of the *shakuhachi* on a classical music program on the radio. I thought, 'That is truly a Japanese person's sound.'"

It was this moment, after all the journeys through Europe, the Middle East, and India, after hundreds of miles of walking the Himalayas in Nepal, and of touring by motorbike all through the mountains of Japan, that Kogan Murata felt he had finally found his path in life, the path of "blowing Zen," of the Buddhist bamboo flute.

"And then at some point I decided it was necessary to have a guru," he says. I smile: he uses here the Indian term instead of the Japanese *sensei*. He's using it in its proper context. The root word in Sanskrit is from the verb *gur*, "to lift someone up."

"I went to a very famous player. He had played with the London Philharmonic. But," Murata says, shaking his head, "he wasn't my type. I knew when I saw his house. It was spotless, sparkling, and westernized. It wasn't my image at all. Also, he played the short one," referring to the standard *shakuhachi*, a term that refers, I find out, to the length of the bamboo.

Today's *shakuhachi* is a modernized version of the bamboo flute played in ancient China, made more similar to Western-style flutes with the coming of the Europeans. It is more symmetrical inside and can be disassembled, which changes the way the flute sounds. Murata finds it is too high-pitched and annoying.

"Then I heard of Koku Sensei; a friend had lent me his cassette. I went down south right away and I met him. And his house was fantastic. Wonderful."

"How?"

"It was all run-down and tatty! Made of wood, earth, and paper. So I decided right away. I asked to be his disciple. And he accepted me."

That was June, and by November he and Sayaka had moved far away, to the southern island of Kyushu to be near his new teacher.

I've seen Koku Nishimura's photograph, on the cover of the only recording Murata has of him, made in 1964. Just his visage is enough to make you stop and look closer. With a very long flowing white beard, heavy white eyebrows, and kindly eyes, he is the very image of a Japanese master. Though Nishimura lived in our own times, as I find out more about his life, it's easy to imagine such a person living a century ago.

He made his living as a wood-carver, and was an accomplished painter as well. He received his *kyotaku* flute training from a Zen monk of the Rinzai order whose name, Tani Kyochiku, literally translated means "Insane Bamboo." For ten years Nishimura walked over Japan as an alms-begging monk, and he made over two thousand *kyotaku* flutes by hand. He also held a black belt in Okinawan karate, and a black belt in Japanese fencing, or *kendo*. Murata tells me that he was "a true genius," and knowing Murata's zero tolerance for anything fake I imagine that Nishimura was one of those rare humans you meet only a few times in your life.

On their first meeting, Nishimura, who was then in his eighties, said to him, "Go find this exact kind of bamboo, and don't show your face here until you find it." He specified the age of the bamboo, the species, the length between the joints, and thickness of the walls of the piece Murata was to get. Then he sent him on his way. That was it.

But, says Murata, he never found the kind of bamboo his teacher had asked for.

Knowing how ubiquitous bamboo is in Japan, I ask, "Surely it can't be that hard to find?"

Murata's eyes widen, in mock indignation, a kind of "How *dare* you?" to his expression. "I looked every day, riding my bicycle around for two months and I could not find a single one."

"Well, did you find the groves he told you about?"

"Yes!" he almost shouts, leaving the implied "You

idiot" to his tone of voice. "That's not the issue. Bamboo is everywhere! The dimensions must be exact. I didn't *really* understand what a *kyotaku* was, that's why I couldn't find one."

"Could you find such a bamboo now?"

Suddenly smiling, Murata says, "Right away, of course!" snapping his fingers. "Before, I had no eye! That's the point. I was almost blind."

Eventually Murata went back to his teacher, admitting that he couldn't find it. "There was nothing I could do."

It turns out that Nishimura was fully aware that he wouldn't be able to find such a piece of bamboo. "It's a sort of test," says Murata, seriously. "You know, about Zen, right, when you want to enter a temple for training?"

In fact I have seen such a test illustrated in a book of beautiful black-and-white photographs published in the mid '60s: the would-be novice monk waits sitting on the cold steps outside of the temple for more than a week. "They just tell you, 'Get out! Go home. Don't come here.' As I said, it's a test."

I let on to Murata (though not stating it quite this strongly) that I have always thought treating potential students in such a way is autocratic and absurd—humiliating the person who wants to learn to meditate.

"No," says Murata, "it's very important. You have to

establish that you really want to do it. Otherwise it's a waste of the teacher's time. And your time. Anyway, you have to be crazy to play this kind of flute. If you're not crazy, forget it."

"So are you saying," I ask, knitting my eyebrows together, "that just by playing, you became able to *find* that specific kind of bamboo?"

His voice quiets, and with a softness that you might even call affection he murmurs, "Yes, yes, that's true." Then he says, looking up at me, "You probably don't understand, do you?"

I admit that I don't.

"It's how much you *love* it."

In my experience, the word "love" is not often heard from Japanese people, the preference being for terms such as "like," leaving the meaning implied.

"But," I say, "to play the flute and to find the correct kind of bamboo are different, right?" I ask.

"No! No difference at all. To play *is* to love. It's not just 'playing the flute.' You have to play with every part of

Murata tells me excitedly about how many cabbages he grew that season.

you, with everything in your heart. Just to mess around is pointless. You have to blow a hell of a lot, and then you begin to understand the bamboo."

As I absorb what he has said, he adds, "Anyway, I passed the test, and my *sensei* said, 'Here, I will lend you this one until you can find the right kind of bamboo yourself.' I was completely surprised. 'Really, Sensei?! Thank you so much!' It wasn't until years later that I found out that usually people have to buy the teacher's hand-made flutes for five hundred thousand or even a million yen [$5,000–$10,000]!"

"So," I ask, "what was your first lesson?"

"He didn't 'teach' me anything. He didn't say, as I had expected, hold your fingers here or shape your mouth like this. He simply told me to go home and play only this one note for the next half year. It was the lowest and most difficult one. He said, 'Don't waste your time coming back and forth.'"

"Only one note?" I ask.

"Yes, it was like he saw my entire character in one glance, like he was holding me in the palm of his hand, turning his head this way and that. He saw what I needed. And every time I came for a lesson, he watched me approach, carefully. Often he just said, 'Go home, don't come here!' My attitude wasn't right."

Murata tried every day just to make a sound for two months. For the first year he couldn't even reach all the holes with his fingers, they were so far apart.

"But why didn't your teacher show you how to hold it, what to do?"

"That's the Zen way: they don't teach. You are supposed to simply *do* it. It's like a *koan*. It was only once in three years that he spoke about how to hold my fingers or how to play."

"So when you went over there, what happened?"

"We just drank tea, and talked."

I try to imagine this. He had moved hundreds of miles, packing up everything—Sayaka agreeing to come along as well—and he and his teacher would just meet occasionally to drink tea.

"But what did you talk about?"

"We'd talk sometimes about Zen, or he'd tell me about his teacher, or about the history of the *kyotaku*, or sometimes 'just nothing' talk. But there was still some teaching there. He might just once slip in some important thing, with me barely noticing. I had to think hard to figure out what the message was behind one of his stories."

Eventually, Murata says, he learned the songs by listening to the recording he had. "I must have played that recording one thousand, or even two thousand times."

"And do you make up your own songs, you know, or just 'jam' sometimes?"

"I have no interest in that. Old tunes have centuries of refinement. I play those. If I'm in a bad mood, I can play those tunes as a person in a bad mood would. Another day, I play them as a person in a good mood would. There's plenty to discover in that. It's impossible to play them perfectly, of course, but to get *close* to perfect . . . there's a whole world in that.

"Some people write one new song after another. For me— I really don't know about other people—that would be shallow. There are perhaps forty 'classic' tunes. I've chosen about seven. I can play them over and over. I can spend the whole day doing that."

I shake my head, amazed: the humility in playing only seven songs. When I think of how attached I am to the idea of improvisation, I realize how profoundly hypnotized by twentieth-century American culture I have been, how I had thought any other way would be unbearable.

~

Murata has a wonderful style of written English. Though it's not his first language, his enthusiasm jumps off the page. I received this letter several years after Murata had moved south:

Cynthia, Andy, my Dearest!!!

Oh my Buddha! We haven't had a pen for long, long time to you, almost four years long. We moved here to this village two years ago. What we have done here: rebuild old musty farmer's house, cultivate rice pad, garden, field, join the community, of course blow the flute . . . etc. Quite same as before. My Buddha! We rent a big house with nine rooms! And a big wasted barn for 10,000 yen a month [$90]. Big deal isn't it!? So we have to get the Yen. We didn't care much about money because as you know we are so-called "stingy" by nature. Ha ha ha. But we need at least 20,000 yen a month . . . uuum too hard!

So I, Kogan Murata, began strolling house to house with the bamboo flute to beg money or food as a *komuso* monk. A beggar! Yes! I'm a beggar. Proudly a beggar. I find myself: I'm a *komuso* by nature since the beginning. Must be a mission! Yes because I feel so happy. Can't stop blowing the *kyotaku* more than one hundred times a day. Thanks Buddha! People gives me a charity or donation with sum of 10,000 yen on the average. Honorable Buddha! In addition,

Sayaka and Murata live on about $3,500 a year, taking self-sufficiency to a level I had not thought possible.

it's a good lesson for the flute. So I can't hardly stop being a *komuso*, maybe for life. To joyful life which we're going to. . . . Life is too short.

Well, brother and sister! Rice pad gets color to yellow, harvesting is just around the corner, but who knows? Possible zero? No problem! Sweet potato is big harvest . . . Burp!

You can come here to visit anytime. Please do so! You're always welcome!! You can come here and go to a hot spring with us, or go hiking or farming. You must come! This is almost an Order. (Sorry for being bossy.) My neck is getting long waiting for your arrival.

Anyway, thanks to write us a letter. We only hope you two good healthy and be happy!

xxxxxx Sayaka and Murata

Needless to say, I obeyed Murata's order. It had been several years since I had seen either of them. My partner Cynthia and I had recently returned to Japan to live for the second time. But their new home was far from where we lived, and it was mid-winter before I managed to get myself all the way across the country to the southern island of Kyushu. I arrived at Murata's house among the rolling hills of manicured tea plantations in the late afternoon. As he had written, the house was sprawling, and way too big. They had cordoned off a small room to heat, and with the lights low, and the warm and slightly spicy smell of charcoal filling the room with peace and intimacy, I spent the evening listening to the sorrowful minor tones of Murata's flute.

I remember Murata saying then, "My teacher told me that I should be able to play the flute in such a way that if I were playing next to a very sick person, or someone dying, they should not be annoyed by my sound in any way. That's how gently I should play."

That night, I think I finally understood the idea of a Buddhist "lineage," something intangible, a resonance that gets handed on from teacher to student across the centuries. This sound is a transmission of something that goes all the way back to the Buddha, to Shakyamuni himself. And yet, as Murata tells me, the playing is about *now*, about this instant, disappearing even as the sound is

Legend has it that in eighth-century China there lived a Ch'an (Zen) monk whose bell would ring a sound so pure that those hearing it would be led on the path to enlightenment. One of his disciples decided that he would try to make a flute that would imitate the sound of this bell. Soon after the teacher would ring the bell, the monk would blow one note on the flute, as if echoing the sounding of the bell. This story, Murata says, is the origin of the name of this kind of flute, the *kyotaku*, whose characters, somewhat poetically interpreted, mean, "bell that makes the mind empty."

Buddhist meditation and the bamboo flute stayed linked as the culture crossed over from China to Japan. And in this so-called "blowing Zen" two of the most important aspects of Buddhist practice—the chanting of sutras and awareness of breathing—were brought together in the tradition of flute playing as a form of meditation. This form of self-training was then joined to two even older spiritual traditions, the walking pilgrimage and the practice of alms begging, both of which had been fundamentals of Eastern spiritual disciplines for centuries before the birth of the Buddha.

All of these—breathing, chanting, walking and begging—came together in the tradition of the flute-playing *komuso*, or itinerant begging monk.

made. And for all the Buddhist books I've read and teachings received, listening to these sutras exhaled through a piece of bamboo is the first time I've had a direct bodily understanding of the utter impermanence of everything. The sound is here. Disappears. And it's gone.

~

Murata's teacher spent ten years as a *komuso* and his teacher before him lived his entire life as one. In turn, Murata too decided he would don the reed hat and begging box and play these plaintive songs on the streets of modern Japan. When Murata goes out as a *komuso*, he cuts a striking figure. The kimono is gray, silken-looking, and spotless. I smile at the transformation from the plaid work shirts and jeans he often wears. He takes the wooden donation box, painted with the characters for "Without Existence, Without Extinction," and places it around his neck. Lastly he puts on the large rattan hat, obscuring his face entirely. Murata explains that in the period when some *komuso* acted as spies for the shogun, this head covering was a way to maintain secrecy—to see and not be seen.

Murata then goes to a local town and, standing in front of a house or store, plays just one sutra. He stops, then pulls out a pure white paper fan, his movements as precise as a Noh dancer, simultaneously graceful and stark. If you choose to place a coin or bill on the fan, this is the time to do that. Then he places the fan inside of the box, bows, and moves on, leaving the incense of the flute's haunting sound still curling around you.

Though the figure of flute-playing monk has almost completely disappeared from the Japanese landscape, there are still those among the very aged who remember when they were a common sight. When I ask Murata if he explains to younger people what a *komuso* is, he says, "I don't explain. When I'm playing, I don't talk to people at all. I only play. That's the only thing that matters then. If I receive money, if I don't receive money, if they slam the door on me, if they yell at me, shoo me on, none of that is important. The reason to play the flute is to advance your ability to better perceive emptiness. You are playing for yourself, not to entertain another person, or to have them pity you. You certainly don't do it with the object of making money. That's why it doesn't matter at all how people react. As my teacher says, 'To play is good. That's all.'"

The cultural practice of alms begging, I've learned over the years, is a way to connect those who are full-time meditators to the larger community. And for me, the presence of a monk embarked on a lifelong devotion to meditation reminds me of my own practice, and I imagine that might be one of the purposes of having monks out in public: to remind us of the importance of our inner life. As Murata explains, alms begging reduces the desire and clinging of the person giving, and also works to humble the begging monk. The walking pilgrimage is also a form of self-training, breaking the habit of laziness and self-indulgence.

Is it theater? Is it religious practice? Is it working for money? Our categories, I think, are not up to the task.

I ask Murata now, here in his current home in central Japan, a little bit more about his actual *komuso* practice. He tells me that the summer is usually best, even though it is hot. "People usually have their windows open in their house."

Sayaka, overhearing, laughs, "It's completely different than practicing at home on the tatami mat."

"How's that?" I ask.

"Well, it's a lot of stress, isn't it?" she says. "You're in that kimono out in the sun, and you think, 'It's too hot!' But you have to keep going; people are watching you." She laughs as she sketches for me Murata's suffering out on the pavement.

I ask Murata how he knows when he can stop his rounds for a day.

"I can feel when I've got enough money" he laughs, "by lifting the box. Then I go back to the car and head home, or pick up a beer."

"A beer?!" I almost gasp.

"Yeah. It's hot, I'm thirsty!" He smiles.

"But," I sputter, "isn't that sort of at odds with Buddhist discipline and training and all that?"

He laughs at me, and says, in English, "Andy! You are just too *square*!"

I blush. Square! Then Murata says, serious again, "Actually, this is the Zen way. It's not like you think, with the reins pulled tight all of the time. Some periods, of course, are very strict, but others . . . are looser. If things are too strict, you can't continue your practice." I remember then what Murata has said dozens of times: continuing is everything.

Murata spent six years studying with Nishimura. Near the end of this period he received a license from his teacher. Its elegant calligraphy, with the teacher's red seal on it, admonishes him in beautiful formal language to comport himself properly, and to observe his manners with strict adherence. He carries this license with him always, along with a folding, hand-bound book of "sheet music," which is more like a vertically written list of syllables, a mix of musical notation and sutras to be "sung."

He was also given a new first name, "Kogan," which means to inspect deeply, to comprehend illusion and emptiness. The custom of granting new names is a practice in several traditional Japanese disciplines. It functions, I believe, as a talisman and a reminder, and a connection between teacher and disciple.

"My teacher was always observing me," Murata says, "from the moment I walked into the room all the way until the moment I left. That is the role of the guru: to watch your behavior, your attitude, seeing what you are thinking inside of your head, to see if you understand . . . or not."

"Wasn't that unpleasant?" I ask, imagining that kind of scrutiny.

"Hah! No such thing!"

"But it didn't give you stress?"

"It did! Absolutely. Stress! But he needed to see what way I was going to behave in the future. That was the problem he was looking at. That's why the teacher is checking you, to see if you *really* have that intention to practice. . . . " and Murata looks at me and raises his eyebrows playfully, as if he were a teacher and I was a student, him tempting me to say, "Nah, not really. I'd really just like to stretch back and relax."

"And that's why the teacher asks you the same question again and again. Sometimes the answer changes, as you get closer and closer. That kind of question-and-answer was very interesting. Thrilling. He taught me so many things."

"Huh? I thought you said he didn't teach you anything."

"I was talking about the bamboo flute! He taught

me very important things. Blowing into the flute isn't the problem. It's the *essence* that he taught me." Then Murata shouts, "This!" and holds up his fingers in the shape he uses to cover the holes, " . . . this is just *technique*, just making some sound. He told me, 'If you think about technique, it won't be the real thing.' He told me to just *forget* about technique. Throw all that away. It's only playing, and continuing to play that has meaning. That's it."

And then Murata adds, "When I asked him, 'How should I play this part?' He just said, 'Blow until you understand.' He almost shouted at me, 'Until you get it, play until then!' That was his answer. And even today I still don't understand. That's why I keep playing."

He looks over at me and says, "It's very Zen, isn't it?" With a laugh in his voice. "But interesting. *Very* interesting."

~

Sayaka and Murata's home near Murata's teacher, however, had a lot of downsides, especially for Sayaka. Since it was so close to the city, most of the neighbors commuted by car to work every day, and, as Sayaka said, "Everyone was so, so busy." It was difficult for her to make connec-

tions with the community around her, something she values deeply. It occurs to me that this might be the fundamental loneliness of workaholic Japan. Their house was also close to a noisy main road. And Sayaka's father was beginning to age, and they wanted to live closer to him to provide for his care.

So they packed up again and started looking for a new place to live. This time the search for a house was even harder, in part because after the poison gas attacks on the Tokyo subways by a religious cult of urbanites who had moved to the countryside, rural people were even more cautious about renting their houses to people they did not know.

Murata and Sayaka were able to find temporary lodging in the mountains of central Honshu, the main island, and they spent much of the next year driving around the adjoining prefectures. Murata commented to me once during this process that the period of finding abundant cheap houses in the country was "over." It was one of the few times that he had anything but ebullience in his outlook.

That hint of pessimism, however, didn't last very long, and when we spoke next, he had found an even better location, and not too far from Sayaka's dad. The house where they live today adjoins a large vegetable garden plot, has a spectacular view, and almost two acres of rice fields nearby that Murata can rent. "Sometimes," Murata told me, "you just have to look at the owner in the eyes and really *plead* with them. Sometimes, you just have to beg."

~

"It is a wonder to grow rice!" Murata exclaims. "Exciting!" We are next to his rice paddies, three flat square expanses of brilliant green surrounded on all sides by some of the highest mountains in Japan. I can see that he's utterly happy. I myself have loved gardening for years, but it was not until talking with Murata that I understood how deeply a person can go into the experience of growing their own food. In an almost feverish tone he tells me how growing rice is different at different elevations; different depending on the soil, depending on the variety of seed. He has to be alive to all the changes: how cold and heat interact with sun and rain and humidity, each variable playing itself out on the rice plants. In this way, Murata binds himself to the earth. He is in conversation with how the totality of the life-world is *this* year, pulling upon his knowledge of how it was last year, understanding so much more than "rice" as he does it. With this much to "read" in the world, I catch myself thinking (though only for a moment), who needs books?

Murata has invited me to help him and Sayaka with this year's rice planting. It's June, months after the rest of Japan has already gotten its rice seedlings in. Since they aren't trying to rush their rice to market at the earliest possible date in order to get a higher price per kilogram, Murata and Sayaka plant their seedlings in June when all of Japan used to.

Sayaka, wearing her black waterproof boots and sitting on an overturned milk crate in the middle of the

It was not until talking with Murata that I understood how deeply a person can go into the experience of growing their own food.

Murata has invited me to help him and Sayaka with this year's rice planting.

muddy field, is going through seedlings, choosing the healthiest ones for planting. Their little boy, Kohei, is having the time of his life running through the watery rice paddy and falling over sideways into it, shrieking with joy. Meanwhile Murata pulls a beautiful old implement, a huge four-foot-wide rake with long teeth, through the soft mud to make rows for planting.

Even though I protest that I know nothing about rice planting, Murata insists I try it. And so, with my bare feet in the warm mud, I make my way along the lines he has scored just below the water. I've rarely felt more clumsy. But Murata is relentlessly encouraging, calling out, "All OK!" and "No problem!"

After I've put in twenty or thirty feet of a drunken-looking line of tiny green plants I ask him if this is really OK. "Do it any way you like!" he shouts again across the plateau of muck. And then, fearing that I'm rushing, he calls out: "Slothfully, slothfully!" I'm not immediately sure of the meaning of the words he's using—*chin-tara, chin-tara*—but I deduce the meaning from his explanatory gestures. "It's like this." He juts his head way forward, his eyelids half closed, and takes plodding, small steps. He exaggerates the movements more, laughing, trying to look like the caricature of a lazy slob. "*Chin-tara, chin-tara!*" It's almost a mantra for him. "Lazily! Dawdling! Go slower!" he yells. "Sluggish! Don't hurry. Rest more! Take a break!"

When I use this phrase around other Japanese people later they laugh out loud. It seems that Murata may be the only person in the world who gives this word a positive connotation.

Later on Murata says to me, "Here, look at this." He holds some rice seedlings in his outstretched palm. For Murata everything is palpable, observable, and direct. He is showing me the seedlings grown by his neighbor for use in a mechanized rice planter, a lawnmower-like machine that is driven through the rice paddy, putting in four or five plants at once.

"See, compare," Murata says, pointing to the yellowed, sickly looking plants. "They're weak." Then he bends down and picks up a few seedlings that he has grown for planting by hand. "These are green and have strong roots. Since those others are grown for a machine to plant, close together and early, he needs to make up for their weakness by using all kinds of chemical fertilizers and pesticides. I plant them far apart and late and slowly. I can't grow as much. But I *have* time. The other way takes money and machines, so after all that he only breaks even."

This makes me wonder about the economics of Murata's rice farming. As we sit now in the shade of a tree drinking some cool roasted barley tea that he has brought in a stainless steel thermos, I ask him how much his rice fields produce. Now that we are talking numbers, I start to understand the potential for what he could be making, but isn't. Each year, he says, he grows about fourteen hundred pounds of rice. Considering the three small fields we are looking at, that seems like a lot. He doesn't, however, technically sell it, he says. The arrangement, as best I can understand (these complex, intertidal zones between gift giving and business are quite common in Japan) is that besides the two to three hundred pounds of rice Murata and his family eat in a year, there are four or five families that "receive" this rice. "It's half gift; a kind of barter," Murata says.

The families give him the equivalent of about $1.80 a pound, about a dollar a pound cheaper than the going rate for organic rice in Japan. The families, all friends, help him out in kind. "With some clothes or something . . . " he says. "For me, that's enough."

"And what if," I ask (kind of embarrassed to be so business minded), "they didn't want to buy from you? Would you go to the organic cooperative to sell it?"

"I just don't do things like that. I only sell to friends."

I tilt my head in question.

"As soon as I go to the cooperative," he says with a frown, "it's just money talk. Only. I would be in *business* then. I'm not interested in that. Soon everyone's talking about making money. "His voice lets me know how unpleasant this is to him. "And I'd also have to sign a contract with them, and keep producing it. It gets like this—" he grabs an imaginary rope around his throat, tilting his head sideways, as if being hung from a noose. In English he lets out a cry, "Choking me!"

"But the way I do it now, I am completely free. Those families I sell to could tell me that they didn't want to buy my rice anymore, and I also could stop selling. That is the best relationship, I've come to believe."

I ask him about the costs and benefits of growing rice organically versus the way the man in the field next to him does, and I find out he's never figured it all out. What's the yield comparatively per unit of land? How much does his neighbor sell his rice per kilo? How much does Murata save by doing so much by hand, and not using chemical fertilizer? "I don't know." "I'm not sure." "Never thought about that." He's not just preaching disconnection from marketplace thinking. It's real inside of him.

"Yes, but what if next year, a big typhoon came, and blew down all your rice just before harvest?" I ask. "Do you have any backup?"

"Ahhh, something will work out," he says. "I have confidence."

"But what would you do?"

"I could go back to the *komuso* life. It's *easy!*"

"Oh? You're not doing the alms begging any more?" I ask with dismay.

"No. I've got no time for that now. I'm devoting myself to growing rice."

I've been thinking all these years that he's still wandering from town to town, reviving this vanished tradition. I've caught myself getting attached to permanence again.

But, I ask him, is he saying that alms begging is an easy way to make a living? How could he possibly mean that?

"Yes, I could make three thousand dollars a month doing that. Simple."

Wow, I think: here's someone who could make three thousand dollars a month doing something he actually loves to do, and it's a real thing, and he's not doing it. He explains that these days he has a family, and cannot go "on

tour," using the English (I smile at my image of him mixing rock guitarist and wandering feudal-era monk). "Also, I can't just leave my rice paddies here for all that time."

And he doesn't need much, he says, telling me about one time in the mid-'90s when he and Sayaka went to make some cash cooking udon noodle soup at a tourist-oriented crafts village. Between the two of them they saved eight thousand dollars in five weeks. Then Murata looks at me and says, "We lived on that for *three years.*"

Although I can't really believe it, I do, having spent many days at their house, watching them eat only what they grow, wearing clothes they received for free, paying virtually no rent. I can actually imagine a life now, in the twenty-first century, using very little money. Then Murata says with a smile, "I don't mind using money. I just hate having to go through what it takes to produce it!"

He then adds, "Anyway, selling rice cheap is fine. If I have two hundred and fifty thousand yen for a year, that's enough."

"Wait a minute," I say thinking about how little twenty-five hundred dollars a year is. "So you are living on *less* than what you were living on in Kyushu, when I visited you there eight years ago, and you didn't even have a child then?"

"It's about the same. I get occasional jobs playing

concerts for the flute. That might bring in a hundred thousand yen a year or so."

I remember attending one of Murata's concerts. Absent are all his usual intense explosions of emotion. He speaks and holds himself formally. I find out that most of the people in the hall have never seen a *kyotaku*. Because of the very small number of people who play the *kyotaku* these days, it seems that Murata could potentially make a significant amount of money doing concerts as well. Yet he doesn't try to scour up engagements. If a call comes Murata may or may not decide to schedule a performance. He's not hungry. This, to me, is so extraordinary, since in terms of money, he has less of it than almost any person I know.

All over Japan I can see, and Murata surely sees, that other rice farmers leave most of the work to the machines and the weed and fertilizer problem to the chemicals, so it's obvious that growing rice without so much labor is perfectly possible. You could say that Murata spends all those hours doing something that, from one perspective, doesn't need to be done. But it's the same way he lived in India: he is not in a rush. He graduated from the school of no hurry.

Then Murata says, contemplatively, as the angle of the sun throws longer shadows across the rice seedlings we've planted, "To continue, that's meaningful. Forward, forward, even a little bit, as long as you don't stop walking. Experience tells you everything. Playing the bamboo, that's what I always think. If I were to stop, I wouldn't have made anything of it. The rice paddy is the same. Whatever you do, it's all about practice: you can't just think about it, or just look at it, or dream about it—even though that's fun—you have to *do* it."

～

We've come back from the rice fields and are getting ready for yet another of Sayaka's delicious meals. Taking off my shoes in the entryway before stepping up into the house, I notice a large green refrigerator. It's dusty and looks unused. I open it and find it's empty and unplugged. It must have been left here by the owner of the house. So I ask Murata how he decides what machines he uses, and which he does not.

"What I need, I have." (And by now I know that Murata doesn't use the word "need" lightly.) "I use a car. A friend gave me a CD player and radio. I use that."

"So you aren't using the refrigerator?"

"There's no reason for me to use it. What would I put in the refrigerator? I don't have anything I need to preserve."

Kogan Murata • 127

"Nothing?" I ask, incredulous. "No milk, no cheese, no eggs?"

"I mean . . . marmalade. Once you open marmalade," he says with a voice that could almost be described as awe, "You have to eat it *every day!*"

I think about that a little bit. Their bread doesn't go bad because they bake a fresh loaf on top of the wood-stove every day. The vegetables come right out of the ground and onto the dinner table. Then Murata adds, "In the winter, really every once in a while, I eat some cheese. When it's cold it doesn't go bad, right?"

"But . . . don't you just sometimes want to go into the supermarket, get something interesting, just for enjoyment?"

"Like what?"

"I don't know, something different, a special treat just to change your mood a bit?"

He laughs, "My mood changes every day. Every day the weather is different, right? The seasons change. Just that is enough."

There's a long pause while I look again at this extraordinary person. The change in the weather is enough? He's laughing. Happy. Amazing.

Part of me wants to just leave it simple, like that. But then the upwelling of counterarguments threatens to capsize me. "But many people—me, for example— like to travel, like to eat out, just to get a shift in our feelings."

Without even waiting for me to finish he answers, simply, "It's a habit."

"A habit? Is it a bad habit?"

He laughs at me, "Oh, it depends on the person!"

Then, kindly, he adds, "Actually, I also did these things too, when I was in my twenties and thirties. I had money at the time. I went to restaurants, I went to India and Europe. Now, no more. The reason why: I have no money. That's all. If I had money, I might go . . . " his voice trails off at the end of this last statement, thinking it over, " . . . achh . . . too much . . . it's too tiring! I've had enough."

"Tiring?"

"Yes. Going over here, going over there. Tiring! Carrying your heavy baggage everywhere. Better to just laze around the house, *chin-tara, chin-tara.*"

After considering for a bit, I say to him, "I think that most people are destroying the world simply because they want to keep changing, getting something new. I'm probably one of them. I'm talking about carbon dioxide and global warming and things like that . . . " Murata nods his head but doesn't say anything, waiting to see where I'm going. "I think you've solved some big problem that most people have. So I want to know how you solved it."

He laughs, "Back! Go back to the past. Well, I mean, maybe, if you keep your lifestyle back to the way it was fifty years before, maybe you can solve the problem." And then he says in English, very clearly. "Don't spend." and then repeats, "Do. Not. Spend."

Is the answer that simple? Maybe it is.

"But, Murata-san, don't you need to have a lot of internal power to accomplish this? I'm talking about controlling your wanting . . . "

"Ah yes, I know that: 'I want to do this, I want to do that.'" And then he adds, surprising me, "It's because of having too much information. I don't have much information, so those things don't bother me. I don't read the newspaper, listen to the radio, watch television. If you do you get *sooo* much information."

There's a pause, and then he says, "Before, I was the same, when I was twenty or thirty. I had the same thinking as other people, exactly. I'd make a lot of money, and I'd go off on my motorbike, or go off skiing."

"So do you ski now?"

"Nope. It costs money. I gave away my skis."

I shake my head, really impressed at how many things he can give up. His exuberant happiness is a testament though.

"But now," he continues, "I've cut the information, so I started not to feel . . . ," he searches around for the

right word, "that motion of 'the world.' I've placed myself apart from it. That's the best way, I think: cut the information."

"You don't even read the newspaper?"

"No. Once a month, twice a month, I go to the library, look at the baseball scores, how are the Pittsburg Pirates doing? See that the Tigers won, or the Giants lost . . . " he says laughing, a bit embarrassed, as if he had committed a minor transgression. "I do have a little interest in that."

"Every day the weather is different, right? The seasons change. Just that is enough change for me."

Walking to the rice paddies with his son, Kohei.

And then he adds, after a pause, the only sound the calls of far off crows, "But computers, cameras . . . I have no more interest in those things."

"Was it difficult?"

"No!" he laughs. "It was easy."

"What changed you?"

"I told you! I don't need it."

I bring myself up to his level of energy, raising my voice, "But you didn't need it before either when you were twenty or thirty!"

"Before, I *felt* I needed such things: skis, a motorbike, a camera . . . " He pauses a long time. "I got fed up! Maybe that's it. It's a pain in the ass, right? If you have a camera, you have to buy film, then you have to develop it, and it takes money to go skiing, and you have to do maintenance on your bike . . . "

Even though I realize that I'm sounding like a cliché, I ask him, "But don't you think you ought to know about what's happening in the world, stay abreast of political information, at least, in the newspaper?"

"I'm not a political type of human being. . . . Yaaa . . . it's better to get myself to the rice paddy. I'm just not interested . . . Although whether that's a bad thing or a good thing, I don't know."

I've listened to everything he's said, yet I still feel something isn't quite answered for me. Then I remember that I have never seen him, here at home or in other places where we've met, without that bright orange book of his, *The Words of the Buddha*. "So is it the teaching of the Buddha that said it's better to let go of your craving? Is that it?"

"Yes, yes, it's better to cut it . . . or to say it better, you should *control* it." And then he pauses, and adds, "What Gautama Buddha said was really correct, I have come to believe that more and more."

"So, is that the main cause of the change in you, what he taught?"

"Yes, that's true. There's also that."

"There's *also* that?" I ask. I have to laugh. He's withholding the secrets of the temple? Maybe that's what they mean by the phrase "the Zen trickster."

"Anyway, the very worst thing, as the Buddha said, is *attachment*. And when I put his teaching into practice, I decided I thought this as well. It's about—little bit by little bit—trying to reduce your cravings and greed for things." He repeats himself, "Just a little bit at a time."

I'm a bit embarrassed to be asking such a student-to-teacher kind of question to my friend, but I ask anyway. "One of the things in the world I spend a... on is books. Now you go to the library, and... the books, and return them, but I just... actually *have* those books around, just... want to read it again someday, I have it..."

Then deciding to get serious with... there's mirth still in his voice, he looks... eyes wide, "What do you *really* need?... that is absolutely a necessity for you?"

"Well . . ." embarrassed again, "love . . ."

"It's not a camera is it? And it's probably not tha... book either, is it? Maybe love . . . I think it's love." Sayaka at the sink, watching us talk, starts laughing to herself. Murata continues, "The fewer things you have, the better. Reduce your baggage as much as you possibly can. When you get rid of your things you get easier in yourself, and you decrease your suffering more and more. But 'I *want*, I *want* . . . ' That's the beginning of suffering."

I look up at the sky turning pink, high in the mountains of Japan, and I think, what does Murata "have"? The sound of the flute, disappearing, no more than vibrating air; the seasons changing; his time with his family; the life cycle of rice. I remember a line from a New Year's card I got from him once: "Blue sky, white peaks, snow fields,

it's a perfect winter these days! And a nice warm wood-stove." Is he deprived at all? He doesn't look it.

After our lively dinner with their son, Kohei, asking a stream of questions about fish and fishing and different beetles, we move into the adjoining room, and ...ta play several songs on the flute.

...contemplatively, he tells me about searching ...ue sound." Although he says he's never heard ...lieves it exists, and that looking for it is the real ...of the bamboo flute player. "The true sound can't ...ound in one or two years. Ten years is not enough, ...enty years is not enough. The real thing takes a minimum of thirty years. That's why you have to be mad. You have to give it all your heart, as my teacher said, otherwise it'll never be the real thing."

"But," I ask, "what is wrong with doing it as a hobby, a part-time thing, after getting home from the office or something?"

"You wouldn't understand at all. Better forget it. It's a waste of time. It'll never be the real thing that way."

I'm not sure I completely agree with Murata on this, but perhaps I am thinking inside my own culture's tendency toward dabbling. And, after all, isn't turning away from "just messing around" what mastery means?

❧

A few years after Murata left Kyushu, his teacher, Koku Nishimura, died. Murata shares a few memories with me of the old master, and then gets quiet. Finally, he says, "Well, he has gone." There's a very long silence, us both sitting quietly together, feeling the presence of death. Then Murata says, as if to himself, "It is the making of effort that has meaning; not *becoming* something, but just making effort toward it. Just to continue; that's the only purpose. It's not what you have done, the important thing is what are you *trying to do*. The result, that will be OK, you can just forget about it. As my teacher said, 'To play is good. That's all.'"

"What about other people, aren't you playing for them too?" I ask.

"No. If someone happens to hear me by chance and they get relief from their suffering, then it's a good thing. But before it can be something which is good for others, if it isn't a good thing for yourself, it won't work."

"So if it's just for someone else, and is not actually helpful to you, then it's bad?"

"Well, rather than say it's bad, I'd say it's an impossibility. Anyway, that's all difficult. How about you knock it off with these difficult questions, OK?"

Before we turn in, Murata, who's been holding his long beautiful flute in his hands the whole time, blows a few more quiet tunes, and I hear the night silence. When he finishes, I ask him what's really on my mind, seeing this good life he has. "So why don't other people choose this way of living?"

"Hmmm . . . " He stops. "I wonder why. . . . Maybe it's me that's different; I'm just not serious. Japanese people are serious, aren't they? Always straight ahead. I just want to play."

"What about your friends from when you were a boy?" I ask. "They loved to play just as much as you. What happened to them?"

Suddenly sober, he says simply, "Cogs." There's a pause. "They became cogs in the big machine. It's like Charlie Chaplin in *Modern Times*, exactly. They became interchangeable parts: and if you're a part, you have to keep turning and turning, and never stop . . . until you're replaced."

Then he adds, "As far as an ideal goes, it's not."

And then he adds, after some consideration, "You know, those guys, even now they *also* want to play, but they're in some habit, and they just repeat the daily routine again and again. *Yaaa* . . . but I don't know about other people."

"And what about your brother and sister, what kind of life do they live?"

Murata laughs, "Air conditioning! Briefcase!"

"But clearly at one point you decided not to go their way."

"Well, it's not interesting. Just imagine it: going to the office every single day for thirty years. For me, I couldn't bear it! If it were an interesting job, say being an artist, you could do it. But for an ordinary person . . . and I am completely ordinary, I can't paint pictures or be an artist . . . " Then he adds, as if he's made up his mind, "Maybe people are doing exactly what they want to do. That's why they are doing it. It's very simple. If they didn't want to live that way, they wouldn't."

Then Murata surprises me and says, "What do *you* want to do with your life, Andy? Time is racing by. Already, look how old we are! What do you *really* want, Andy?"

Well, I think, maybe I don't really know! And then it occurs to me, although I'm a little too shy to say it out loud, that part of it is writing this book, putting it into people's hands.

What will happen with Murata in the future? Probably he'll live out his life "the same as before," as he says.

And what will happen with me? Such talk, I know he would think, is pointless. To continue, to move forward, that is what has meaning. Forget about everything else.

5 Asha Amemiya

"Striving to excel." "Doing better than our parents' generation." These mantras have been spoken into our ears since before we knew what they meant. Whether in Japan or in the U.S., society values achievement. While this view of the purpose of life is reinforced at every turn, when we adopt that view, what do we lose? And how does the collective trance of our society cause us to make choices we're not even aware of making? And if we do choose a different path from that of the culture surrounding us, how does our choice affect the next generation, the children in our house? Spending time with Asha Amemiya and watching how she raises her kids, I got a picture of how enriching it might be to have a lot more "good enough" in my life.

"If you don't have a whole lot of unsatisfied people, the economy stops dead, doesn't it? And then the entire society is in trouble."

I'm speaking with Asha Amemiya, mother of three daughters, batik artist, rice farmer, and all-around tough customer. We are reclining comfortably on the soft wooden floor of her small house tucked into a remote corner of Kochi Prefecture, just trying to stay cool. The July heat is intense. The insects outside are shrieking hypnotically in the flamboyant green of the southern countryside, and all seems right with the world.

I ask her to tell me what she means.

"For example, a good computer comes out, and people say, 'Hey, that's a good thing, and convenient, and useful.' And they buy it, right? And they are satisfied . . . for a time. But then a new one comes out, a new variety. And it has all kinds of improvements, right? So of course, you want it. The one that you've been using, the one you've been thinking, 'Huh, this is really good' . . . well the next one is *even better.*

"Since you want it, you have to work even more." And then, nodding her head knowingly, looking at me with her eyelids half closed, "It takes money to buy, doesn't it?" Her attitude saying, "They ain't gonna give it to you for free, right?"

And then she says, "But if you keep chasing that kind of thing, there's no end to it. Next, next, next, next!" Her voice gets thin, pinched, almost hoarse, demonstrating how wound up people get: "The better one, the better one, the *even better* one."

She looks down at the ashtray in front of her, picks up her tightly rolled "bidi" cigarette that has gone out, relights it, and says, "A lot of people think if they start off down that road, that there's definitely gonna be a good thing at the end of it, that *some*where there'll be a point where they'll be satisfied. They don't understand that it's neverending. Once you start heading down that road,"

she says speeding up as she speaks, "it gets faster and faster and faster and faster. And you have to go along with that pace.

"But to me . . . Enough! It's a pain in the ass. What do you say?" she asks, looking at me, "*Pugyou!* Oh, that's Bengali isn't it? Or, wait a minute, is that Nepali? It's what you say when your stomach is totally full. 'That's enough. I don't need any more.'

"If too many people say, 'It's good enough just as it is,' then the system—what is it you call it?—'capitalism' stops turning, and like I said, it's a big problem."

When Amemiya says "It's good enough as it is," she really means it. She's prepared to let things be, just as they are. Her house, for example. It's an old house, and it has in no way been gussied up. You'd never find it in some coffee-table book of rural chic. It serves its purpose: it keeps out the rain, there are some bedrooms, a workroom, a kitchen, a bathroom and a toilet. When I arrived, her middle daughter, Shanti, was repairing the *shoji* screen doors. One (or several) of the cats had torn the paper, jumping after the shadow of a moth at night and the doors had ripped. Amemiya hadn't let it bother her, so it was Shanti who took it upon herself to fix them.

The paper screens make me think of something I read about the philosophy of Japanese gardens and the houses that they're designed in conjunction with. "Don't make such a solid wall between you and the outside world: let it be permeable." Being in this house, I often feel I am partially outdoors: the rain on the roof, the sounds of the wind, the cicadas constantly yammering. The place feels very much "as is," in the good sense of that phrase. The chickens squawk noisily nearby, the area in front of the house has its fair share of weeds, and the tatami mats have loose fibers from much use. And don't step on this floorboard in the corner here; it needs repair. I can hear her voice: "It's *fine*." I'm surprised to find how much all of it puts me at ease. I can let my mammal self be.

But the things that are important to her, she bolts them down like a rivet on a battleship. The food she feeds her family is safe. No pesticides, no hormones, nothing genetically modified, no additives, preservatives, nothing. With her partner, Koichi Yamashita, they grow almost everything they eat. She wakes up before anybody else in the family, preparing three rich, varied, nutritious meals a day for all five of them.

Once when I came here during rice-planting season she went out in torrential rain, wearing her sturdy second-hand rain suit to plant the seedlings in the muddy rice paddy, up to her ankles in muck. It was hard work, but she did it without complaint.

Her friend from her years of living in Nepal, Atsuko Watanabe, describes Amemiya thus: "Her life now is sometimes hard: the physical labor is tough, the house is old, she's not exactly blessed economically. Nevertheless, each thing she takes as it comes and it's enjoyable for her. When she left Nepal and was preparing to come back to Japan and she had finished with all of her packing and preparation, she had just a tiny bit of money left. She took all of us out for tea; even down to the tiniest last coin, she used it all up, having fun. That's the feeling of being with her. No matter how intense the physical labor is, or if her children become sick, no matter how tight a place she gets into, she's the kind of person who can find joy in her life. Even smoking a single cigarette, she really enjoys it."

As Amemiya and I talk, her three daughters are constantly nearby, asking questions, making food, cleaning up, eating ice cream, or correcting their mother's mispronunciations of Bengali words that come up in our conversation. The family returned to Japan after more than a decade in India, and the two older daughters still sometimes banter back and forth with each other in Bengali. It's a comforting hubbub of voices, echoing the cadences and chatter of the insects in the thick green of nature just outside the open sliding door.

Here the important things are in place. The green mountains are resplendent, the conversation is good, art and music are part of everyday life, and her daughters are extraordinary human beings. They are forthright, well-informed, sharp-witted, full of lively laughter, and not the least bit shy. The eldest, Himalie, has studied years of Indian classical dance, and, last night, to her sisters' encouragement and clapping and singing, she graced us with a performance. Her younger sister Shanti visited Ghana, West Africa a little more than year or so ago. Giving a speech on it, in English, she won first place in the prefectural English speech contest. These girls are more cosmopolitan than most city dwellers. There's a real ferment in this modest house.

All three girls, I find out, were born in India, which Amemiya says is a much safer place to give birth than Japan.

I raise my eyebrows and ask her what she means.

"Well, in Japan, they do all kinds of things to you and the child in the hospital without asking you, even if you don't want them to: pumping you full of drugs and inoculations and things like that."

Like many of her unequivocal statements, this too is emblematic of her "don't give me any crap" personality. I ask her if it was her years in India that made her so strong, and she laughs her scratchy-voiced belly laugh, "No, I've always been strong!"

When Amemiya and Yamashita returned to Japan, they settled in a small village in southern Shikoku that invited them to join in a village revival program to resettle depopulated rural areas. One of the reasons they came back was to have the girls be able to learn their mother tongue. But also by the 1990s, says Amemiya, "India had changed so much there wasn't any need to be there at all. The spread of television and cars, new houses— it was getting to be as bad as Japan!"

One of the main reasons that drew her to live in India in the first place was the different ideas Indians have about the flow of time. "We were freer and had more time in India," says Amemiya. "In India, people think that if a job doesn't need to be done today, it can be done tomorrow. In Japan, if a job *can* be done today, people think it *should* be done today—even if it's painful and feels strained or forced. Overall, Japanese people are more restless, and hurried, so there are lots of functions you have to appear at. Like for example today, I had to show my face at some event at the preschool, even though I didn't want to—I had to go. Even if I don't intend to keep the same pace as people here, I

"A new computer comes out with all kinds of improvements. So because you want it, you have to work even more."

Asha Amemiya • 137

It's mid-afternoon and the sounds come in waves through the steamy air: the soft murmur of the river, the undulating buzz of insects.

often just have to. In India, there's none of that kind of stuff. The difference is as great as that between getting on a slow local train and getting on the bullet train."

When I ask her what she thinks the reason is, she says, "Well, the effect of the heat is one thing: India is hot. But don't you think the principles they have are different? The focus of thinking in Japan is economics, or it has become that way recently. Even politics is more like a form of economics than an attempt to realize an ideal society. Politicians don't have any principles in Japan."

"What do you mean by that?"

"Think about it: normally if you believe that we should have a certain kind of society, or if you believe that a new policy would be good, or correct, you think, 'How should we make it a reality?' And for that reason you become a politician. But Japanese politicians go into government only for power and authority.

"In India there are millions of people who are thinking about what kind of a society is ideal, and some of them become politicians. But in Japan, that doesn't happen. In India too, it's beginning to change. In the five-thousand-year history of Indian culture there hadn't been that much shift, at least in terms of values. The idea that becoming rich is a *good* thing is very recent. It started in the 1970s. But it was in the late '80s that it really accelerated and city life became busier. Becoming a merchant, doing business, and rising in the world were suddenly thought of as *good* things. Indians of a long time ago were just different, it seems to me."

I ask her if she could give me an example.

"Well, just look at Gandhi! His way of living was meaningful to people. Why, you have to ask, why did so many millions of people look to him, thinking he was wonderful, supporting him, saying, 'I will follow your way of thinking'?"

In fact Gandhi's ideas about the centrality of hand

labor to living a satisfying, meaningful life affected her deeply. "Gandhi really understood industrialization and its effects because he saw them firsthand in England."

That's right, I think. He was there as a young man in the 1890s, a time when the harshness of this kind of production was at its worst. Or, perhaps I should say, at its most visible. And then Amemiya says, "That's why he was so focused on making your own cloth."

Before she met Yamashita, Amemiya spent almost two years studying the techniques of hand spinning, weaving, vegetable-based dyeing, and other fabric arts in different textile centers in Nepal and India. It's easy to forget that for centuries textile arts were far more highly developed in India than they were in England. In fact, the British did much to destroy the Indian textile industry—often with shocking brutality—in order to create markets for factories in England. Still, some of the techniques of textile-based handwork and the values that came with them managed to survive, and it was this thread that Amemiya was able to pick up on. "I would go to various textile centers, villages where a certain style of dyeing or weaving was well developed, and ask at the local government office about where I could meet and observe craftspeople at work. I think," she says, laughing, "they were especially helpful because I was a young, single woman."

Much of her recent work is done with a wax-resist dyeing method most commonly known today as batik, an Indonesian word. However, Amemiya tells me, batik was originally an Indian technique that spread to Indonesia and was subsequently lost in India. Its revival there, she says, is due in large part to the work of the poet and philosopher Rabindranath Tagore (1861–1941).

I ask her to show me some of her work in batik, which she does only after a fair amount of importuning on my part. In one piece, an undulating orange and red-hued sunset creates a sense of dramatic movement behind a massive trunked tree. A poem by Tagore, rendered into Japanese by Amemiya, flows down the right side of the cloth hanging. Another piece is a watery image of bubbles breaking the surface in abstract movements of chocolate brown and ivory white. One of my favorites is a spiraling red and orange composition in which tiny particles—that might be either flower petals or leaves spinning in the wind—transubstantiate into streaming Bengali script. The poems accompanying the images speak of the joys of gazing into the round, moonlike shape of an infant's face, and of the life of young girls and women in agricultural society, things which Amemiya feels for strongly.

Amemiya's love for rural India is evident in her voice when she talks about her years there. The family spent more than ten years in the state of West Bengal after Yamashita got a job teaching at the university founded by Tagore in the small village of Shantiniketan, 115 miles north of Calcutta.

Tagore, who won the Nobel prize in 1913, wrote more than fifty volumes of poetry, composed hundreds of songs as well as musical dramas, wrote a wide range of essays, and was an accomplished painter and choreographer. But perhaps most important to Amemiya was Tagore's educational philosophy, which was based on the idea of the "cultivation of sentiments."

"At Shantiniketan, hours of every day are spent in helping children and young adults become more sensitive using a lot of different methods, including singing, making drawings, and reading and listening to poetry. The point of this is not so much the work itself but helping the child cultivate her receptivity and finer sensibilities." Just as in the U.S., a century ago most educational bureaucracies saw schooling as primarily an employment-training program, and scorned those such as Tagore who insisted that education should help children become more full human beings.

Rather than Tagore's ideals forming Amemiya's it would be more correct to say that there was a "sympathy" between them—to use one of Tagore's key words—in the emphasis on learning directly from nature, in perceiving more closely the life cycles of plants, insects, birds, and seasons, and in knowing that the mind works best when unhurried.

Once Amemiya introduced to me the phrase "the cultivation of sentiments," I could see its beauty and value not only in the way Amemiya raised her children or made her batik, but some years later, in the extraordinary people I met when I visited this village where the family had spent ten years of their lives.

Walking the shaded streets of this quiet rural town situated on the vast agricultural plains of northern India, I could feel the spirit of Tagore's vision in the huge spreading trees of colorful red and purple flowers, many planted by the poet himself, and in the earnest groups of students discussing philosophical or artistic topics seated outside on the broad lawns next to the elegant old buildings. There was a peacefulness in the very air.

One can imagine a line coming down through time, through Emerson and Thoreau, and the transcendentalist philosophers—who were themselves influenced by Hindu Vedas—coming through the writings of Tagore and the group of people around him, manifesting in a community they established that later enriched Amemiya's and Yamashita's aesthetics and perspective on life, and was passed on to their children, living today, who are teaching it to me, in this house, now.

As Tagore wrote in an essay entitled "A Poet's School":

> We may become powerful by knowledge, but we attain fullness by sympathy. . . . But we find that this education of sympathy is not only systematically ignored in schools, but it is severely repressed. From our very childhood . . . our life is weaned away from nature and our mind and the world are set in opposition. . . . [W]e are made to lose our world to find a bagful of information instead. We rob the child of his earth to teach him geography, of language to teach him grammar. His hunger is for the Epic, but he is supplied with chronicles of facts and dates. . . . Child-nature protests against such calamity with all its power of suffering, subdued at last into silence by punishment.
>
> —Rabindranath Tagore, *Personality*, 1917

Noticing the date, I have to sigh, to think how deadening education has become in Japan, with all its mechanizing tendencies, and how Japan's "success" (as measured of course only by test scores) has become something pointed to by the advocates of mass-production education all over the world. Working here as a teacher I've seen so many children—especially girls—becoming frightened and apprehensive, so afraid of making mistakes that they retreat into a shell of silence and shame.

So for me, I'm heartened to see how Amemiya's daughters are turning out, so vibrant, alert and full of laughter, with an independence of thinking that is the fruit of how their inborn creativity has been nurtured and strengthened. I'm sure they'll have no trouble getting whatever kind of employment (if that's what they choose) in any field they want to work in.

I can see Amemiya's values and her love for rural life in the poems she has dyed into her many cloth hangings. Several that she has chosen were written by a twentieth-century haiku poet, Santoka, who wandered the length of Japan in complete poverty, begging for each day's food, and sleeping outside in all kinds of weather.

One haiku hints at both the joys and sadness of a solitary monk on a pilgrimage in the winter:

© Koichi Yamashita

Amemiya studied wax-resist dyeing, or batik, in India.

Even in my empty
begging bowl
A piece of hail.

Translating this poem, and
thinking about it a while, I feel like
I understand Amemiya's sensibility more and more: the hardness of
the human world—no alms for the
starving monk—but there is still
the consolation of the natural world
bestowing something delicate and
small. Yet the hailstone also indicates that it is surely going to be a
cold night, and without any money
for a room it will again be spent without shelter, sleeping
outside.

I think about Amemiya's life. "Not blessed economically" is how Atsuko puts it. But she's enriched by the
life-world around her.

On one very long piece of cloth in light brown Amemiya has transcribed the entire Heart Sutra, with its dozens of "nothingness" characters repeated again and again.
I ask her about her reasons for choosing this, and she
mentions the Japanese Buddhist practice of the copying
of sutras to attain merit as one kind of training, but when

I try to find out more, she gives only vague answers. As
I try to explain my reasons for pressing her, Yamashita is
looking on from his small desk area by the window, a bemused smile playing on his expressive face. Amemiya says
to me that I shouldn't try to know so much, "The vague-
ness of language is one of the interesting things about
Japanese. You have to use your imagination."

I protest that while I certainly can imagine many
things, it won't do for my readers to have only the writer's
own speculations.

"Well, fine then," she says, "just write, 'When I asked
her why she copied out the Heart Sutra, she just smiled
and said nothing. This is Japanese culture!'"

Yamashita laughs out loud.

～

During their years in India, Yamashita and Amemiya often journeyed northward to the Himalayan kingdom
of Sikkim, now a part of India but still retaining its Tibetan Buddhist and Lepcha tribal minority cultures. In
this region of steep mountains and deeply cloven valleys,
they explored trekking trails and traveled to gompas, or
Buddhist monasteries, documenting rituals, customs,
food, and clothing. This work they later published in the

cultural guidebook they authored together, *Visiting the Eastern Himalayan Foothills.*

In Amemiya's writing, I again find the part of her that is drawn to the slow, the gentle, and the beautiful: she writes of the mists that cloud the tea plantations around Darjeeling, or the sound of a hard rain on the rooftops of an old mountain town, or the green of the highest tree branches spreading against a clear mountain sky, or even the simple pleasure of drinking a cup of tea in the middle of a crowded bazaar while gazing out purposelessly at the people passing by. She has subverted the implicit hurry of the guidebook form, which seems to always be goading you onward. The book lingers rather on myths of the Lepcha people, the symbology behind the color-drenched Buddhist rituals, and tea harvesting, processing, and brewing. Throughout, I find Amemiya's line drawings, some on how to put on the local gowns and clothes, or of traditional kitchen tools and how to use them, and diagrams of thatch-roofed hut construction. It's part travel guide and part loving testimony to this little nook of the world that they happened upon and want to share with others.

In one passage, she muses for the reader about life at a monastery where many pilgrims are staying:

Wherever I look they are spinning their prayer wheels constantly, saying mantras while walking, chanting sutras all day long, day in and day out. They do not stay for just one or two days as we do, they plant themselves here for weeks at a time. It seems to me that rather than their faith being just one part of their lives, their lives are deeply embedded inside of their faith.

For people from the big cities caught up in working all the time, probably they envy the life of these pilgrims. Or maybe, on the other hand, such dedication to one's faith, and that only, is something people of today just can't do. These are the things I think of, coming to this place.

～

"You Westerners are just like the Indians!" Amemiya complains in a loud voice after I've asked her yet another (to her, unreasonable) question. "You're always asking 'Why, why, why?' I don't know why I like the color blue, I just do. You ask me why I hate wage labor. I don't know why I hate it; I just do."

It's mid-afternoon now, and it's even hotter than

before. The sounds come in waves through the steamy air: the soft murmur of the river down in the valley, the undulating buzz of insects, *chucka chucka chucka,* crescendoing, *ya ya ya ya*, getting louder and then softer, as if the sun's intensity were turning the volume knob up and down on the great cosmic amplifier.

Then, looking over at me, with a "hey, wait a minute" kind of look on her face, she says, "Why is it that you want to write this book about us anyway?"

Caught off guard, I reply with even clumsier than usual Japanese along the lines of, "Well, one reason is that I've always been interested in ways that were practiced a long time ago and . . . "

But before I can finish, she interrupts me, "Don't say 'ways that were practiced a long time ago'; say instead 'ways that have been practiced *since* a long time ago.' The way you just said it makes it sound like they were gone entirely and we're reviving them. That's not true."

"Well," I say, trying to get my balance, "how do you decide which ways of doing things you want to continue, and which to discard?"

"First, you have to think, does it involve using money or not?" As usual, she is decisive, clear. "Then you look at whether it is natural or not. That, and whether it causes suffering and pain to others . . . or not."

As I'm jotting down her answer she looks up over to the kitchen where her youngest daughter Kanchen is at the sink and shouts to her, "Hey!! Are you playing around, or washing the dishes like you're supposed to, or what?"

I'll admit that the tone is a bit rough to my ears, but the warmth I feel all the time in this household clues me in that I don't have to hear it that way, and I can see that the girls don't either. There's an intimacy to the directness. And I've suffered Amemiya's upbraidings myself ("Your questions are bad!"). Personally, it's a bit of a relief in this hyper-polite country, where every eggshell is overlaid with another eggshell. And it makes me think as well of the samurai ethic, where the absence of explicit protestations of affection do not imply a lack of love.

Curious about how the choices Amemiya and Yamashita made have affected their daughters, I ask them if I could ask them a few questions in order to add their words to this book as well. Happily, they agree.

I talk with Amemiya's middle daughter, Shanti first. She's in her mid-teens, and as we speak, she holds one of the kittens from the recent litter.

"What do you like about this kind of life?"

She grins, "Living with cats!"

I smile. Not quite what I was looking for, yet. I try again, "Compared to your friends, how do you feel your life is different?"

"Well, there's no TV. But as far as living in an old house, everyone around here does that. My parents think about it differently, though: they *want* to be living this way. Also," she thinks for a long time, cuddling the kitten, hesitates, then ventures, "I think my sisters and I are a bit stronger than the other kids."

"In what way?"

"Psychologically."

"Why is that?" I ask.

"It's probably because I was brought up in a more wild environment. Also our bodies and bones are tougher, more solid. The food we eat is better."

"And do you want to live in the country when you grow up?"

"Definitely. But maybe not *so* far out into the country. And maybe not quite *this* wild!"

"Does your older sister want to as well?"

Shanti smiles a sly smile, "Aaah . . . I think she's the city type."

While Kanchen, the youngest daughter, in her last year of elementary school, is still too young for much critical reflection on this different way of life that her parents have chosen to lead (or at least to articulate it to the gigantic American with the hard-to-understand Japanese) she does say that watching cats is more fun than watching television.

All of a sudden, another cat who's climbed up into my lap digs its claws into my thigh. "Ouch! Damned cat!"

They both just laugh out loud.

~

By my third visit to Amemiya's house, Himalie, the eldest, is in university. She's living far away in big-city Osaka. Her

Amemiya's daughters are constantly nearby, asking questions, making food, cleaning up, or correcting their mother's mispronunciations of Bengali words that come up in conversation.

Asha Amemiya • 145

father gives me her contact information, and the next time I am passing through that city, I call her and she graciously agrees to give me some time to ask her a few questions.

One of the realities of urban Japan is that it's quite difficult to find any public area to meet that is free of mechanical and electric sound. We meet at what indeed turns out to be a noisy restaurant, with clinking glasses, blaring, high-pitched "energy music" over the speakers, and the clamor of large groups of students out drinking and making the general uproar. Still, Himalie seems to me to retain the calm of her rural upbringing despite the racket. She's fully an adult now: self-possessed, perceptive, and, like her mother, direct. Her love for drama and dance that was nurtured in Tagore's village in West Bengal continues: she recently finished playing a lead role in *West Side Story*, choreographing the dancing for the whole company as well. She still pursues her study of Indian classical dance, and she says she is writing poems and short stories, and even a novel. I think again about that phrase, "the cultivation of sentiments."

After we order, I ask her about her upbringing, and how she sees it now.

"I know that city life is materialistic, and people are often insincere, or even cold-hearted, it's true. Also there's a lot of confusion and turmoil. And while coun-try life is really more friendly and harmonious, and really beautiful—and perhaps that's the way people *should* live—sometimes there's a lack of stimulation in the country for me. It's also not easy at all.

"Say if you want to eat a chicken. You have to get a small chick, feed it, raise it until it's big enough to eat, kill it, and then get the meat to eat from it. Or if you want to eat a tomato, you have to plant that seed, grow it, wait two or three months, and then finally, you can eat it. You have to be ready to accept that if you are going to live that way."

She adds, after some consideration, "For me, that life is a little too insecure." As I'm jotting this down, she looks up and says, "But maybe I'm saying that because I just don't have the courage to do it."

I say to her, "You know how your mother often says, 'It's fine like it is'? What do you think about that?"

"Well, for me, I'm aiming upward. If they say 'It's OK as it is,' it just stops right there. There's no growth!"

"What do you mean by 'growth'?"

"Well," she says, reconsidering, "there's *some* growth for them: they have certainly gotten better at farming, but you know what I mean, more and better things."

"What kinds of things?"

"Well, a better environment to live in . . . but perhaps for the two of them, that environment is the ultimate, the best. People might look at the life I grew up in and say, 'Wow, that looks good,' but they don't know that it can be hard sometimes. There were times I didn't have anything to talk about with my friends because we had no TV, and I was teased in school because I was born and grew up in India. Japanese people can look down on India, and I tried to hide the fact of where I was born from my classmates. I had a real inferiority complex about it. Also my choice of university was limited because we didn't have much money. I also wanted to study Hindi and I couldn't afford it. There's a risk to that kind of life. It's too unstable for me.

"But on the other hand, if all the convenience stores and supermarkets disappeared, other people here in Osaka wouldn't have a clue what to do, not a single clue. I know how to plant rice, how to keep chickens. The other university students don't even know where their food comes from. They couldn't even imagine that a person like my mom exists in Japan."

Although she's critical of some of the choices her parents made, I have to remind myself of the almost universal tendency for grown-up children in their early twenties to focus primarily on the faults of their parents and not the struggles they went through to make their kids become what they are. I think that she may see the whole set of choices differently when she gets older.

Still, Himalie's the one who has had to pick up two or three part-time jobs to carry her through her time at university. I imagine one of her classmates who has plenty of money and can just breeze through her university years, going shopping and out to restaurants with her abundant free time because her father worked his six-day weeks, and late most nights.

Interestingly, the job that Himalie has accepted for after she graduates next spring (which was apparently quite competitive to get) deals with the very problems created by absent parents in workaholic Japan.

"Most children's time with their parents is limited, *extremely* limited," she says. "When both parents are working the children can't develop well, and have a lot of problems. Some of them become 'shut-ins' who don't leave their rooms ever, and others get into crime."

We get into a spirited discussion of the role of the father in the family, and how strongly she feels that he must be around, at least for dinner, to help the children grow up well. I ask her why some men don't just put their foot down at the office, and go home at dinnertime.

"It's not as easy as you think!" she says. "The boss would say to him, 'But what are you going to do about the work you have?' His work would then have to be done by his office mates staying until nine or ten, and then he might be the first to lose his job in the next downsizing."

"But Himalie, I know you said earlier that you thought it was unfair for parents to burden their children with the insecurity of surviving on so little money. Don't you see how that choice your parents made to be at home a lot when you were growing up has made you as strong as you are, and that in some way your life is more secure because of it?"

"That is so. . . ." she says, her voice trailing off into thought.

We continue like this, back and forth, both of us knowing that we won't, at this table, come up with an answer to this massive system of time deficits and market economics. But, for me at least, it's refreshing to be able to talk about it so directly with someone willing to challenge me, and with someone who feels the human costs so acutely, and wants to do something about them.

One thing I'm particularly struck by is her compassion. She remembers her own culture shock, coming back from India and trying to adjust to school life in rural Japan. "And I could even *speak* Japanese! But the children of immigrant laborers living here in Japan, from Brazil or Korea, they have so much trouble in school. Their parents don't have the skills to teach them the subjects they are having problems with, and it's really hard on the kids."

It is children like these, and others who don't fit into the regimented and ultra-competitive educational system of Japan, that Himalie has chosen to help in her career. Like her father, who has taught all his life, she has always been interested in education. Her new job is with a company that helps the families of children who aren't making it, for whatever reason, by providing a personalized curriculum and guidance.

As we are finishing we talk a little about her writing projects and the theater, and I try to point out to her what I see so clearly: the benefits of the way she was raised—her internal self-reliance, her feistiness, her critical thinking itself.

After we say good night and I wish her good luck with her new job, I think to myself that it's true, her parents' lives are tough in some ways. And certainly that affects their children. But our highly diversified world economy makes it easy for us as individuals to ignore how the system shifts the difficulties "somewhere else," to the farm worker stooping in the mono-cropped fields, to the Chinese peasant sickened by pesticides and dying early of cancer, or to the factory worker breathing fumes who makes the things we do not make for ourselves.

It brings me back to the way Amemiya decides what things she will and will not do: "Does it cause pain and suffering to others?"

~

It's summer again, and I'm visiting Amemiya and Yamashita's house. And again the insects are loud. We're just finishing lunch: cooked cucumbers in a creamy broth. I would never have thought of something like this, but it's fantastic. In a nation of exquisite food, Amemiya's cooking is not only delectable, it's really unique. She's made do with what's in season, minus what they weren't able to grow successfully this year, which this season, she tells me, was quite a bit. Almost all the corn was eaten by crows and there was a blight on the tomatoes.

"So what vegetables *do* you have?" I ask.

"Cucumbers, green onions, carrots, green peppers, leeks, potatoes," she says. "And the eggplants are coming in a week or two!"

"Don't you sometimes have the desire to just go by the store and pick up some eggplants? I saw them on the way here in big bags, and cheap."

"*That* would be bad-mannered!" she exclaims. Then more softly, "There are flowers on the eggplant bush," the delight of seeing those pretty light-purple flowers audible in her voice, "and soon we'll have eggplants! It would be rude to the eggplant bushes—just ugly—to go out and buy them, don't you think?"

I laugh out loud. It's funny, but she also does mean it. They're part of her community; she feels the relations of common courtesy toward them.

Then I ask her how she feels about having so many weeds to cut, and with them roaring back so quickly. "Don't you feel, doing that year in and year out, 'Damn, this is a pain! I'm too tired!'?"

"Sure I do. Sure. But there are all kinds of disagreeable things in life, aren't there? I just think, 'That's my job.' Otherwise, if you started thinking the way you're talking about, you don't even clean up after yourself! You think, 'I did that yesterday, why do I have to do it again today?' It's better to say to yourself, 'If I cut back the weeds, then the eggplants will get big, and then I'll be really happy.'"

Later in the afternoon, as I am looking through my notes, I glance across the room and Amemiya is stretched out on the floor, reading a book, occasionally looking out the open door at the green, smoking her cigarette. Because of the heat, everyone's laying low. She turns a page, reads some more, then looks up again, gazing into the smoke

The lushness of the Japanese countryside can hardly be exaggerated.

Asha Amemiya • 149

wafting around, lost in thought, at ease in her body. To my eyes, she seems utterly content. I don't see such faces in the massive and glamorous department stores, fourteen stories high and crammed with every sort of possible stimulus that offers . . . no, promises to slake our thirsts.

In other Japanese houses, I think, the loose fibers of straw coming out from the tatami mats might be intolerable. But without money to fix them, it doesn't matter so much to Amemiya. For her, maybe just keeping ahead of the weeds to grow the food is sufficient for the day. A huge black butterfly with light yellow markings floats lazily in the heavy air just outside. This too is impermanent. She doesn't try to change everything to suit a prefabricated idea of what is comfortable. It feels very radical to me. And I realize how in my own life I've been far more fussy about what I "need" to live than really is necessary.

I hear other sounds in the background too: quiet water sounds, crickets, birds chittering in the branches. It's another "argument" going on behind whatever she and I are talking about, a more persuasive point of view. Sometimes it's just simple silence: the lack of any sound at all, or rather it is the lack of any machine sound. I think about how much humming, buzzing, roaring, accelerating, revving, and beeping I have slowly gotten used to in Japan without even noticing. In the late afternoon, the weather changes and the soft sound of a summer rain comforts my ears. I feel the intimacy of the sounds as the rain and light wind rustles in the trees, and the old house settles under the impact of the weather, with the susurrating downpour enveloping us all around.

As Amemiya and I sit together now, sipping tea from some nondescript ceramic cups and eating a few plastic-wrapped sweets that one of her neighbors gave her, I ask, "Why do you think India changed so much?"

She thinks for a while and says, "All humans are the same that way, aren't they? They get one good thing . . . ," she puts the tone of a little guilty pleasure in her voice, "and they want more."

I pick up one of the sweets that we are eating, "You mean something like this?"

"Mmm hmm!" she says, savoring the sweet flavor, raising her eyebrows.

Then, musingly, she says, "To make money is interesting, or it seems like it would be. It's like a game, that 'business' thing. And a game is interesting, right, once you start doing it. It's just like gambling.

"In India a long time ago, it was a society without capitalism (whether they used that kind of word or not)—a world of not having money. For all those years their values about that didn't change. They lived with the feeling of 'For us, life is good the way it is.'"

I ask her, "But do you think they really were satisfied?

Weren't they thinking, 'I'm poor, I really want to have a bit more money!'?"

"As far as it goes, everybody feels like that, not just Indians, anybody in the world who's poor; they want to become rich. But for the Indians of that time, living in peace, and their family around them, simply happy . . . " —there's a calm and settled tone to her voice—". . . it was fine.

"I think there was some difference between that and being poor in Japan and thinking, 'I've *got* to become rich, do some business . . . that gambling feeling, like I said before. In India back then, the barber's son or tailor's son, every day cutting people's hair, making clothes, they were able to survive with just enough to get by. They felt, 'I can live on this.' A Japanese person in that situation would be saying, 'This is miserable for me! I hate it!' These two feelings are a bit different, I think."

Then she cautions me, making sure I'm getting it right, "I'm talking about India a long time ago! As for today's India, I don't know. But some years back, with all those people excited about Gandhi, they just thought, 'OK, those rich people are those other people, and we are us.' With that kind of feeling they were satisfied; they were able to make it." She lights her cigarette and says, "When you think about it, satisfaction *is* happiness, isn't it? Don't you think so?"

As I'm scribbling her words down, she adds, "Ahh, anyway, this kind of talk gets to the point where it's just words . . . it's not so interesting."

"No, I don't think so!" I say. "It's interesting."

"Yeahhh, but it just becomes a bunch of words, only. There *is* a way of thinking, but as for speaking it, you could just go on saying it forever. Why don't we just switch topics in your 'interview' here?"

She means it, I understand, so I just leave it alone.

"So do you think you have changed in the twelve years you've been back from India?"

"Well, that guy," indicating poor Yamashita working over there at his desk, with his sad contemplative face, "he's changing more. He likes that kind of thing, you know, the computer. And he's also got a fax machine too. I like the old dial telephone." (For his part, Yamashita maintains that these things are only for his anti–nuclear waste dump organizing.)

"*This summer we have cucumbers, carrots, green peppers, leeks, potatoes. And the eggplants are coming!*"

Being in this house, I often feel I am partially outdoors.

"So why don't you like the computer and the fax machine?

"They're *too* convenient."

"Too convenient?" I say, with laughter in my voice. "What do you mean?"

"There's no need to write a letter any more."

It's true. I sometimes miss receiving an envelope, handwritten, on paper, in the mailbox, that sensory experience.

"Also," she adds, "convenience just speeds you up."

As obvious as it sounds, when I hear her say it, I wonder that I've never thought about it this way. I guess I, too, have gotten conned into thinking that the convenience machines give us will free up a lot of my time, and then I can use that time to slow down or something. Tools, I consider, are never neutral. Whether it's a hammer or a computer, a tool affects the way you think and behave, and sometimes even your values. Maybe convenience is just a faster conveyer belt and it hoodwinks me into thinking I can cram a lot more into my already crammed days.

"So, why do you think so many people get caught up in this?" I ask.

"I really don't know," she says, laughing, although perhaps somewhat bitterly. "I wonder why it is? Maybe it's just that humans are that kind of animal; they don't really want to move toward satisfaction. Or maybe it's just that the place where I'm satisfied is different . . ."

"So," I say, jokingly, "are the people who've figured all this out just smarter?"

"No," she laughs. "Not smarter. Just lazier." And then she adds, after a moment or two, "Us lazy people just ruin capitalist society."

Although she offers this last comment partially in jest, I know that Amemiya is continually thinking about the question of, to use her expression, "What makes an ideal society?" And I like how she is so hardheaded about it. To my mind, one of the things Amemiya articulates so clearly is that there's always a psychology to economics, and there's a moral aspect to it as well. It's a reminder for me that even though the kind of life she lives in the country is so rich—with its slow pace, full of the thrill of nature—there's no reason it has to be gauzy or wispy like a fairy tale. Because the Japanese countryside is so deeply appealing to me, I have to watch that I don't slip into that dreaminess myself. Still, looking out at the many rich greens of the valley, I ask Amemiya why she thinks more city people don't want to live out here as well. From her answer, I can tell that she thinks my question is pretty naïve.

"It might be impossible for them! I mean they have that 'It's so convenient' lifestyle. When they go off on the weekends to the countryside they may ask themselves if they might like to live out here. But then they put all the elements on the balancing scales. You know what I mean, those scales?"

I nod my head.

"They'd have to change their current way of life. So instead they might just continue to do a little 'nature thing' on the weekends, and find satisfaction." She pauses, "Well, not satisfaction, but it might allow them to endure their city life."

"That's the issue, right there," I say. "Those scales …"

"Yes," Amemiya says. "Which side of it becomes heavier really depends on that person's determination."

"So don't we need to find ways to help people make their determination stronger?" I say (thinking to myself, I admit, about this book).

But Amemiya shakes her head. "It's about whether that person himself *really* wants to do it. There are desires in people for each way. They've got children, they've got

a house, they've got a job, and they've got to make a living, don't they? It's not so easy to just climb aboard this trend of 'country living' and throw it all over in an instant and change everything." She's almost scolding me. "First of all takes *a lot* of courage; it's a difficult thing. I mean, if it's after you've finished your working life and have a pension and then you go and do it, well that's fine, but people who have a job, it's hard.

"Nonetheless," she says, focusing my attention with the tone of her voice, "even considering all that, there are people who do decide, 'Dammit, I'm going to do it.'

"But," she adds after a moment, "if everyone were to come out to the countryside, it'd be a hell of a problem for us. We'd have to kick them all out!" She laughs, lights a cigarette, looks out the open door, and then says, "Aaaanyway, everyone has their own path."

"So then," I ask, "Amemiya-san, if somebody, just a regular person wanted to make some changes in their lives, detach from the system somewhat, what would you tell them?"

"Well, if you want to, just do it a little bit, and only when you want to. Don't force it. When you get off the train, and it's noon, and your stomach's empty, well, maybe you brought your bento box, you made it at home and you can eat that, but if you didn't there's no need to just clench down and suffer. If you have a little money, you can buy some lunch. Or, for example, water. Just water. When you go out, you bring water with you, in an old bottle. I mean most people just buy it, right? They don't go through all the trouble of bringing it from home. So normally, in ten days, you buy a bottle of water all ten times, and you might realize, 'Now that's a waste, isn't it?' So for just two days of those ten, you think, 'I've got a bit of time, I'll make some tea at home, cool it down, put it in a bottle.' And you bring it with you. That's what I'm talking about."

As I think about it, I catch her drift. Her example, I think, could be a kind of metaphor for a lot of changes we each could make. Just planning ahead a little bit—that is to say, making a connection between our present and our future—can really reduce our dependence on convenience, and thus our resorting to waste.

"So in that way," I say with a smile, only half joking, "will capitalism slow to a stop?"

"If it does, it'll be interesting!" she smiles.

I laugh. "Interesting? How?"

"Well, all the changes. . . . " She's really delighted; you can hear it in the tone of her words. "Each person, with their tiny little will—you need a will—the world will change, and you will be able to see that. It would be interesting." Then after a pause, she adds, "But . . . probably it won't change, right?" Then, a little bit of a faraway sound coming into her voice, "Though, yeah, it might change . . . "

She's probably looking at the same facts I have been of late, which is why people are saying the system we're in is "unsustainable." So it *might* change. At some point, it's going to have to.

6

Akira Ito

Every so often, perhaps looking up at the stars at night, each of us turns our attention to the bigger questions. What is the universe, and how are we part of it? What has the past given us, and what part should it play in our lives today? We may give these questions some deep consideration on occasion, but it's hard to connect them to our day-to-day life. Getting a chance to meet and learn from the painter, writer, and philosopher Akira Ito, I began to connect these very different worlds. Both smart and wise, a scientist and an artist, highly talented and exceedingly humble, he has created a work of art out of his own life. Through his many pilgrimages to Nepal, India, and China, his documentation of the folk arts of traditional cultures, and his inquiry into the intersection of theoretical physics and Chinese philosophy, Ito has, I think, understood something essential about existence itself.

My editor at the *Japan Times* and I steal a quick and amused glance at each other as we step onto the crowded Tokyo subway car behind Mr. Ito—him dressed in blue and weather-faded peasant garb and conical straw hat, the quintessential mountain hermit of yore among the stylish and busy urbanites. He is wearing a rustic backpack made of stout wooden branches and thick hempen rope that bind a large cardboard box to his back. Though small and in his sixties, and though the box is heavy with glass-framed paintings, he moves with sure-footedness through the packed car. He, Ms. Yamaguchi, and I are on our way to have dinner at an Indian restaurant that he has invited us to after the closing of his exhibition of watercolors and handmade books.

As the train rocks back and forth under the world's largest city, Ito keeps his balance with his load like a rooted rope of kelp seaweed in heavy surf, talking excitedly about the title of my recently published article on him. I'm embarrassed that the part he likes the most is the headline, "The Unified Field Theory of Folk Art," the one part I did not write, it having been assigned instead by the staff at the *Japan Times*. He feels that it brought the two parts of his life together in a new way.

When we exit the subway Ito leads the two of us through underground passageways full of commuters, up staircases, and into a huge subterranean shopping mall where we make our way down a long corridor of boutiques lit by fluorescent lights and speakers blaring tinny J-pop music. He guides us unerringly amid the noise and haste to the small restaurant. The moment we step in the door the ambience changes completely and we are surrounded by the smells of spices, the quiet tones of a sitar, tasteful Indian décor, and the tactful waitstaff of a relatively upscale Tokyo establishment. From rustic peasant artist in the big city, Ito morphs in one breath into the distinguished and gracious gentleman with impeccable manners who makes one feel entirely at ease with oneself. He then proceeds to charm the urbane Ms. Yamaguchi, a thoroughly modern Tokyo intellectual, with literary references and tales of his recent travels in China. His weathered farm garments remind us, however, that we are with someone from an utterly different world.

Although Ms. Yamaguchi, has, I'm sure, seen a lot of good art in her day, she is behaving the same way I am, still deep in the enchantment that happens to all of us when art has contacted that rarely touched place inside. As she and Ito talk over samosas and thick milky chai, I think back to his exhibition at the gallery. On the blue walls in the low and quiet lighting hung Ito's many paintings illustrating the life of a Japanese man of letters living in the mountains, and the forest plants and creatures in the circle of life around him there. On several tables he had displayed copies of his richly colored children's books, a single-edition book of watercolor paintings of wildflowers from the southern island of Shikoku, and his small, handbound volume explaining how theoretical astrophysics and yoga practice (as well as classical Chinese philosophy) can, together, explain the working of all energy in the universe, from the quantum level to the big bang.

But of all the quite different works at the exhibition, the most moving for me was the smallest: a hand-sewn volume that fit into a box about the size of two packs of cards. The book, a loving documentation of traditional Nepali papermaking processes, displays Ito's affection for the ways of life of traditional rural peoples.

"I made this," he told me at the gallery, "as a way to try to support their way of life at the time that industrially produced paper was coming into Nepal from factories in other parts of the world. I had been doing research on handcrafts in the Himalayas in the 1970s, and I devised this project as a way to introduce Nepali methods to Japanese craftspeople, artists, and collectors."

By gathering funds from "subscribers" in Japan, Ito hired Nepali artisans to make the paper, carve the woodblocks, produce the prints page by page, and sew the pages together to produce a boxed edition of a few hundred copies.

The paper itself is baby soft, and so pleasing to the touch that I felt myself relaxing just holding it in my hands. In the gentle images on each page, I find women walking mountain pathways with straw baskets on their backs, while the trees, the river, the yaks, the clouds, and even the rocks of the mountain themselves vibrate with Ito's energetic line. Nepali men in woolen caps harvest branches from saplings which, on another page, are soaked in a rushing river and then beaten against rocks. Like the meshed fibers of the supple paper, the people seem completely woven into the energy of the landscape.

In this book I can feel what Ito cherishes. The pictures are of the peasant life of Nepal, yet the influence of Japanese folk art is evident as well. The entire process of boiling and pounding the fibers, sieving the pulp in screens under a thatched roof, drying the individual sheets in the sun or by the fire, are rendered in such an intimate and inviting style, yet the book has enough information that papermakers in Japan could use it to replicate all of

In addition to his daily yoga practice and devotional chanting, Ito spends his days writing, studying the Chinese classics, doing calligraphy, and handbinding books.

the techniques, and at the same time feel a sense of connectedness with others doing similar work far away.

Bringing his skills as an illustrator, a writer, and a book designer, and being the son of a traditional craftsman himself, Ito manages to have the book "say" (without saying) that in these mountain villages of Nepal, the daily life of the people, their artisanal craftwork, the specific local culture and the entire life-world are enmeshed into one single fabric. I think to myself that the project of this book is such a creative and nourishing way to accomplish actual cultural preservation and save traditions from extinction: financially supporting craftspeople so that they can continue to do their work, while at the same time both documenting the craft for posterity and introducing it to people in another country. It revitalizes both parties.

As Ito said to me once, "The *good* things of the past, that's what we must preserve. They have passed through the hardships of history to become a tradition, and we who are alive today must treasure them, and take care of them for the future."

Palm Wine and the Ganges of Heaven

Without a single lightbulb, the night sky of
Mithila village is a darkness of pure lacquer black.
Onto that, the radiance of the stars is fierce

everywhere. The downpour of their chaste and brilliant rays bathes us as we tip back glasses of palm wine. Extraordinary! The alcohol content is low, but after a number of cups we are overtaken by a mild intoxication. It is as if the Milky Way was the Ganges of Heaven cutting across the sky with the luminescence of flowing palm wine. The number of stars is so countless, and they close in upon us so, it feels almost as though we'll float off into the universe. But no! In truth we are already afloat in the universe's flow.

—Akira Ito

~

When I finally arrive at the end of the bus line that Ito-san's directions indicate, I feel like I might have arrived at the end of the earth, which is a strange sensation as I am less than three hours from central Tokyo, one of the largest cities in the world. Still, the many conveyances—subway to express train to slowly chugging local—transferring at ever more rural stations, the slow winding bus rides over steep canyons with rushing rivers, and eventually the final half hour on the bus with me the only passenger, the last junior high school student having disembarked at the last seeming habitation, all of this combines to produce a gentle loneliness and, like an old forest with its dark, overhanging boughs, the promise of coming upon something unknown.

When I step off the bus, I find myself near a solitary bus shelter with a single, rusted, round sign, tilting slightly from the weather, indicating the route name and number. On the other side of the bus turnaround are the stairs of a decrepit Shinto shrine and a steeply wooded mountainside behind it.

The bus driver finishes his cigarette and climbs back into his seat, and the loud bus trundles off. Presently a man wearing the kind of yellow hard hat often worn by a construction laborer comes putt-putting down the single lane road on a motor scooter. I think maybe it's some out-of-work timber worker now seasonally employed in the cement industry, but when he stops the scooter and takes off the absurd helmet, I see that it is Ito-san, greeting me with a warm smile.

Besides my unusual friend, I see nothing of particular interest at the bus stand, but Ito immediately comments on the abandoned futon mattresses next to the shelter. Five well-maintained futons, their fabric slightly faded in the sun, have been placed for the next garbage collection in a neat stack by someone who evidences the customary Japanese countryside orderliness even in the placement of their refuse.

"Ho ho! Perfect condition. A grand harvest!" Ito pronounces. "This would have been very useful last week when the Tibetan lama came and I had all the guests! But no matter, he's coming back next month. Great!"

I volunteer to carry a mattress while Ito ties two to the back of his motorbike, donning once more the construction hard hat with the cupped chin strap. He points up the hill along the narrowing road through the woods and gives me rough directions as he putts off ahead, dropping off the first load and coming back for a second.

When I get to the end of the pavement, Ito packs the second load of futons into a solitary storage building, parks his motor scooter, and leads me off onto a narrow path through thick woods, going seemingly nowhere at all, until, after cresting a small rise and curving down to the right we see a quite large three-story house made of dark brown wood, with a blue sloping metal roof, sliding wooden and paper doors, and a low porch in front.

I put down my bags, and even though I've hardly shaken off the city and all the traveling from my brain, Ito says, "Ah! There's still enough daylight. Let's see if we can find some mushrooms in the woods for dinner tonight." In the light duff under the trees Ito finds seven or eight different edible varieties, all of which he can distinguish authoritatively.

Coming back from India, Ito said, "I decided to quit that Tokyo life and live in a mountain village myself."

Now it is after dinner and we've finished the udon noodles that we made by hand. The October night is fully dark. Augmenting the darkness is the deep burgundy color of the wood and the physical size of the house that separates us from the world outside in a substantive way. Beyond that, the woods.

Presently, a villager in his forties drops by for a visit, a working man who does shifts at a fire lookout tower (which Ito refers to as a "star viewing platform") in a direction that Ito indicates to me with his hands, off in the dark. Then, to my surprise, Ito takes out a bottle of whiskey, and I find myself in this male world of sitting at a table, talking, drinking scotch. Though, as with everything with Ito, there's something slightly different here.

As we drink, I try to imagine his life: an electrical engineer in a petroleum refinery until the age of twenty-eight after growing up as the son of a traditional craftsman in a small town. He tells me more details about his boyhood, and I can only shake my head at the hodge-podge of influences. "I was born in 1935 into a family of paperhangers. My father was an artisan, doing handwork making sliding paper doors.

"They gave me a militarist education in school," he says, matter of factly. Calculating backward to figure out when Ito was born, I realize he was being trained for fighting in Japan's Imperial Army. "But when I wasn't in school," he says, "I spent a lot of my time dancing in the fields with the grasses and flowers, or going fishing. Other than that, I spent time drawing pictures."

"What kinds of things were you drawing?" I ask, imagining his current botanical work.

"Mostly fighters, tanks, and warships." We both

laugh to think of it. "But at home my father was a devout Buddhist, and would recite sutras every morning and night. I could hear them from where I slept, and I had many of them memorized from hearing them so often."

Early on Ito showed promise in mathematics and the sciences so the family decided to send him to high school, something his elder brother, who was to take over the family business, was not permitted. College, however, was impossible—"We were too poor," Ito says—so after graduation, he went to work as an electrical engineer in a petroleum refinery. Like so many in his generation, he was caught up in the postwar expansion of the Japanese economy and left his small town to receive training in Western science and technology. The changing economy of the heavily populated countryside could no longer give work to its sons.

This change from the hand work of his father's generation to the industrial salaried work that Ito took up seems to me archetypal of the wrenching shift the entire society experienced in the shock of the postwar period. But Ito did not follow the path of so many others of his generation. At twenty eight, he gave up that high-status life as an engineer, its money and its security, to begin a journey that led him through being an itinerant artist and philosopher, and later, to living in this house in the woods near the slopes of Mt. Fuji in order to follow in the foot-steps of the Chinese mountain literati of ancient times. His choice to try to wrest freedom from a society not accustomed to granting it easily says to me that Ito was somehow able to break the dual trances of achievement and money that so many people today are living snugly inside of. "When I quit my job, I knew if I didn't do what I really wanted to do then, that when it was time to die I would be left with regrets," he says.

As we talk, I notice that Ito's eyes show a softness and compassion, although somewhat tinged with sadness. His treble voice seems to come from far back in his throat and is often marked by a hesitation, a slight pause before choosing the right words, as if he is constantly checking to be sure that what he says will not unintentionally injure another. He is generous to a fault, and his hollow cheeks remind me of his many fasts. His sparse, triangular eyebrows, his gray wispy beard and spotted skin, and the way he carries his head slightly forward remind me of his age, but underneath these surface things, one can always feel the glow of energy coming from him, something I imagine is a result of his years cultivating his interior resources.

Ito now goes over to a wooden cabinet and pulls out a small object to show me and his neighbor. When he brings it into the light, I see that it is a book bound in dark-blue cloth in the traditional manner, with an accordion fold, as all books in Japan once were. Its title is *Pictures of a Long Ago Journey*, by Takeshi Motai. As he hands me the book Ito says, "This may sound strange, but though I never met him, this man was my teacher."

Motai, an illustrator and painter active in the late 1940s and '50s, has been a source of inspiration through most of Ito's life. When I open the book, I find a style of painting that is rough, abstract, and brightly colored, showing a naïveté that reminds me of children's drawings, and a sympathy with their world. Yet this effect somehow manages to be in no way mannered or forced.

Looking at this book I recognize that Ito has also chosen this innocent way of portraying the world in his own artwork. It is a way of seeing and drawing we all practiced at one time but abandoned once we became older. Ito's choosing this style shows a humility, even a tenderness, not in fashion in our times.

Ito explains to me that Motai's paintings hearken back to a journey Motai took in his youth, when he boarded the Trans-Siberian Railroad in 1930 and made the long overland journey to Europe at twenty years of age. Almost all of Motai's drawings from that period were later burned in the firebombing of Tokyo in World War Two, so he made this one book of paintings simply for himself and his three children.

"Can you imagine," Ito says with awe in his voice, "that without photographs or sketches, he painted them from impression and memory only?" The book, I next find out, was never published in Motai's lifetime. In his archiving of Motai's work in the mid 1970s, Ito discovered the original book of paintings among Motai's papers and arranged for its publication as a hardback, conventionally bound art book.

After its publication, Ito reconstructed and rebound the book in an accordion style with this handwoven cloth cover. It takes even more discussion, translation, laughter, nighttime, and scotch to understand that this accordion binding was the *original* form for the manuscript that Motai himself hand-bound, years ago when he painted it in 1943 in the middle of World War Two. Ito has re-animated the form back to its original source. I like the metaphor: rescuing the spirit out of mass production and, through care and precise work with the hands, making it come alive again.

In the first plate, the sky is a murky blue and a boat low in the water sits moored alone in a harbor, illustrating Motai's departure from the southern Japanese port of Hakata. As we page through the book, Ito reads the caption, "The sounds of strings and voices singing are fading into the smoke of the land of night."

Now the three of us slowly pore over the richly colored images and Ito's story begins to merge with that of his teacher's in my mind. For Ito, at thirty-five years old, decided to retrace Motai's journey himself, boarding the Trans-Siberian Railroad to Europe and starting a two-year journey to study the art of the world. While it could be said that we all retrace the paths of our forebears, Ito made this explicit in his life. The sense of the two men's lives fusing into one is heightened by the lack of subject pronouns in Japanese, and I often lose track of which journey Ito is telling me about as we move through the book.

He turns the page and now we are in Korea. A boy monk gestures to a couple who are dining while sitting in an open pavilion. Ito tells me the boy, who holds a wand of incense sticks, is singing a song of the four seasons.

"I really like this kind of place," says Ito, "it's a *ryotei*, a traditional restaurant, in a traditional building. The food is probably so as well, don't you think? And the people who are eating there and living nearby are continuing to live the way they have from long ago."

The villager breaks in with a laugh, "Ah, just like you Ito-san!"

"Me?" Embarrassed, Ito laughs self-consciously, "No, I'm just imitating!"

～

It has been almost ten years since I began to contemplate the universe of energy, or *ki* (*chi*). One day, I hit upon the idea to create a serial work of paintings on the theme of "A forest and the circling sun," linked with this contemplation.

In this work I wanted to capture on paper the drama of the lives of various creatures in the forest, particularly hoping to express my awe of—and thanks to—the plants for the creation of all the foods for all the beings of the forest that they make by way of photosynthesis from the showering unto the earth of light energy from the sun.

In each season, while I sketch and put down the shapes and forms of plants, flowers, animals, and bugs, embraced by the life of the forest, I sometimes experience a complete unification with the forest and all its life. These times are truly times of bliss for me.

Picking tea leaves on a rainy July day for fermented bancha *tea.*

As a vegetarian and abiding by the yoga precepts, I literally depend on plants for all my food. When I recently wrote an innocent story about a feast on wild plants, the story by the Buddhist poet and philosopher Kenji Miyazawa was playing continuously in my mind: "We all eat other lives to nurture our own life. When our turns come, let's allow ourselves to be eaten unbegrudgingly."

Though I keep it in my mind to try not to do any harm to any creatures, and to feel affectionate toward all of them as though they were part of myself, it is hard to imagine and feel the sense of pain of plants, and I regret that I have often acted as a tyrant toward them.

Plants in the mountain benefit me beyond their direct gifts of themselves as food. The small stream from which I draw water for my house has never dried up, most likely because the forest trees upstream maintain the water in it. And in the winter, the forest all around me supplies me with fuel in the form of fallen logs to heat my house with the woodstove. The warmth of a wood fire is soft, and is quite different from the heat provided from gas or kerosene. Wood heat warms one all the way to the center of the body. The warmth is a gift from the trees of the forest. I've even overlooked the fact that the house itself is made of wood.

When I look at my life in the mountain village in this way, I keenly feel that my whole life depends on plants, and this thought adds to my awe and reverence for them more and more.

The harvest season and autumn colors will soon come to the mountains of this village. Many animals are waiting for the ripening of acorns, horse chestnuts, and wild grapes. Deep in autumn, leaves which have finished their tasks turn to shining red or yellow, and go back to the earth while giving off their wonderful fragrance.

Knowing the shortness of my share of life, and feeling it keenly, watching over the falling leaves, I sometimes wish that I also will disappear altogether like the leaves. Until then, I hope that I can live in peace, and in health, and with the support of all the plants.

—from "The Boons Bestowed by Plants" by Akira Ito

[TRANS. ATSUKO WATANABE}

"Born of nothingness and returning to emptiness, the universe is ceaseless change."

~

Ito's neighbor is kind of a rough sort, not a mountain philosopher or poet. Yet Ito makes him feel welcome with his typical kindheartedness, and the three of us share the night together with the villager's brusque personality, Ito's halting attempts to adjust to a world he is not quite suited to, and my own persistent questions.

With Ito's narration we follow Motai's journey of memory as it overlaps and mixes with that of Ito's. Night scenes predominate: a Christian festival of lights in Eastern Russia; the green interior of a sleeper car of the Trans-Siberian Railroad with bunks as it crosses the vast Russian Steppe. Motai then comes down through Europe, and stays for a year in Paris, painting.

Now Ito brings out another book from his cabinet, this one hardbound with a spine. It is entitled *Ton Paris*, and is a facsimile of Motai's beautifully illustrated journals, with the young Motai in an enchanted Paris of 1930. This too, I find out, was collected, annotated, and published through the offices of Ito-san. By looking at this period of Motai's work, I can see that he was an accomplished draftsman and could paint sophisticated, lifelike renderings of people and street scenes, but that he chose this later naïve style on purpose.

Ito picks up Motai's *Pictures of a Long Ago Journey* again, bringing us south from Paris down into Italy, and now we are in a sun-drenched Naples with laundry flapping on the balconies of bright yellow buildings. Seamlessly Ito shifts to his own story as he meets up with a friend at an art academy in Milan, both of them looking at the paintings of Hieronymus Bosch, Goya, Brueghel, van Gogh and, especially Gauguin.

As we page through the images from Motai's travels, I feel steeped in both of these men's lives as they overlap each other, imagination and memory mixing in layers. To me, it is one of those moments when actual mystery comes alive, sitting as I am in a dark house in the deep woods, immersed in another language with this older man, and scotch in between us. How improbable that I would ever see such a book, a book never intended to be shown—painted in a burnt-out Tokyo of 1943, by someone now dead for half a century—and yet it is here, a resurrected document, one stake stuck in the ground against the fierce onrush of time.

There's a companionship as well, as both Ito and I meet in the love of the adventures of travel and also of the echoing resonances they leave inside of us. We seem to both be reveling in the abstract nature of the past itself, the pages of the book acquiring potency in his telling. Now both men's journeys are over, but through it all something remains, the residues of time, the brushstrokes in stories and paintings each of them left behind, if only just a few.

~

Some years later I get to meet Motai's son, Izumi, after being given his address in California by Ito. Izumi was only nine when his father died, and at age twenty he made his way to the U.S. to study art, and returned to Tokyo for some years after graduation. Yet now here he is sitting across from me at a sunlight-drenched Chinese teahouse in Berkeley. Graying at the temples, Izumi is the epitome of the handsome and impeccably mannered graphic designer. As we talk, he recalls fondly the days in the early 1970s when Ito was a guest in the family's home, archiving the elder Motai's work.

"Yes," he recalls, "when I went off to America to art school, we closed up the old house, and I put all my father's paintings, drawings, and manuscripts in some tea boxes. Do you know what a tea box is?"

I shake my head, and he says, "A tea box is a completely airtight wooden box with tin lining, about this big," he holds his hands apart about two feet by three feet by three, "and they used to store freshly harvested green tea in them for transport. It was those tea boxes that saved me in Ito-san's eyes. If I hadn't done that, who knows what would have become of me!" He laughs.

"And it was a good thing we put all those old paintings and drawings in there, because the paper after the war was a quite poor quality; it decays with age, yellows, and falls apart. Almost all of his paintings were on that kind of paper. You'll have to remember, I was twenty at the time, and not too responsible. I just packed it all up and put it in a closet in the house in Tokyo and off I went to San Francisco. Can you imagine what Ito felt, opening that closet and coming upon all that work?! It was a treasure trove for him."

After coming back from his first journey to Europe and India, Ito was put up by the Motai family in Tokyo. Izumi had returned home after finishing art school, and he now tells me stories of the lively bohemian parties Ito would throw in the quiet Tokyo residential neighborhood. It was this period when Ito embarked on the painstaking process of curating and cataloging all of the elder Motai's paintings, writings, and journals. Working in conjunction with editors and publishers, he began to arrange for the republication in books and magazines of the almost-forgotten master's works, adding his own essays and commentaries. By reintroducing Motai to the Japan of the mid 1970s, Ito was sharing something he felt was worthy of saving and making it available for future generations—"preserving the good things of the past."

As Ito studied Motai's writings, archived his works, and made copies of his paintings, he steeped himself in the artist's influence, and this is how Motai became Ito's "teacher," even though he had passed on almost two decades previously. Many nights Ito would drink saké and excitedly tell Izumi and his sister Koyomi about why their father's work was so excellent, or bend his head over a mathematical proof he was trying to work out.

Listening to Izumi's tales of Ito, I fill in with my imagination what those days might have been like, with Ito in a topknot and north-Indian garb inviting all kinds of strange people not ordinarily seen in that neighborhood to come over and drink or play Indian music, the neighbors not knowing what to make of any of it. I shake my head, because for me Ito has always seemed the quintessentially restrained older gentleman. But when I see a book of his paintings from that time, a picaresque of ski accidents and hot spring mishaps, I can begin to picture a younger, slightly wilder Ito.

Izumi has brought with him to the teahouse a large tome of his father's illustrations. Turning the heavy pages, I can see again Motai's influence on Ito. The ink drawings, mostly dating from the late 1940s, seem more like woodblock prints with their simple, rough-edged lines, and they match the mood of their subjects perfectly. There are lovely whimsical images of animals dancing at festivals, of two grasshoppers arm-wrestling as a pair of curious smiling snails look on, and of a fox taking a nighttime walk with a skin flask full of saké.

It was also at this time that Ito began to publish his own writing more widely. His poetic essays on woodblock printing and on Nepali and Tibetan culture and religion would run occasionally in one of Japan's foremost arts and literary magazines, and he was also asked to provide—in the form of prose poem and ink drawing—the monthly cover to a journal of news of the Indian subcontinent. Over the decades he contributed hundreds of such pieces, giving the publication a recognizable and unique aesthetic.

During these years, although in his late thirties, Ito lived like a student, or so it seems to me, getting part-time work in factories or polishing bamboo. Sometimes he and his friends would live in dormitories, and travel by boat back to the subcontinent whenever they had enough money saved up. Ito once told me that it took about half a year of working in Japan to put together five thousand dollars, on which he could live for almost four years in India and Nepal. I consider that this was right smack in the middle of the biggest economic expansion Japan had ever seen, which is to say that Ito and his friends could have gotten wealthy along with the rest of Japan if they had wanted to. It seems like a nugget of wisdom to me: If you don't need it, don't take it.

~

It is morning now at Ito's house in the forest. First he shows me his eclectic morning ritual, including changing the water in the little cups in front of each of seven deities, from the folk sprites Kappa and Tengu to several bodhisattvas and Gautama Buddha. He then offers rice and incense at his little altar for his mother and father, who passed away in the late 1980s. He makes offerings for the health of the rice farmers of the south and for the hunters of the north.

He then leads me through a series of yoga poses he has put together, adding in postures borrowed from sumo wrestling, explaining what the health effects are of each. Then Ito lights a stick of incense, and while hitting a big bell with a piece of turned wood, he chants several sutras, one with a sweet lyrical tune, and one more dirgelike with a grinding *chung-chung-chung* rhythm to it, similar to those I often hear in Japanese temples. We follow that with a short period of silent meditation.

When we finish, he invites me up a very steep flight of dark wooden stairs to the second floor. I see immediately that he has given over the entire floor of this large house (previously a building for the raising of silk worms, he says) to his study, library, and art studio. Although he is deep in the mountains I find here the life of a true intellectual. As Ito sits at his desk and begins to look through his papers with his reading glasses slid down on his nose, he indicates that I am welcome to look through the bookshelves.

I sit on the floor beside his bookshelves, the autumn sunlight pouring in from the windows on all sides and begin pulling down volumes here and there. In one section, I find several whimsically illustrated books of fairy tales and nursery rhymes in German and in English: Mother Goose, of course, Hans Christian Andersen and the Brothers Grimm. It's so funny, I think to myself, to find these in the mountains of Japan. On the next set of shelves, copiously loaded down with books, I come upon Japanese translations of the great Chinese classics of Taoism—Lao Tsu and Chuang Tsu—as well as Confucius and Mencius. On another shelf, I find several collections of Japanese poetry perfectly bound and fitting snugly into the slip-cover boxes, the end pages of translucent glassine paper. The beauty with which the books are bound, the context, the person who owns them, all come together to produce the richness of the experience of holding them here, now.

On another wall, I discover a long shelf full of small, hand-bound volumes. I ask Ito-san about them and he tells me that they are his "picture journals." As I page through them, he says, "Ah, I remember. That was indeed a good period. For several years I tried to write down a single image to encapsulate each day." Indeed there are 365 pages to each volume, with each page showing a quick line drawing and sometimes a few lines of text.

Looking through these small but strangely moving sketches, I see years of time, each day marked and made conscious. I wonder what I would understand of my own life, of life in general, if I did this myself. I remember what our mutual friend Murata once said to me about Ito. We had been speaking about one or two of our acquaintances that had given up on pursuing their artwork or their creative careers. I had asked Murata why.

"Have you ever seen Ito's workroom?" he asked. "He has such a huge amount of drawings and sketches. It's like a mountain! Those people who think that being an artist always has be glorious and shining—they're the ones who give up. You've got to be like Ito-san. Just keep walking, on and on, creating your work."

One hand-bound book that particularly catches my eye contains a series of original watercolors centered around the life of a single but massive persimmon tree, from its first emergent leaves to the harvesting of the

luscious fire-orange fruits. In one of the paintings the artist, a younger Ito of twenty years past with jet-black curly hair, is sitting on a second-floor balcony amidst a flurry of cherry blossom petals, eating a bento box breakfast and gazing at the tree in the first flush of springtime, light all around. In another, he is perched in the thick brown branches of the tree, gazed at by mythic-eyed birds straight out of central Indian tribal art. On the next page, a brown bear takes the place of the human in the branches, snacking on the succulent fruit in the half-moonlit night. In one of the last illustrations, the young Ito has tied a rope around his waist and hangs from the branches harvesting the bright orange globes, hundreds of which populate the now otherwise barren and brown scraggly branches of the big tree. Like much of Ito's work, in these paintings the very vibrations of the air and light hum through the brushstrokes like thousands of tiny white threads caught on the wind.

"My own inner eyesight was not sufficient, so I decided to train myself as a yogi."

Akira Ito • 169

The handwriting that narrates the tale is warbly and full of energy, compelling. Looking at this book, I think of the line from Ito's article about life in the forest, "In each season, while I sketch and put down the shapes and forms of plants, flowers, animals, and bugs, embraced by the life of the forest, I sometimes experience a complete unification with the forest and all its life. These times are truly times of bliss for me."

～

Growing like thunderheads all summer long, the trees and plants of the woodlands thrive and cover every bit of the mountain until they finally begin to lose their momentum, and in the dark shadows of a forest that has gone through its adolescence and prime, one feels a touch of sadness.

The forest in September is so abundant in foliage that underneath everything is darkened. However, in winter, the trees lose their leaves and you can see through the woods very well. Then the dramatic transformation that a mixed-species forest goes through every year in early spring is truly extraordinary. Young shoots growing from the branches of trees burn like light-green flames, and before long, the forest which had been empty is filled with green leaves. Walking over the pass that leads to my house and observing the changes, I understand the Buddhist phenomenon of "existence emerging from nothingness" and the phenomenon from modern physics of "energy transforming into matter." I understand that these abstract, philosophical ideas represent exactly what is happening here.

"Energy transforming into matter" is the process of photosynthesis—sunshine energy, with carbon dioxide, creating organic compounds, that is to say plants creating leaves with the energy they have taken in. "Existence emerging from nothingness" can be seen when shoots and then leaves appear from the bare branches of the trees using that potent energy-nourishment. And then in autumn they fall off of the trees and return into the forest, or into the original state of "emptiness" or "nothingness."

Thus in the forest I am able to learn that these phases of the circulation of energy, the "formation and disappearance," are common to all phenomena of energy, and this understanding can advance my work in the contemplation of the universe as a phenomenon of energy.

—from "To Learn from the Forest" by Akira Ito
[TRANS. ATSUKO WATANABE]

~

Now it is after lunch, and Ito tells me what had originally started him off on his first pilgrimage. After quitting his job at the oil refinery, he worked for a few years in book design and publishing. But though he was skilled in that technical world there was a question he had to have answered, a question about life and death itself that was planted in him in his childhood, and which eventually caused him to throw all that over and start out on the road.

He recalls to me that pivotal moment at ten years old: "It was near the end of the war in 1945 and the town next to mine was heavily firebombed one night. My family was evacuated and although I escaped unhurt, I became terrified of death. My question was: 'When will it be my time to die, and where is it that we are headed after death?'

"Then, when I was twelve years old I read an article in a children's science magazine entitled 'The Earth's Very Last Day,' which described how the sun will some day expand and explode, and burn up our planet completely. This article had a big impression on me because of the experience I had at the end of the war. I thought 'This kind of thing is really going to occur,' and from that time on I wanted to know everything I could about the cosmos."

Ito then takes from his desk an illustrated chart that shows the progression of his inquiry into physics and cosmology through time. In one very small sketch, a tiny figure stands on the edge of a sphere. The words say, "The end of the cosmos (watching)." This one rough drawing immediately communicates the sense of a miniscule person in the vast universe, looking out at emptiness. The density of information conveyed in such a small space and with so few lines is remarkable to me. Other illustrations in the chart take on issues of entropy, phase changes of matter, and infinity. He tells me that he always uses images for thinking—"Drawing is a way of reasoning on paper." And it's true, his illustrations allow me to go beyond the limits of verbal rationality. Here is ontology and epistemology as well as theoretical astrophysics, all on his little chart. It does something more, and something other, than words alone.

And what does it mean to be "a philosopher," especially outside of the structure of a university? Looking at Ito's life, it seems to me that it is a bold attempt to understand the world, as big as it is; to understand

still studying techniques at that time," he says. "My heart hadn't yet changed that much."

Listening to him, I understand that Ito is very much a pilgrim, and that travel is one of his primary ways of knowing. It may seem obvious to say that one must see the world to know it, but for a philosopher, someone who wants to understand the human in relation to the universe, journeying is an unparalleled way to do it.

It was also on his first journey to India that Ito first met his lifelong friend and future collaborator, Shucho Takaoka. They traveled together trekking in the Himalayas, visiting *gompa* (Tibetan monasteries) and exploring Buddhist art together.

Looking for an Observation Platform for the Things of the World

When I was a child, I always liked to climb a hill near our town to look around at all the scenery. I could climb on the ruins of the old castle tower and look out over schools, temples, the shrine in the woods, and the saké factory chimneys. Even today all the details of the town are inscribed on my brain.

As I got older, my horizons broadened and I began to think that there must be some place

While archiving the work of the artist Takeshi Motai, Ito lived with the late artist's family. There he wrote and illustrated a children's book for the family's daughter.

ourselves, as complicated and broken as we are; and to find some wisdom in this swirl that will help reduce the amount of suffering—both ours and others'.

In pursuit of the question of where we are headed after death, Ito decided in 1970 to quit his job in publishing, leave Japan, and look for answers in the way that many before him had, in the worlds of spirituality and art. Following in Takeshi Motai's footsteps, he traveled through Europe, and then overland through the Middle East, through Afghanistan and Pakistan heading toward India. "I took twenty-two months on this journey, moving without any hurry, although my plan was only to be gone six months."

In India he focused on a study of Buddhist art, especially Tibetan *tanka* and woodblock prints. "But I was where I could get a grand view of the whole world. Geographically, the earth is round, so an easy place like that cannot exist, but still I thought there must be some high place where I could see the world with "the eyes of the heart." I left Japan in the early summer of 1970 and traveled to Europe. I climbed the Moscow Tower and the Eiffel Tower and Mt. Blanc, and although they all had great views of their respective locations, they were not what I was looking for. I saw Mt. Ararat as I crossed the Middle East, where Noah's Ark was thought to have landed, and that seemed to be a good place to look out over the world, but I couldn't get a visa so I was forced to give that up.

Entering India I headed in the direction of Mt. Everest, and on my way, I came to the Buddha's Eye Temple outside of Kathmandu. It is the world's biggest tower that contains some relics of the Buddha's ashes. On the four walls of this tower, the huge compassionate eyes of the Buddha are painted. These merciful eyes look out over the whole world to save all living beings from their sufferings. I climbed up to the platform of this huge tower at sunset and crossed my legs, widened my eyes in all four directions, and surrounded them with my prayerful imagination. I realized that this had been the world-viewing platform that I had always been looking for. I felt how the Buddha's affectionate and compassionate eyes were watching the world, enlightened innocent eyes that could see the true nature of all objects without missing the most enormous or the tiniest thing anywhere in the world.

And I realized that my own inner eyesight was not sufficient to see the world. I decided to train myself as a yogi and set off for the yogi's most holy land, in Rishikesh on the skirts of the Himalayas.

[TRANS. ATSUKO WATANABE]

Translating any of Ito's work into English is always difficult; the words send me to my Japanese dictionary again and again. He always writes in such a literary style, regularly employing characters not much in common use anymore, and his particularly poetic turns of phrase are hard to render into English without harming them. Even the sounds of the words themselves echo the topics he is writing about. When he writes about woodblock carving, for example, the syllables in the original Japanese seem to re-create the sound of a chisel being hammered into hard wooden blocks. Native Japanese speakers as well always remark about the beauty of Ito-san's prose. And as I read his writing about craft, about being an artisan, I see that when he describes a technique it is more than just instructions or a purely technical discussion for practitioners. For him, the "how" of a craft cannot be divorced from the heart of the craftsperson. It is the core of their life, and the handwork is not simply a means to do something; it *is* the meaning itself.

Tibetan woodblocks are carved in a much different way than Japanese ones are. On the first day of my training in Kathmandu with my Tibetan teacher, I went to the workshop and observed the tools that they used. For carving the wood plate they only used the flat and round type of chisels while Japanese use a variety of chisels including a woodblock knife, which cuts a smooth and streamlined curve. The characteristic nature of Tibetan carving is that it is done with lots of little cuts, exactly like the ticking of the second hand on a clock. It takes a lot of time, but this is exactly what makes the work fascinating, what gives it that "flavor."

When I finished my final assignment after several weeks of training, I showed it to my teacher. He praised me by saying that I had done it quite quickly. But hearing his words, I felt like my impatience and hastiness—so common to a Japanese person—had been exposed and I felt embarrassed. I realized keenly how accomplishing this kind of clock-ticking cut is not simple or easy at all.

After my initial training, I took some time to leave Kathmandu and travel around Nepal. I went with a friend to the Langtang Valley, known as one of the most beautiful valleys in the world. We visited one particular temple located in a tiny village of no more than twenty houses where people had been going for almost a thousand years. There they had several woodblocks, and it was the custom for the pilgrims to bring a piece of paper and rub a print from these old and holy wooden blocks. The pilgrims could take this image home to decorate their houses, or to use at times of festivals and ceremonies, and the donations received would be a source of income for this temple.

Tibetan woodblocks are not made by artists; rather they are brought into being by craftsmen and by monks. Having made the crossing of all these generations of refinement, the woodblock prints have attained a high level of sophistication. Then, through the process of rubbing the paper on the wood, a kind of unity is achieved—a weaving of the wood and paper and ink.

Tibetan woodblock prints have thus been created from four elements: the depth of the artisan's spiritual faith, the harmony of the materials with each other, the heart of the individual craftsperson, and the powerful wood-carving skills of the Tibetan people as a whole. By tightly binding these four elements with each other, the very beautiful world of the woodblock print has been created. It is not just a form of art.

In one temple I visited, every morning the chanting of sutras woke me up. There I saw the women circling around a stupa where some of the Buddha's ashes were interred. Moving forward little by little, they would advance on their circular pilgrimage, each time making a full-body prostration. They would lay their bodies out fully on the stone, stand up, move one inch forward, and lay themselves out once again, moving forward one notch at a time. It was exactly like a clock cutting out the seconds, like the cutting of a chisel, one little notch at a time.

And it had the same interior quality given by the woodblock prints.

—from *Tibetan Woodblock Prints of the Himalayas*

Reading this, translating it phrase by phrase, I'm starting to understand a bit of Ito's fundamental sadness. He is running against the current of this era. He struggles in his essay to render this culture and craft of Tibetan woodblock prints and the values embodied in them to a modern society that, at least from its outward appearances, does not seem to care. And I think this explains Ito's melancholy to some extent: so many beautiful things in this world are disappearing, and he feels that loss keenly.

Ito now shows me yet another hand-made book, a series of brightly colored paintings from Benares, India, one of the oldest cities in the world. It is as ancient as Babylon and Jerusalem, over thirty-five hundred years. There the pink sandstone towers of Hindu temples line the Ganges, and hundreds of thousands of pilgrims bathe at the edges of the massive river as it cuts through the sweltering central Indian plains. To my eyes, Ito's paintings from Benares are, of all his work, some of the most vivid and intense: a funeral procession wends its way through the old city in a crowd down to the river; two very small children, almost infants, with the most open and vulnerable faces, look upon each other in a field by a large-eyed cow; three sages, Brahmin priests, sit on a platform by a glowing Ganges in the late afternoon under a white canopy, discussing earnestly with each other.

Seeing Ito's characteristic wavering line, I remember asking his old friend, the potter Gufu Watanabe, about Ito's theory of art.

"He believes that the best art is rough, simple, and artless, and that is better than to have clear, clean lines. The idea is that nature itself is good, so wood is better than plastic. It's not 'perfect'; it doesn't tire you."

I tilt my head in questioning, "How can art 'tire' you?"

"Because humans *are* nature, of course. The surface of the earth is uneven, full of dips and bumps. It is mixed and incomplete. If you think about the world of pottery, fine celadon and porcelain ware are like jewels—they don't let you sink in, feel at ease, and relax. The tea master Rikyu said that the seat in the teahouse where you sit should have the feeling of the earth itself. Similarly, perfectly completed work is not to Ito's liking. He likes slow and soft movement, rough, like the *shoji* doors opening, *shhhhh*. He avoids complexity of expression in his drawings. That's why he prefers handcrafted and unsophisticated art, things made by common people. Without artifice or professionalism, the essence of an expression can shine through."

~

As Ito traveled around India with his friend Takaoka, he says, "I began to understand what it was that the Buddha taught, how exactly to escape from suffering."

"But hadn't you always been interested in Buddhism?" I ask him.

"Yes, since I was a child. My father was a very serious Buddhist. But at that time, my understanding of Buddhist teaching was not so deep. It was mostly words, the surface level, not the essence."

"I think it's interesting," I say, "that you got a deeper understanding of Buddhism in India, which is a Hindu country, while Japan is a Buddhist country."

"Japanese people often don't get the true nature of Buddhism. It's difficult to do in the twentieth century. Japanese people learn Buddhism formally and from books, but that is just surface-level information. It doesn't possess the power to have them really understand it on that deep level.

"Also, through their daily life they get trapped in habits and patterns. Buddhism isn't a calling for them. They don't do the actual training, the practices, and so they don't open their eyes to the innate place that you can see by cultivating that part of the heart. To get the

Photo © Yoshihiro Aoyama

Buddha's message you have to prepare the inside of your own mind by doing meditation. And the kind of people who do that in Japan are few.

"But if you travel in India, it's all naked. You can see it in everyone, you can see the very quality of the human being directly—that suffering exists, and that divine and sacred things also exist, and all the happy things too. They are all in a jumbled-up, mixed-up mess."

I think of all the chaos and misery I saw in India myself, and also of all the many, many sacred places, and the central part that ritual plays for millions of people, and I nod my head. He continues, "In India it's all visible to you. It's not just words anymore. And you say to yourself, 'Ah, that's what the Buddha is talking about; this is suffering, and this is the road to being saved from suffering.'"

And then Ito takes out from his collection a cedar box of precise joinery and opens it slowly. Inside, wrapped in blue and red cloth, is a marvel. Three scrolls lie in a row next to each other, perfectly fitting the small wooden case. "Pilgrimage to Sacred Buddhist Sites" says the calligraphy label on each.

"This work was commissioned by my father. He was in his eighties at the time. Because he was a paperhanger, he knew how to properly prepare and mount scrolls. He said that if I documented a Buddhist pilgrimage, he would

back the paintings onto scroll paper, and produce a book in the old Japanese style."

Ito removes the first and rolls out several feet of it on the low table where we sit, and it occurs to me that this is the only modern scroll I have ever seen. Yet by the very format of it I get carried back into the past. The gray and black paintings accompanying the vertically written text are quieter than the others but capture a meditative spirit, and some of them even manage to capture the sacred. It is also, I notice, a variation on the traditional "Life of the Buddha" series of images that one sees in temples all over the East.

I think of Ito making this work as not only part of his own pilgrimage, but one for his father, a devout Buddhist who never got to leave Japan and was nearing the end of

"My father said that if I documented a Buddhist pilgrimage, he would back the paintings onto scroll paper and produce a book in the old Japanese style."

his life. It also has the peculiar quality of being an overlay of the ancient past and Ito's own life as he traveled to the sacred sites of India, treading in the footsteps of Gautama Buddha.

And again the tactile nature of the actual work contributes powerfully to the effect. The strong but smooth paper backing and the heavy, black ceramic scroll posts around which it is wrapped both underscore for me its most striking aspect, the fact that this work exists only one place in the world. I hold it in my hand.

~

"You can't imagine what it was like in the late 1970s in Nepal," says U.S. Buddhist scholar Hank Glassman, an associate of both Ito and Takaoka's. "Pages were being ripped from ancient texts and sold to tourists one sheet at a time on the streets of Kathmandu." We are talking about Ito's second long journey to India and Nepal, from 1977 to 1981, which came at the invitation of Takaoka, who was embarking on a large-scale cultural preservation project of Buddhist iconography in Nepal. "Nepali Buddhism exists solely in the Kathmandu Valley. The rest of the country is overwhelmingly Hindu, and there was little recognition of the value of that ancient culture. Takaoka

and Ito recognized the situation and set out to try and rescue what they could."

Takaoka, who at the time was photographing Nepali Buddhist art for conservators and academic researchers in Japan, once recalled for me a conversation he had with someone who came to his apartment in Kathmandu trying to sell him torn sheets from centuries-old manuscripts. "I told the man that what he was doing was wrong, and he looked at me sadly and told me he knew it himself, but his old way of making a living had disappeared and he had no other choice in order to support his family."

Partly as a result of such experiences, Takaoka initiated a cultural preservation project and invited Ito to come to Nepal to be its artistic coordinator. The project would document the 108 manifestations of the Buddhist deity of mercy and compassion, known as Kwan Yin in China, Kannon in Japan, or Avalokiteshvara in Sanskrit. After years of research, and with the help of Nepali monks, artisans, and academics, as well as a group of other Japanese collaborators, they produced a very large-format book on thick yellow handmade paper, hand-bound in blue Nepali hand-spun cloth. Each page displayed a finely detailed woodblock print of a lithe dancing female deity holding dozens of symbolic objects in her dozens of hands. This was accompanied by two slim industrially printed volumes, one edited by Takaoka on the religious and historical background of these images, the other edited by Ito on the handcrafts and techniques of woodblock carving and papermaking.

To fund this massive six-year project, Ito and Takaoka used their connections in the worlds of arts and culture in Japan to find financial sponsors, who would receive a single finished copy of the book. Although these supporters might have had life circumstances that prevented them from traveling to, much less living in, Nepal, they were able to learn of another strand of Buddhist culture and at the same time support a work of real cultural preservation.

The 108 Kwan Yins book project implicitly said that cultures are not preserved in artifacts, but in techniques alive in the hearts and hands and minds of people. By means of the project, Ito and Takaoka showed the woodblock carvers, the papermakers, and the hand binders, as well as the fabric spinners and weavers and dyers who made the fabric for the cover, that their work was valued in the world, that people would pay for it, even pay *more* for it than for something made by a machine.

The two men also inspired a whole younger generation of Japanese people who helped them with their project: Nakamura, Atsuko, Amemiya, Gufu, among others. The bonds they made then have also lasted a lifetime, many of these people keeping in contact with each other for over twenty-five years now. Ito and Takaoka both, I

realize, played very much the roles of elders and guides for the generation born after the war. Kogan Murata, a friend from that period, once told me, "Ito-san never, never puts himself first; that's what I learned from him. He is always humble, and always praising the other person. 'You are good, you are good,' he is always saying things like that. 'Go ahead, keep going, do it your own way.'"

Ito also began his study of yoga during this journey. "This was a real turning point in my life. I studied at the well-known Shivananda Ashram at the sacred city of Rishikesh, where the Ganges leaves the Himalayas and pours out onto the vast plains. This was 1978, and one could say that my mid-forties was relatively late to start yoga practice. But because I kept at it, doing the postures, training myself with Zen meditation and doing breathing exercises, slowly, bit by bit, my powers of concentration increased. I was able to . . ." he pauses, "to see beyond the surface of material things. And because of that I was able to understand the *meaning* of those Himalayan and Indian rural villages I had visited."

As Ito wrote in one of his monthly magazine essays, "Yoga means 'the practice in order to understand the identity of the essence of the cosmos (*Brahman*) and the essence of the self (*Atman*).' The aim of the practice is to reach samadhi, a state where the cosmos and the ego are unified."

Then Ito tells me of a remarkable thing that happened to him. "It was after I had been practicing yoga and meditation for some time. I was on a long, long train ride from the southernmost tip of India all the way to Delhi. Suddenly, there on the train, I started receiving a spontaneous transmission, a divine connection, like I was being spoken to by the goddess of compassion herself. The vision I got was of a thousand hands and a thousand eyes, like Kwan Yin offering to us her many, many hands with an eye in the center of each one. This continued for almost thirty hours.

"I later understood the meaning of this vision. It is the eyes that do the work of perceiving, of seeing, and the hands that do the work of holding things and of express-ing things. Because to live is to suffer, and all living things suffer, I decided that as much as possible I wanted to give to others, to lessen their suffering, and I knew from this vision that I was to use my eyes and my hands to work for that purpose.

"Thus I use the imprint 'Thousand Eyes, Thousand Hands Workshop' for everything I publish or make, the paintings, the books, the woodblock prints. Even in writing poems or essays, you are working with your eyes and hands to express that compassion and kindness in words. I vowed then to not increase the suffering of others, and that would be my way of making a living as well."

After a moment, Ito adds, "I had one other important experience on that journey. I traveled to a small village on the northern shore of the Ganges river, a small village called Mithila in the northern Indian state of Bihar, to do research on their paintings. This was a village that was almost totally self-sufficient and not so oriented toward economics. They did not even have electricity. They lived from the soil and made their own food; even the tools they used every day they made for themselves. I lived with them and saw how they worked with their hands. [Translated literally, what Ito says is 'how they caused their hands to work.'] I had an awakening then, that yes, *this* way of living really was good for humans. I understood clearly that this was what I had been pursuing all this time, and that when I went back to Japan I would quit that Tokyo life, and would live in a mountain village myself."

~

When Ito returned to Japan, the Motai family had sold their old house and his dear friend Izumi had moved back to the U.S. With some sadness, he understood that those days of reveling and all-night discussions of art and poetry were over. A friend told Ito that he knew of an old silkworm building that had been out of use for many years in the vicinity of Mt. Fuji that he could live in. So Ito moved his few possessions and books there and began one of the most productive periods of writing and painting in his life. He was almost fifty years old.

One of the books he published then was a book for children about a small girl who saves a huge tree from being cut down by her father, who doesn't understand how all the forest creatures depend on it. The father had intended to cut it down to give the trees of his cedar plantation more light—that is, to produce more money. "This tree belongs to all of us," the little girl cries on one page, her arms around its trunk. Ito explains to me that this story was based on a true event in the vicinity of his house in which a local woodcutter had in fact cut the huge old tree down, unaware of how attached Ito had been to it, and so Ito wrote this children's book as a kind of memorial or homage to the tree, and as an expression of thankfulness for the blessings of plants. There is much between the lines of this lovely book that speaks of the loss of old ways of life, and of the sorrow he feels as humans destroy the beautiful life-world around them.

He also published a longer narrative book for adults—part of his examination of the work of compassion in practice—on taking care of his mother and father in their last years, and of the process of their dying.

This was also the period when, he says, "my heart began to turn from India more toward China," and he began an intensive study of the Chinese classics, particularly of the *I Ching*. These ancient texts inspired him to adopt many of the recommendations on "the life of the mountain literati," such as doing calligraphy for hanging scrolls and playing the Chinese table harp, the *qin*. Without models for living as an artist in the materialist Japan of the 1980s (at least one who rejected commercialism), he looked back in history to men who faced similar incongruencies between their hearts and what society expected. He found these answers in the writers of Tang-dynasty China.

In his new home he spent his days painting, bookbinding, studying both ancient Chinese philosophy and modern theoretical physics, as well as in deep contemplation of nature. This was in addition to his daily yoga practice and devotional chanting.

Ito is also a prolific letter writer and I have had the pleasure of receiving several of them over the years. They always include margins filled with birds and frogs and moths, and once, an illustrated story of a badger and a young bamboo shoot. In his letters, all the pages are glued to each other, so that they open as if they were scrolls. Each is dated with the year since the birth of the Buddha.

A House Full of Mosquito Nets

My house in the mountains accommodates seven mosquito nets. Among them, the blue green one is rare and old-fashioned. Its mesh is not only closely woven, but is also torn and poorly ventilated. Even in daytime it's dark inside, and its darkness recalls my old memories as well as makes me feel I can dream old dreams.

I've been fond of mosquito nets since I was young, so when I moved to the mountains I asked my friends to send me any they were not using. As a result I received many at once. The hemp net, severely damaged and seldom hung recently, used to hang in my parents' house. My mother patched a big hole in it the year before she sent it to me. The slightly wild patch and its rough seams reflect her painful state of mind as she was experiencing senility.

On hot summer days the first floor, with the windows thrown open all day, is cool and pleasant when the crisp air from the stream near the house passes through. As I sit downstairs under the mosquito net, I enjoy listening to the ups and downs of the cicadas' calling. A deep drowsiness comes to me unnoticed and I become unaware where I am or what time it is. The mosquito net gives you such a deep sleep. The older I get the more I value the nets because I believe a good sleep is the best way to keep your health, and as I age to have a good sleep has become more rare. Napping in the wide mosquito net listening to cicadas chirp in the early drowsy afternoon is worth a thousand pieces of gold.

The net which brings a blissful sleep in the afternoon turns into a yoga ashram in the morning and the evening. Mosquitoes bother my mind with their biting and buzzing during the practice of yoga, but the net protects me. After the evening yoga asanas, I bathe in the clear water drawn from the stream to the east of the house and scrub my skin with a rough vegetable-fiber brush. Then I return inside the net and I meditate for awhile. This is again one of my blissful times.

Now, mosquito nets have another utility besides a practical one. That is when I tackle my greatest lifetime assignment: understanding the cosmos. I crawl under a net and look up. The drooping net's ceiling is quite similar to Einstein's idea of curved space, which has a saddle-shaped negative curvature. Looking up at it, I contemplate the field of energy or the nature of space. But generally I fall asleep before a good idea visits me; so I have not come to a great discovery yet.

Eventually a cricket perched on the net starts chirping, and autumn cicadas join the song, and the emotion of reluctant parting arises in me, "Ah, the season of the mosquito net is passing so swiftly!"

[TRANS. ATSUKO WATANABE]

~

In the late 1990s, after twenty years' absence, Akira Ito revisited Mithila, the small village in Bihar, India. He stayed at the same house he had long ago, and the grandchild of the person he stayed with then looked after him again. In preparation for the conference of the Folk Art Society of Japan he wrote a short report of his visit:

The Folk Paintings of Mithila Village:
Returning after a Twenty Years Absence

Walking around the village I saw much had changed. I was sad to notice that the arbor where I had strung my mosquito net to sleep two decades ago had been replaced by a brick building. In fact, everywhere newly built brick houses and tile roofs have been replacing traditional thatch, and I could see the increasing disparity between the rich and the poor.

I bought many of the paintings that the village is known for to give to people at our upcoming conference, as well as to introduce other people in Japan to the beauty of their work. These are the same paintings I had come to see twenty years ago. In the more than three-thousand-year history of these distinctive paintings, it is only recently that they have been painted on paper. Traditionally they were painted on the walls of the house and were thought of as

Akira Ito • 183

"women's work," in the same way as cooking, cleaning, and doing the laundry was, and so girls would learn how to paint them as they grew up. These paintings were always regarded as offerings to the gods, and it was not until recently that were they thought of as decorative, or as "art."

About thirty-five years ago now they started to paint on paper. This was also the time that the paintings started to be thought of as decorative, as a kind of adornment. As they became popularized and were turned into folk paintings for sale, the original spiritual nature of the art became more and more diluted. It seems to me that if the painting wasn't being made for a god, it could be drawn with a more carefree, easygoing feeling . . . that is to say, more lightly. And by the time of my visit, most villagers had completely given up painting on the walls in order to make commercialized versions on paper for sale.

I felt also that the culture of the village had become more unmannerly, and more rough and noisy, and the village itself seemed less well cared for. I wondered, "Had the influence exercised by cash income from the folk paintings begun?"

With three thousand years of history and tradition, the Mithila folk paintings were the communal property of all the people living in this region. The villagers had a share in this fortune in their day-to-day life. When these paintings began to be painted on paper, this communal property became something that could be converted into cash. The paintings became material objects owned individually, and a big gap in income was born between people based on their talents as painters, or other things such as caste and class. Artists whose work was popular became rich, and they then became the target of jealousy from others.

Long ago the artistic vigor and talent was focused on beautiful displays of artwork for festival days or at weddings, or as paintings for the gods themselves. But now this energy has all swung around toward making paintings as items for sale, and the quality of the original wall paintings has been neglected. I wonder if this is unavoidable in the ordinary course of things.

Everywhere in the world you can see this common property, our cultural heritage, being turned into money, and this is just one example of it. For the purposes of turning everything into economics, the nature and good culture of the whole earth—which are our common property—are being destroyed, and even the continuance of life itself is threatened; this is our era.

And now, sitting with me, Ito lets out just a little bit of his disappointment at what's happening on this earth. "For the sake of money, and for the sake of 'economic activity,' people try to change things, products, works of art—everything—as quickly as possible. To win at competition, everyone tries to make new things as quickly as possible. Even though it is the nature of the universe to change, the 'change' originated by human activity is too violent and rapid to accept as just natural. The scale of change that has occurred in the last fifty years might be equal to that of the previous hundreds of thousands of years. It's as if the entire globe is turning into toxic gas and trash. Floods of cars and airplanes, the acceleration of transportation, mass movement of merchandise, the forced cultivation of vegetables in all seasons, excessive lighting and air conditioning, and limitless information: the change is much too violent and intense. The human body and spirit cannot withstand this kind of acceleration. This is what I hate the most.

"For the sake of this changing, the world is being

ruined. And it is based in greed. I don't want to get involved in it. It's better to be poor."

~

I remember the very first time I met Akira Ito, some years back, at Tokurinji temple in Nagoya, during the annual Festival of Flowers, held every April to celebrate the birth

Ito's eclectic morning ritual includes offering rice, water, and incense at his altar, followed by a series of yoga poses, the chanting of sutras, and a short silent meditation.

Akira Ito • 185

Ito's gray beard and spotted skin remind me of his age, but underneath these I can feel a glow of energy, a result of years of cultivating his interior resources.

of the Buddha. Amidst the huge billowing cherry blossom trees, Nepali and Japanese people gather for eight days of music, food, and ritual. Takaoka is now the abbot, and together with Ito, they coordinate the bustling festival with its "Kathmandu Bazaar" full of handmade crafts, including pottery by the Watanabes, a tea stall staffed by Osamu Nakamura, an evening concert of meditative bamboo flute by Kogan Murata, lively Nepali music performances, and a Buddhist ceremony in the main hall of the temple attend-

ed by the many monks and Buddhist students from Korea, Vietnam, and Bangladesh who lodge at the temple.

Every evening after the festivalgoers had left, Ito would sit in the second-floor gallery where his paintings exploring the life of the forest were hung, take out his *qin*, and sit down for his nightly practice. Working patiently through his finger exercises, he would play three quiet tones at a time, producing sound first with the fingernail and then with the fingertip.

After he had finished one set, I mentioned to him how Westerners often prefer to be taught just a few things and then be allowed to fool around, to improvise. In fact (I admit) I was struck by the tedium of repeating such simple, repetitive three-tone intervals. I imagined how easy it would be to start picking out tunes and save myself the laborious and frustrating years of "basics" that the Asian method usually prescribes.

"Yes, that's true," he replied with characteristic calm. "Both ways have their merits."

I could see from his expression that he was completely at peace and not frustrated at all. For his goal wasn't to start to learn tunes to play as soon as possible, and perhaps it was beyond "music" itself. As I watched his meditative movements I saw a man satisfied with his life; I could feel it simply being near him. And with a bit of a pang I realized how rarely I had seen that in a human being. Watching his simple, patient striking of the strings, his tacking away in a long-established pattern, I found myself becoming open to a world that I never noticed was there.

Ito tells me now, in his sunlight-filled studio in the woods that his practice of the *qin* is a way to understand the fundamental fabric of the universe, the movement and vibration of energy itself. "Energy is vibration—of course you know that. A painting is the energetic vibration of light particles, and music is the energetic vibration of sound. The connection between these two means of expression is extremely deep. So this is why I have taken up the *qin*. Until I began this practice, I had done only visual communication, but in playing the *qin*, I am able to feel the reverberations of the strings through my fingers, and thus contemplate the true nature of things through the finger tips and the ears. Playing the *qin* also connects me with the expansiveness of time: I can feel that the ancients also felt this same resonance, and I experience a connection with them.

"The more I studied their writings as well, the Taoist classics, Lao Tsu and Chuang Tsu and the *I Ching*, the more I realized that those philosophers' view of the universe was very similar to mine. Although in pursuit of my understanding of the cosmos, I've read many Western physicists, including Einstein and Hawking and Feynman and Schrödinger, and even Spinoza's *Ethics*, I still felt that there was something that Western science and philosophy does not quite understand.

"I read the Indian texts as well, including the Rigveda, and I've studied a lot of Vedanta, the Hindu theory of cosmology. But much of my research is very practical, exploring energy through yoga and meditation. In line with that, as it was recommended in many Taoist commentaries, I decided to take up practice of the *qin*. And by doing that I have come to understand things about the action of energy that I could not in any other way, not even in painting."

When I consider that Ito is trying to untangle the mystery of the nature of all things and all life, I admit to taking a step back. It's quite a question, "How do we know such a thing as the universe?" There's a certain gargantuan courage to it.

"In the vast spaces between the galaxies, most people think that there's a complete vacuum of nothingness," he says. "But even there, there's a very thin spread of energy in between; a fine field. Everywhere has energy. In fact there *is* nothing but energy. There may be materials, but even below that, everything is energy. The universe is nothing more and nothing less.

"And finally, about fifteen years ago, after many years of study and practice, I started to be able to see this myself, to see past the surface of physical objects and down underneath, into their energetic essence. This is what I had been pursuing since I was a boy when I experienced the air raid and read about 'The Earth's Very Last Day.' What happens when we die?"

∼

Born of nothingness and returning to emptiness, the universe is ceaseless change. In the process of this change, from time to time, and by sheer co-incidence, existence or "being" makes its apparition. But it is not permitted to exist permanently. Although "life" is but a phenomenon in the midst of this change, it hungers for permanence and seeks the maintenance of pattern. Even though ultimately the universe is headed in the direction of absolute nothingness, life attempts to move in the exact opposite direction. Thus it is an irrational and absurd kind of existence.

In the East, it has been recommended that we should live in such a way as to attempt to overcome this irrationality by trying to actually experience the state of becoming one body with the universe, by obeying this basic law of ceaseless change heading inexorably toward nothing-ness. This is often spoken of as "The transitory outlook on the world" or "Natural idleness."

To speak in general terms, the West has placed great importance on "respect for life," as well as on those things that are immutable and things that last forever. In the East, as a way to stay in touch with our own spirit, predominance has been put on obeying the basic law of ceaseless change headed in the direction of absolute nothingness.

∼

Sitting now with Ito by his desk, I look over at what he calls his "contemplation corner" where he does his meditations. On the walls he has put illustrations of all these physical properties, which he is investigating—the pulsing of energy inward and outward creating quantum particles, a diagram of the way gravitational waves and electromagnetic waves overlap each other, as well as the illustration of Hindu meditation diagrams (*yantra*) and the eternal spiral of yin and yang. During his meditation practice he gazes at these, taking in through his eyes this work of his hands, this way of understanding by means of imagery. Doing so he attempts to grasp the things in this world that are beyond the visible. He is trying to extract the spiritual from the most material of phenomena. And by years of meditative contemplation and decades of serious study of this question, he hopes to understand the very nature of the universe (something that may perhaps be beyond our human reach) and what that has to do with the biggest question of all: what it is to no longer exist, to die, to cease.

Although I've been taught that all matter is made of atoms, electrons, and protons, with huge distances between them, and that these then are made up of subatomic particles that are not strictly solid either; and although I also know, as Einstein proved more than a century ago, that neither time nor space are absolute facts but are elastic, are relative; and though I understand (on some level) concepts such as yin and yang, "emptiness," and the idea that the human body has energy meridians *(ki)* running its length, once I put down my science book or text on Eastern philosophy, I—like most people—simply return to consensus reality: time and space exist, and are absolute, and material objects are as solid as they appear to be. But Ito is attempting to go beyond this barrier, trying to bring it all together and really *comprehend* all of it on the deepest level. I admit to him that I still don't really get it.

"Well, to put it simply," he says, "energy is always in a process of expanding and contracting, from the largest level of the cosmos to the most minute of subatomic particles. But even as energy expands, the potential for the contraction is building and building. A rubber band is a good example: if you stretch it out, without fail it will manifest a force that pulls it back. The more you stretch, the more that force accumulates. It eventually hits a peak and then it begins to return. This is the unbendable rule of the universe: if something manifests, it absolutely goes back to zero, to *nothing*. Another way to say this is that energy turns into material things, then back into energy."

"But, Ito-san," I ask, "how does this relate to your own spiritual practices, to yoga, or meditation, or the way we should live our lives?"

"Well, if you recognize that energy obeys certain rules as it changes, and if you understand that this thing called 'myself' is a phenomenon of what we call 'life,' you start to wonder what kind of relationship this 'life' has with the fundamental law of energy, which is to expand and contract. It is the nature of life to try to keep entropy at the lowest level possible, but the main flow of the universe is the increase in entropy and toward eventual extinction and disappearance of everything. If we thought about this as a river heading from the mountains to the sea, the phenomenon of life is to go upstream against this, in a backward flow, like an eddy in the river. That is why life is full of suffering and pain, as the Buddha said. But in the end, you must join the main flow of things: you must die and return to nothing. So if you really correctly understand this, you will see that your 'self' is existing in the middle of a much larger phenomenon, and that going upstream against it will bring you pain and distress and sadness. Then you say, 'Ahh, at some point, I myself will have to be extinguished as well,' and you can prepare yourself . . . prepare yourself for death. It is a process of observing reality as it actually is. If you detach your selfish mind by meditation, you can identify yourself with the principles of the universe. For myself, what I do is think about this. But I not only think, I try to contemplate it, deeply."

I realize, listening to him, that not only is Ito trying to understand all this, but through his books and lectures and essays and illustrations he is trying to describe and communicate it to others, this idea that most people feel is beyond explaining, so that our own fear of death and the suffering that results from it might, if only a little bit, be relieved.

≈

It is midsummer, and I am visiting Tokurinji temple again. I know it's possible that this may be the last time I see Ito-san. It's been more than a year since he received his cancer diagnosis, and lymphatic cancer is very difficult to treat. The prognosis is not good. As we talk, I can see that regardless of the pain he is in, he maintains his gentle kindness and consideration. After dark, Ms. Noda, his friend the fabric artist who has been caring for him tirelessly, suggests that we walk down to the forest beyond the temple to see if there are any fireflies. Ito can still walk, though slowly, and we make our way down the dark path through the woods, even though beyond us, on all sides, the industrial behemoth of the city of Nagoya surrounds.

As we get to the very darkest part of the path, we begin to see the shy and intermittently glowing green lights dancing around. Ito comments that there are not as many as before, or as we hoped, and Noda-san agrees. The three of us know that the planned road will come through nearby here. Still it is a beautiful night, and we are here, loving a vanishing world, glad for what is left.

For myself, I vow to do what I can to preserve what I am able, and to pass it on to those who come next.

≈

Akira Ito passed into the infinite on February 9, 2007.

7 Wakako Oe

So many of us don't fit in the world we are given. Yet "being true to yourself" is not easy either. If we go against the mainstream currents of society, too often we end up solidifying the ego. This is even more true for those who make art. So . . . how can we navigate a way through this thicket that feels natural to who we really are? Meeting the puppet carver, calligrapher, experimental painter, and environmental installation artist Wakako Oe, I was able to find the beginning of an answer to this question, as well as some clues on what it would really mean to "step lightly on the earth." It turns out to be a lot easier than I had thought.

I'm sitting in a movie theater next to Wakako Oe. Not even looking at her, I can feel how powerfully she is moved. She asked me specifically to attend this film with her: it's about how Japan came to have a constitution that forswears going to war.

On the way over here in the car with her husband, Masanori, driving, I had raised my one concern with her. "Wakako-san, I'm in support of that clause of the constitution as well, but what about the fact that the U.S. imposed this on Japan for its own designs, not from any kind of real belief in peace?"

"That may be so," Wakako replied, in her typically deferential manner, "but the

191

fact that we now have such a precious thing is extraordinary, and we should cherish it and never allow it to be taken away."

The film renders the tense times in the 1930s leading up to World War Two. The main character, a young lawyer, is pursued by thugs from the military police and is beaten and tortured for refusing to stop his speeches against the militarists and warmongers. Later, in bombed-out Tokyo, as the U.S. Occupation forces are preparing to draw up a new constitution for Japan, the lawyer, now a constitutional scholar, convenes a group of other liberal and left-wing politicians and thinkers. They write a document of recommendations for what kind of government Japan should have and submit it to the Occupation authorities. It is this hidden story of the progressive elements of Japanese society's contributions to the final constitution that the beautifully shot movie is seeking to show.

But this is not just a historical movie. For even now, as we sit in this theater, right-wing lawmakers in Japan's parliament in Tokyo are trying to change this most central tenet of Japan's constitution, claiming that since the U.S. imposed this policy on Japan under duress, that Japan must get rid of this sign of weakness, and rearm. And this is the reason, I believe, for the emotions coming from my gentle and committed peace-activist friend next to me here: the specter of a warlike Japan just over the horizon.

~

On our way back to Wakako and Masanori's house from the matinee, I can see snow still clinging to the two ranges of rocky crags that enfold the sides of this wide valley in the southern Japan Alps. When we arrive, Wakako offers to make me some tea from some herbs she has gathered on one of her walks. The tea is strange and delicious, rustic and intriguing, and we sit down to drink it and talk in the sunlight-filled veranda that she has built by hand from bamboo struts and twisted vines. On all sides we are surrounded by her organic sculptures made from sheaves of grain, large tan gourds, bundles of millet, woven nests of roots and seaweed, and stalks of Japanese pampas grass with their feathery, horse-tail plumes.

Wakako is of slight build and though her voice is not strong, her presence is. Her gaze is unwavering and clear, and the soft tones that she speaks in are often filled with mirth and surprise. She seems to manifest an urban conciseness and a cosmopolitan air mixed with the rural richness and warmth of almost two decades of living in the mountains.

As we talk in the afternoon light, I start to find out about her story.

As a university student in the 1960s she wanted to study philosophy, but, she says, she felt alienated by the abstract, theoretical approach of the teachers. "Philosophy is the study and act of thinking, isn't it?" she says. "I went to university to decide what way of life I should choose. I thought that's why everyone studied philosophy!" She laughs, embarrassed by her misunderstanding. "But that theoretical talk wasn't useful to me. I could think on my own, and at least it would be connected to reality."

After she graduated she became a magazine reporter and began covering the antiwar protests of the late 1960s. At that time, the Japanese government was signing controversial security treaties with the U.S. and starting to build up a "self-defense force." When Wakako went with the protesting students to the U.S. Army bases, she found that nuclear weapons were coming into Japan. "I first went as a journalist, but then bit by bit I began to question this too: was it really all right?" And then she adds, "But I wasn't special in this way: everyone did this. It was just part of my generation, and I was part of the flow of those times. I am not an aggressive person at all."

She explains, "You see, the people older than my generation, up until Masanori was in school, they were educated during the war and before, and they were taught

to do what they were told, and to move exactly as they were instructed to move: 'Follow what your parents and your teachers say, absolutely!' That was their education.

"But I was born after the war and by the time my generation came in we were in a period called 'postwar democratization.' We were taught the spirit of the peace constitution: everyone is equal and we should try to get along with each other. The teachers told us that if each of us behaved with that kind of feeling, the people of the world would give us their acceptance again. They said we should think about things for ourselves to decide what was correct, and that it was proper to express that on our own."

I shake my head. I didn't know this about the postwar period, and I think to myself again how often progressive history tends to get erased. How different, I also think, such an approach is from the dominant educational philosophy in Japan, even today.

"When the kids went off I asked myself, 'Wasn't there something I wanted to do?'"

The partially carved puppet heads with empty eyeholes and parted lips lend an air of something slightly ghostly.

"So it was our generation that was at the center of the student movement in the late '60s; we saw the government was signing treaties that amounted to militarism again. Even though we as Japanese experienced the atomic bomb in Hiroshima and Nagasaki, and we had the nuclear-free policy in our laws, even so, our government was accepting these nuclear-armed submarines into our ports." Listening to her I can hear her anger, so rare in her voice, upset at the breach of trust. "We said to them, 'You gave us this kind of education about peace, and the reality is different, is it not?'"

After a moment or two she adds, "And in fact the curriculum changed soon afterward and the next generation was told to make themselves 'useful' to society, to the economy, and industry.

"I guess," she laughs, "we weren't very useful to society!" And then she adds, "That was our good fortune. We really were blessed."

~

She pours me another cup of the wild-crafted tea, and I ask her about this space we are in, this mix of artist's studio and tearoom that is partly inside, and partly out.

"At first," she tells me, "I collected all these wood scraps and leftovers from a prefab housing construction site as firewood. But then I thought, 'Ahhh!'"—her voice rising—"I could make this into a veranda! This piece can be the floor, and then . . . OK, this could be a post here, and then I could hang a cloth, or wait a minute, maybe I could hang this reed blind and it could be a wall . . . and maybe put a stone here." The way she's speaking it is almost as if she was not the person involved, as if these little inspirations were strangers she chanced upon walking in the sunlight. I can hear in her voice how delighted she was with the process as it came to her.

She laughs at herself, "I bring all kinds of things in from the mountains. And even though I started out making a place to work on my pictures, as the seasons change I keep bringing more and more things back, so I never finish it!" She seems even a bit embarrassed by this willful spirit inside of her with intentions of its own.

I look around. On surfaces here and there, partially carved wooden puppet heads with empty eyeholes and parted lips lie at different angles, lending the space an air of something slightly ghostly. They make me think of departed spirits, perhaps just about to speak.

Looking down on us from one of the walls hangs another sculpture: an orange terra-cotta face with a kind gaze underneath which hang long stalks of bright yellow millet. The piece, she tells me, is called *Arigato* or *Thankful*.

This place is part artist's studio, part tearoom, and part theater for these "players" brought in from the life-world all around. Their presence together is soothing and energizing at the same time. I realize that we are literally *inside* of her art. Although the phrase "getting more intimate with nature" has suffered from overuse, I see that in this altar to nature she's created a place where that intimacy is real, and I'm inspired to try to make something like it myself.

~

Masanori has now joined us in the open-air tearoom. They first met each other, they tell me, when Wakako was working as a journalist and going to demonstrations at U.S. military bases. He was at the time a young documentary filmmaker and had just returned from four years in the U.S. Within a year they had decided to travel together to India and Nepal to make films and explore the wisdom traditions and teachings there.

Now the two of them, with their typically vivid storytelling, paint a picture of their first few hours after flying into the Calcutta airport in 1971. "That was an era before Japanese people would go to India as a destination," says Masanori. "They might stop there on the way back from Europe, but nobody was saying, 'I want to go to India.'"

As Wakako tells me her first impressions, I imagine her, a young woman fresh out of Japan on her first trip abroad. "We got in at night. You know, in Japan, the airports are brightly lit. But the Calcutta airport was really dark, and all these porters came up to us wanting to carry our bags. They were barefoot and wearing only loincloths!" I can hear the surprise in her voice as she speaks about it, even now. "It looked to me like they were in their underwear in the dark airport lobby! And they were all almost shouting, 'Yes! Hello, Madam! Let me carry your bags!' and I thought, 'What?! I'm going to give my bags to these people?'"

Now all three of us are laughing at the expense of the shocked young Japanese woman who Wakako was. Masanori adds, "And all of them were saying, 'Get into my car,' 'No, come to my taxi,' 'No, come on this bus!'"

I imagine the two of them, trying to make the best of things, disoriented, tired, but also open, in that way that only happens when you first arrive in a new country.

"We had no idea where we should go," Masanori laughs, "and we thought, OK, for the time being let's just go with this person. We ended up staying on the second floor of this tiny hotel, and in the morning we heard this Indian sitar music coming in. Then, when we went to go out, we opened the door and *boom!*" a tone of startled surprise in his voice. "A whole different world burst open in front of our eyes—we were suddenly confronted with the reality of India."

"What do you mean?" I ask.

"The hotel was right in front of a place where they were serving breakfast to people who had nothing to eat. There were so many people all lined up to receive their food, and they were eating it right there, sitting on the street."

"So," I say, "India was different than you imagined?"

"I couldn't have even imagined any of it," laughs Wakako, "starting from the barefoot people at the airport. You see, I was born after the war. When I was little I saw people planting rice barefoot, but by the time we went to India, Japan was all about high-speed growth, especially of the economy, what they called 'modernization,'" she says, as if in the presence of something on the verge of frightening. "The scenery that I was used to as a child had all changed so rapidly. In the road in front of the house when I was very small there were cows walking down the street, horse-drawn carts were passing, and people were cultivating the rice paddies with oxen. And then, one day, all the cows were gone, the horses were gone, and cars were running down the street.

"Also when I was little girl, I wore a kimono every day. Everyone did. That was only until I was in elementary school. Then suddenly all the girls were wearing skirts. It was amazing how suddenly it disappeared."

Listening to Wakako now, it occurs to me that when people lose things very quickly, especially things they feel are beautiful, it can be bewildering.

She continues, "No matter how I tried—I'm sorry—it was really hard to breathe in Japan at that time. I couldn't keep up. By the time I was a reporter for the magazine, I was wearing miniskirts like everyone else. It was part of my job, going out and meeting people and getting their comments on the issues.

"In Japan in the '60s and '70s progress meant getting rid of old things. But when we got to India, it was all heading in the opposite direction—they treasured their past. I felt a big sigh of relief coming out of me.

"When I saw the kind of scenery that I had known

as a child, I said to myself, 'Wow! What is this?' I had this strange feeling that maybe there *had* been no change in the world.

"You see, before I went to India I thought this rapid change was something I had no choice about at all, and that it was impossible to return. And I thought the whole world was moving that way, the changes coming faster and faster. I had thought I couldn't even survive without climbing on board with this change."

～

"What were you thinking about at that time, when you were in India?" I ask.

"A lot. A lot of things. For one, seeing all those people who were living in poverty, I wondered how they were able to survive day to day. For them, seeing us come there as travelers, it was something they could never even imagine: going to visit Japan. But we weren't thinking, 'We've come here from rich Japan.' Instead our attitude was, 'We are all humans, living on the same earth, and you've let us come here to your country. And now, here we are, breathing the same air, alive in the same place.'

"And meeting, for example, the old man pulling the rickshaw, or the person selling things on the street, they really had so much vitality and self-confidence. And for some person like me on the other hand, coming from Japan . . . first just the heat! And then worrying about the food, it felt like we could *barely* make it there; it all took so much effort. I was young, so maybe it was OK for me, but for them . . . I was amazed: the old people, the children, every last one of them, their chins up, really healthy and full of energy.

"In Japan at the time people didn't seem like that at all. I thought, Where does this vitality come from? What is the source? And then I noticed that everywhere, in the buses or around town they had put up posters of their Hindu gods, and everyone had these red dots on their forehead, and there were little shrines in the walls all over, and people always praying there. And before going on a journey, they would always go to the temple. Everyone would go on pilgrimages as well, taking the whole family.

"I thought, back in Japan it just isn't that way. Maybe we had it long, long ago, I don't know. Sure, when people die we do have a funeral, and there might be village festivals and things like that, but . . . " she trails off, thinking.

"So you felt the spiritual life was the reason for their vitality?"

"Yes, exactly. Because of this larger presence around them, bigger than humans, what you might call 'the gods'—because they could always feel that consciousness they themselves would be lit up. Or that's what I supposed. Without that presence, people can lose themselves, and not know what they're doing, what their values and principles are. They get confused. But because the eyes of the gods are on you, you become visible to yourself; you reexamine who you are."

"And for you," I ask, "did this witnessing of the Indians' relations to their gods begin to waken a spiritual life?"

"No, actually, from when I was very small I was able to sense that 'there is something there.' When I closed my eyes some figure like a grandmother would arise before me, smiling at me. Or when I was walking in the rice paddies I would feel that some grandfathers, or beings like that, were present. Ever since that time, I had this feeling that some kind of beings were looking after me. It was not like 'I deeply believe this,' but more like just a normal and ordinary sensation for me.

"So I had that in common with the people of India . . . or you could say there was a natural understanding between us, about things such as prayer, or what was sacred. The things they held dear, I *also* felt were important. I'm not talking about specific gods such as the particular forms of the Hindu deities, just that there was a pure existence larger than the human.

"The attitude in Japan, however, with all the focus on economics, was that getting prosperous was a matter of such great importance. We were told, 'That's just a bunch of superstition. It's from some bygone era. Why don't we hurry up and forget all that?'"

≈

Then Wakako glances up and says, "Ah! Look at the time. We have to get going here soon."

The Oes have invited me to attend a special event this evening, a party honoring the eighty-eighth birthday of a female poet, and a celebration of her life. I'm not sure what to expect, but I gather my notebooks together and we drive through the winding roads of the valley as Masanori points out the galleries and studios of the many local artists in this region. We arrive, and as Masanori had promised, the building where the event is being held is spectacular. It is an old villa that has been professionally restored, with all the exposed beams polished to a shine and hanging scrolls and flower-arrangements placed formally in alcoves.

While it is beautiful, I can see the difference between this kind of house, restored with some of Japan's new wealth, and the kind of house that the Oes live in, with the earthy feeling of a lived-in dwelling. Still, I certainly appreciate the energies that are put into such restored houses: a decade and a half ago when I first came to Japan such buildings were being heedlessly torn down for office buildings or parking garages.

As soon as we walk in the door we are surrounded by the warm bustle of the many people in the Oes' extended network of friends who have gathered here. There are authors and painters and musicians and carpenters, all talking and catching up. The proprietor who runs this old house now as a restaurant and hotel has made it available for the celebration and has prepared a sumptuous dinner for everyone. I see here another part of the world that Wakako and Masanori move in: the intellectuals and artists who may maintain a connection to the cultural life of Tokyo three and a half hours away, but have chosen to live here in the mountains. I end up sitting next to a man with a full black beard and smiling eyes who has come up from Kyoto.

After dinner I am introduced to the poet herself, a gracious small woman with pure white hair and a very warm presence who gives me one of her books of haiku and calligraphic illustrations. We part and I take a look through the book. As the crowd is milling around, I see Masanori in front of a table of copies of his translation of the *Tibetan Book of the Dead*, printed and hand-bound in red cloth in the early 1970s, one of which he presents

to the guest of honor. It is, to me, a poignant moment as he explains how the book contains instructions to the soul of the person who has died on how to journey through the terrain one enters just after death.

Then the group gathers together in an adjacent room as if for some performance. The man I was sitting next to at dinner is then introduced by the host, and he begins to lay out on a board in front of him some curious small clay and stone instruments shaped like birds, fish, and reptiles with abstract symbols carved into their surfaces. He explains that these ocarinas and other wind instruments were given to him during his travels in the Andes of South America and how they are used by the Indians there to summon spiritual forces.

He lifts one to his lips, and as soon as he lets the first note sound, everything else stops. The high-pitched whistle pierces the air and I feel transported utterly, as if something otherworldly had entered the room. And then, to my surprise, Wakako stands up. She is holding one of

"This one," she says, indicating the wooden man on her arm, "traditionally welcomes visitors."

Wakako Oe • 199

her hand-carved puppets who is wearing a white ceremonial gown decorated with dark green branches of the long-needled pine.

She says a few words, speaking quite formally now, about how dance has been used since ancient times as purification for a space and that this one—indicating the wooden man on her arm with the demeanor of a noble or a Shinto priest—traditionally welcomes visitors. Then she says that, "in honor of the poet on her eighty-eighth year—though perhaps I am not a person of enough skill or ability to take on such a role—I hope you will allow me to offer you this dance tonight."

She walks quietly out onto the straw mats with this alert-looking companion of hers. She is holding his arm, looking at him to see what he'll do. He is looking out into the sky. She is curious about him; his gaze is far. The haunting whistling music begins again and she moves naturally to it, the courtly figure before her. Smiling dreamily she swings about the room, the small crowd of people watching in silence. The music moves from whistles to castanets to the shaking of rattles to a riveting tune on a very small flute. She steps and pauses, turns and sways, filling up the room, carried along in her obvious trance, which, through her movements, she transmits to us. Emotions play across her features, and she seems lost in her own movement. It is not she who is dancing, it is he. She looks at him with love, her expressions swept up in the altered state she has entered.

I think back to her telling me about her sense as a little girl of presences in the rice fields. How does one reveal this to the world? Now I am seeing this dance of the puppet in a new way. This figure of carved wood is a talisman, in the most literal sense of that word: a physical manifestation of the ineffable, of something, which though invisible, is actually "there."

~

Now it is morning, and still quite early. I've already gone out for a walk in the neighborhood, passing the old temple next to the Oes' home with its 108 bells and mossy Japanese garden; not your famous Kyoto Zen temple with its ground staff, ticket takers, and entry hallway for the many visitors, just your simple mountain temple, with its small rock garden, main hall, and abbot's quarters.

Down the road, dark blue irises are in bloom next to the old gravestones and weathered bodhisattvas, the oldest ones just vague shapes receding into the anonymity of

Then I see one of Wakako's most dramatic pieces of calligraphy, a black exclamation of ink that wriggles in formless form, contracting and leaping.

the stones they were carved from long ago. A little bit of mist still hangs in the air. On my way back to the house I come across Wakako's mint and thyme bushes. They are resplendent, blanketing the ground, giving off waves of buoyant fragrance when I run my hands across them.

When I get back, I sit down with her in her kitchen to talk in the morning light. I compliment her on the mint and thyme, and in reply, she brings the topic of gardening to a much more basic level, saying, "Sometimes just to touch the ground is enough for me, even if not a single thing grows from what I plant. Often I'll go outside and just place my hands on the soil, even if there's no work to do on it. When I am filled with worries, I do that and I can feel the energy of the mountains and of the trees."

It seems to me that this may be the same energy that gives such a calming feeling to the sound of her voice.

Although many people love plants, Wakako is *enchanted* with them. Often on walks with her I'll watch her gathering twisted vines from the brush as if she can't help herself. We cannot go far in the woods and meadows in the valley behind her house without her stopping to admire a wild spice or show me a leaf that provided a seasoning to people in these mountains long before exotic spices from the tropics entered the culinary lexicon of Japan. She sometimes has onomatopoetic sounds to describe their flavors. "This one has a *piri-piri* (peppery) taste."

She really participates in the life-world of plants, going beyond simply looking at or studying them.

Wakako often returns back to the house with a whole armload of vines—"exuberant" is how Masanori describes her—that she weaves into shades to go around lightbulbs, (giving the impression of a glowing bird's nest) or a bower of matted fibers to hang from the ceiling. Many of the wild herbs and weeds she gathers go directly into the next meal. On numerous occasions I've enjoyed the dark green or strangely fragrant delicacies that she has served on small plates. When she runs a bath for a guest, she puts a few long spires of a fragrant green herb into the water to provide a soothing fragrance.

Last night before I went to bed, Wakako took some of the huge pile of mugwort leaves she had gathered from the roadside where it grows relentlessly and put them into a clean white pillowcase. She handed it to me, saying, "Here, why not use this as your pillow tonight?" The fragrance was calming, luxuriant, and mildly hypnotic. I mentioned that I had read that sleeping with mugwort under your head helps you have more vibrant dreams, and she said, "I don't know about that, but it should keep your head cool and fresh in the night."

~

In 1977, after five years of living in Tokyo, translating Tibetan Buddhist texts, and teaching, Wakako and Masanori returned to India for a second journey, this time bringing their three-year-old son along. It was a different kind of journey from before. Wakako tells me she felt it wouldn't be good for a small child to be moved around too much, and because they had to be more careful about the food and water, they didn't journey as tourists and stay in hotels, but would set up a home temporarily in government-run hostels for Indian pilgrim families, staying for more than a month at a time. "Every day I would go down to the marketplace to buy rice or potatoes or vegetables, and then I would cook at home, using a portable white-gas stove.

"The first time I went to India, it was such a shock for me, the different culture, and *everything* was a new experience for me. I had so much to learn. The second time it was more like 'everyday life.' The main thing I understood the second time was that I didn't need as many things as I thought. Not at all. I could live with what I could carry in one backpack. With a family, I had thought I needed all that furniture and tables and kitchen equipment and washing machines and a vacuum cleaner! I realized I really can live simply. After that, I thought, 'I could live exactly this way anywhere.'"

Soon after their return to Japan, their second child, a daughter, was born, and Masanori and Wakako were now translating not only Buddhist texts, but modern and ancient Hindu teachings as well.

Wakako says of that time, "When Masanori and I were doing the translations of Krishnamurti or Milarepa or the others, we would read and reread about their mystical experiences, and that thinking would color our whole lives. With everything that would happen to us in daily life, we'd ask, 'How would Milarepa see that?' or 'How would Krishnamurti see that?' And we began to see the world that way ourselves.

"That was a good feeling and a good thing. Yet, especially as a woman who was raising children, feeding children, doing laundry, and having to form relationships with all the people in the neighborhood, there was a gap between myself and the work of translation that I was doing. Eventually, I began to feel that instead of being as 'like Milarepa' as I could, I had to be as 'like myself' as I could.

"That was the point at which I really began to liberate myself. In the end, you have to be honest to what actually feels best to you." She then adds, looking at me and nodding her head, "That's not such an easy thing, is it?"

Indeed it isn't.

It was also around this time that she and Masanori began to feel the pull to move away from the city. Each time they had moved so far, it was in the direction of the mountains. "I looked at my kids—they were three and eight years old then—and I felt like I wanted to have a place where they could grow up without being constrained, where they could be spontaneous. If your neighbor is right next door to you, you have to worry that if your kids are shouting or crying they are creating a nuisance."

As Masanori's reputation as an author in Japan grew, it became obvious that they didn't need to be in the city at all, and in 1982, the couple took the final step, moving from the outermost suburbs of Tokyo to this valley to make a new life.

~

My interviews with Wakako and Masanori are usually interspersed with visits from people in their community dropping by with a question, a gift, or some piece of news. Some people bring their children, others bring out-of-town guests. It's a wonderful variety. Just since yesterday I have met two bright-eyed drummers from the women's African drumming group; a photographer friend of Masanori's who has completed a large-format book of nighttime images of Mt. Fuji; two twin teenage boys, their essays in hand to run by Masanori, who are studying at an alternative school; an antiwar activist professor who tells of confronting—in fact shouting down—several judges who've sided with the government in a lawsuit about the constitution; and a quite shy young woman, Keiko, wearing a brooch from a tribe in North Africa that she lived with for a time. The Oes, I can see, are always ready to make themselves available to all who might come by, modest about their accomplishments, and interested in what others might have to offer them.

Wakako tells me that Keiko is currently researching unusual grains for cooking and experimenting with new recipes because she believes that the Japanese diet of primarily rice and wheat has started to create health problems. Keiko joins us for lunch, which is served today on huge green leaves.

While we eat, I hear about the two huge Festivals of Life that, with Masanori, Wakako was part of. She participated—and she emphasizes that she was not "a leader"; that term would be much too presumptuous—in symposiums and forums on human rights, gender inequality, nuclear radiation, the Japanese military's use of Korean and Philippina "comfort women" as sex slaves in World War Two and, most importantly, on issues of global peace. "At the festivals, it was not just Japanese people, but people from Africa, Europe, America, all of us, *all of us*, crying out for peace. And from our first festival in 1988 a whole movement has grown, including many of the people around here that you meet in our community." Then she adds, "That movie that I brought you to about the constitution, this is only one part of what we need to do to promote peace. We all have to gather signatures on petitions, write letters to the newspaper telling them of our opinions, go to forums and events to educate ourselves, and have art exhibitions and musical benefit concerts as well. It's not just going to a movie."

After lunch Wakako excuses herself to join some women—her apprentices, actually—who are already working out in her rice fields under their straw sun hats. The Oes have invited members of the community to use the rice fields they have recently bought as a place to experiment with the "no-cultivation" method that she practices. I smile seeing Wakako in the rice paddy with her black boots and traditional blue-and-white checked farmer's garb. Working together with the other women she suggests possibilities, asks them questions in response to their questions, and by her simple presence gently encourages them. She talks about what the soil is, what creatures live in it, and how the plants nourish themselves even if we don't step in to try to engineer everything. Some of the women who come by are single, others are raising families. Almost all of them have come to these beautiful

mountains from somewhere else to live a different kind of life from what mainstream Japanese society has set out for them. And because of the choices that Wakako made decades ago, she's available as a guide and elder for them.

I'm sure Wakako would object to me labeling her an "herbalist" in the same way she has objected a number of times when I referred to her as a "teacher." Any kind of ascribing of status to her she immediately deflects. The technique she practices with these women is known simply as Natural Farming because it does so very little to disrupt already existing natural processes. When I first learned about it, I didn't quite get the importance of growing food without digging up weeds or even turning the soil. Also I couldn't understand how letting weeds compete with the vegetables would work.

But Wakako answers my objection by saying that by leaving the weeds be, the soil is not disturbed, and the microorganisms and beneficial insects flourish. In the first years the yield drops, but over time the generations of dead plant matter, roots, and cut leaves build up the soil. While most organic farmers are still relying on bringing in fertilizer and compost, Wakako and Masanori can grow all they need without *any* outside input. They don't even have to use their time and energy carting off materials to the compost pile, turning them over and bringing the finished compost back. "We just give a little boost to those plants that we slightly prefer, the ones that we can bring to our table," Wakako says. They have taken the idea of nonharming, of gentleness toward the earth, to a very radical level. Even the weeds are not enemies. She adds, "The insects, they've been on that piece of land for a very long time, and they had their own food. If we come in and remove it, those 'weeds,' in order to plant our vegetables, we shouldn't be surprised if they eat them. But if we just leave them their food, they'll understand, I think, and tend to leave ours alone."

In fact, she tells me, many people in this large valley are feeding their families using this method, and some are even growing enough to sell for the cash income that they need. I am really impressed how far she has taken this idea of "stepping lightly on the earth."

~

It's evening now, and all the visitors besides myself have gone home. Wakako tells me about the next big transition that happened in her life. "I worked as a magazine reporter, and with Masanori on the translations, but at some point, I just moved from words to images.

"I had my hands full when the kids were around, but when they went off I suddenly asked myself, 'Wasn't there something I wanted to do?'" She pauses, then says, "I knew I didn't want to draw pictures of trees and flowers, but at the same time, I felt like there was something inside that I wanted to express."

She found herself picking up the colored pencils the children left lying around the house. At first she simply enjoyed the rough rasping, scratching feeling they would make on some old pieces of plywood she gathered from a construction site. She laughs, "I wasn't doing 'art,' I just loved the scritch-scritch feeling of the pencils on the wood.

"When the kids came home, it was back to cooking and playing with them. But, when they went to bed!" she says with glee in her voice, "I was just *burning* to get back at it again."

But even more than the sensations of the materials, music came to be the center of her artistic process. "I would get some cassettes from the college students that came here to study with Masanori. Sometimes it was

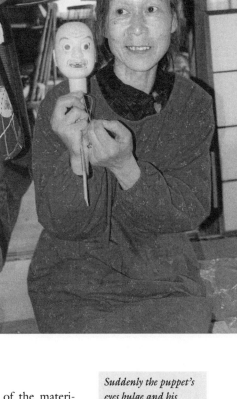

Suddenly the puppet's eyes bulge and his mouth drops open to reveal pointy white fangs.

She laughs at herself, "I bring all kinds of things in from the mountains."

Okinawan rock with traditional Japanese shamisen, and other times, experimental music like Kate Bush, or 'minimal music,' what's his name? Some kind of guy, 'Eee-no.'"

"Do you mean Brian Eno?" I ask her.

"Oh, yes! That's who it was. It wasn't music that I had chosen myself, but something that someone else brought to me: kind of like 'receiving sound.' And each kind of music would pull a different kind of picture out of me.

"First it was just colors that came to my eyes, but there was still no form. I would feel . . . " she pauses, "Here! I need blue. If I put that on, then . . . Ah! Here I need red, and I'd throw that on. The sounds would pull colors from inside of me. Then once I put a color there, the color would start to want to move on its own. So it wasn't at all like, 'I want to paint this here.' There was just music and movement, and the colors themselves would play. It's like dancing, isn't it? You hear a sound and you want to move."

Sometimes in the evening, she says, she would listen to the radio performances of stories by Kenji Miyazawa, the early-twentieth-century poet and Buddhist, and these in turn would call paintings out of her. On other days she would put one of her plywood pieces outside, and the way the trees moved would be the impetus for her choice of color and line.

"During the summer vacation," she says with almost an air of conspiracy, "when Masanori would take the kids to his parents' house for ten days and I was here alone and didn't have to cook, I would have all day to paint pictures. So I put plywood boards all over the house," she says, laughing at herself, "on the first floor, second floor, and outside too, then I would put music on in each place and move around from one to the other. Different types of music call up very different emotions; an incredibly lonely or sad feeling could be awoken, something that had been closed in me. That's why my art, for me, is not really 'painting' or 'drawing' as much as it is giving birth."

Wakako then tells me that a friend of hers who had just opened a gallery said to her, "Hey, let's have an exhibition of your work."

"Then," Wakako says, "I did that exhibition, and then another gallery owner came by and saw it and said, 'Why not do an exhibit at our gallery?' Then someone else: 'Why not at *our* gallery?'"

Soon she had more exhibitions than she could keep up with. As I listen to her speak, I think that it's almost as if she was being carried along with the people around her like that Taoist ideal of "non-doing," without much exertion of her own will. It wasn't like "I want to exhibit," or "I am an artist"—just events and situations naturally coming together. Her approach, it occurs to me, is so much more about relationships: she receives sound, she is interwoven by mountain air and wind, and by the energies and ideas of the many people who pass through her home. What a completely different model from that of the solitary artist creating individualistic works.

When I think of the bounty of artistic talent in Japan and of all the art schools, I can understand why she might have been so surprised and self-conscious about her success. Yet perhaps it is exactly her lack of training, her authentically being open and without artifice, that has allowed her to create work people have never seen before.

Her paintings, she says, started to change as well. "It's kind of hard to exhibit work on plywood," she laughs. "I had never painted on canvas, but someone around here made some frames and stretched the canvas for me. And then another person who was looking at the paintings saw that I was drawing with Cray Pas said to me, 'There are also these kinds of paints, acrylic paints.' They just gave me some and left me to try them. Then someone else said, 'What if you were to paint on paper?'" she says laughing. "Then 'Here are some charcoal inks.'"

Wakako renders each "*And then*" with a rising tone, a "wow" in her voice, as if some unknown deity were casting rose petals upon her. It's the same surprise of discovery I hear in her voice when she walks through the woods.

"I've even tried the juice of the persimmon," she says, "the astringent variety, very green. The juice on the paper is invisible at first, and as time passes, the color displays itself."

When she says this, I think she's talking about a matter of hours or perhaps a few days, but then she continues, "for the first year, there's no color . . . then, gradually . . . "

I smile. I have to constantly recalibrate myself. Slowing down. Then slowing down some more.

"And the interesting thing," she says, "is that working with different kinds of inks and paints, I found each one had a different sensation in my hand: a smoothness, or a sweep, or a rough kind of resistance. I discovered," she says with her voice rising and her eyes widening, "Aaaah! The *feel* of the material I was painting on, and the feel of the kind of paint changed the art in so many ways.

"When I tried paper and ink, for example, I could

finish it in such a short time! Before, with a whole board of plywood, it would take a month to cover the area. But paper! In one or two minutes!" she laughs. "If you go too slow, the paper will rip.

"So with absolutely nothing there on the paper, it's not about, 'What do I want to draw?' But simply to make myself completely empty, . . . " she lets a pause hang there between us, listening carefully to something, holding her breath, then, "Hah! My feeling has become *thus*, and with the brush in my hand, in a single instant I draw it.

"Then," and she leans back and raises her hand with that imaginary brush still hanging in space, "looking at it, I think, 'Hmmm? What *is* this thing?'"

As I listen to her, I notice my programmed way of thinking about "art" start to shift. She's had all this success, but that wasn't the reason for painting. It was more for that moment of discovery, that "Hah!"

She continues, "But then at the exhibitions, I started to feel that saying to people, 'Hey, look at these paintings' must be really tiresome for them, a real hassle" (as if she were pressing people into attendance), "so I thought, 'Let's make this gallery space more like a painter's studio, a place they can relax, as if they were at home.'" Her voice now getting perceptibly easier, more happy, "and then let's just all paint and draw together."

The actual words that Wakako uses are, *kaite morau,*

"to receive their coming to paint with me." The phrase indicates how she seems to feel about it: that it would be a gift if they would join her.

I myself have once or twice experienced Wakako leading a small group who've gathered together to experience her approach to painting, this receiving sound and responding as a dancer would. She led us on a walk outside first, and asked us to talk about what appealed to us. She then had us paint according to that feeling. Her own authenticity, gentleness, and manifest enjoyment in the process create the perfect circumstances for people to relax into their own potential to create. Although she is doing no more than following what feels natural to her, it turns out to be the perfect gift to others.

Eventually, Wakako says, she tired of all the exhibitions and the work of bringing the paintings down to Tokyo, hanging them, and cleaning up afterward. She decided to give it up. Just as she hadn't sought out recognition and "success" from the world, neither did that success and recognition in the fancy Tokyo art world con her into doing something that felt unnatural.

≈

The house is quiet now, the third day of my visit, and I take a look at the actual structure of their home more closely. Something about this place, which the Oes built together a few years ago, seems more like a living being than an average house. The walls of dark brown clay still show the finger marks of the hands that molded them. Outside, high up on the wall there is an Australian aboriginal "dreamtime" animal in bas relief. And just next to the door I notice one small square window with a white wooden frame around it as if it were a painting. Rather than being here to let light in, I think the window is to let art from inside of the house out. On the shelf just behind the glass, Wakako has placed a beautiful celadon ceramic bowl, and inside of that sits a chocolate brown lotus pod with its honeycombed holes. A bright pink and orange hanging cloth sets off the arrangement.

Walking inside to the brick-floored entryway, I notice that Masanori has poured a circle of water that has soaked into the bricks. He tells me that it is a common practice to scatter water in front of a doorway in Japan to welcome visitors, but that he has added the innovation of doing it in a circle to remind us of the circle that is life. It reminds me too of the Zen calligrapher's practice of painting circles with ink and a brush (though of course this one evaporates).

Removing my shoes and stepping up, I enter an area with bright wooden polished planks for the floor and, hanging from the ceiling, Wakako's many sheaves of grain and bundles of herbs.

In fact the house itself is made partially from the woven fibers of plants. By adapting the traditional "wattle and daub" method of construction historically used in Japan, the Oes have built a highly energy-efficient place to live, with walls made of rice straw twisted and then tied into a mesh and filled in with mud and clay. On one wall, they've left a small section of the wall exposed, unplastered and covered with glass so visitors can see inside the wall. Like so many things here, it's an invitation to try it yourself.

Next I walk into the main living area with its high ceilings and light pouring in, and a big brick woodstove to radiate heat in the winter. I pass into the small room in back where Wakako displays many of her carved wooden puppets.

I sit down to look at the alcove. In any traditional room in Japan (borrowing from the tea ceremony) there is always a raised area (a *tokonoma*) in which flower arrangements and a scroll of calligraphy or *sumi* ink painting would hang. Wakako's alcove both calls up that echo and makes an improvisation inside of it. The first thing I notice is the colors: the richness of the browns and earth tones are soothing and don't alienate us from the soil and the woods. One of Wakako's pieces of calligraphy on ivory white paper hangs on the alcove wall, but instead of a flower arrangement there is a sphere woven from branches and twigs. It's more crowded than the austere form of "tea ceremony alcove," but there's something comforting to that as well.

I look around the room and see some sliding doors. Instead of leaving them bare white, Wakako has pasted vertical lines of a poem onto them. Over the poem's brushstrokes she has glued another layer of translucent rice paper, so the brush marks seem to be emerging from the speckling of the door's paper, as if they might be leaves on the forest floor.

I then notice on a low table next to me stacks of very thin paper. There are dozens and dozens and dozens of them, piled on top of each other, each with calligraphy or a painting, or simply her dynamic lines.

When Wakako passes by, I ask her about them.

"Oh those!" she laughs. "Just messing around."

"No, I like them a lot," I say, and try to indicate that if there were extras . . .

She says, without any false modesty, "Why would you want any of that old stuff?"

One she lets me keep is an ink-wash of fireflies glowing in a gray night sky: it's quite amazing how she can make black ink seem to emit light. She also lets me have what appears to be a stack of folded paper towels. It turns out that's what they were before she glued all of them together into a twelve-foot-long accordion-folded work of abstract lines and short poems. It is a modern, though weathered-looking, version of an ancient scroll. The use of white space is extraordinary. One of the poems I find on it reads, "A dream: to whom does it belong?"

Then on another sliding door I see one of the most dramatic pieces, a black exclamation of ink that wriggles in formless form, contracting and leaping. Underneath, in English, in bold but tiny lettering, the words "Who am I?"

I love the juxtaposition of the energy-infused line and the words. I have heard this question, "Who am I?" for many years without really understanding what was being asked. It always felt too abstract for me, and perhaps even a trick of language itself. But this line—just maybe—gives a clue to it. I remember Wakako telling me about her painting process: listening so closely to what's inside of her, painting in an instant, and then stepping back to look at what that line has to show. I suddenly understand that this work of calligraphy, executed in an instant, is a concrete examination of the question, a question which after all lies at the center of almost all philosophical traditions.

~

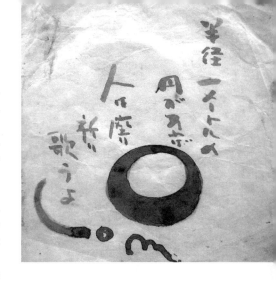

Recently Wakako has been spending more time with chisels and wood than with brushes and ink. When Masanori's father, the nationally known Bunraku puppet maker, passed away, his mother, now almost ninety, was left with a backlog of orders from the troupes that the elder Oe used to provide with puppets. Several times a year Wakako travels down to the small town where Masanori grew up, and in a tiny workshop she "sits at the feet" of her mother-in-law and helps her with the carving.

When I ask Wakako why she doesn't paint as much as she used to, she replies simply, "There aren't many people who carve puppets these days, so there's a need for people to do so."

"But," I say, "don't you feel that it takes away from your time painting?"

"No. It's just a different kind of flow of energy, a different world. Painting with music is similar to dancing, and so is carving: each one is just an expression. To me it doesn't matter so much which form it takes.

"Also," she says, "it's so interesting to watch the faces take shape from nothing." Looking at the puppets that she's showing me, I can indeed imagine the mystery of it: to start with a block of wood and have it slowly become *human*.

She then shows the different characters to me, saying "he is this way," and "she doesn't like that," and I can see that she truly feels their personhood. She holds up one, a clear-faced young man, and then shows me a mask he sometimes wears of a wizened elder, also lacquered in bright, oyster-shell white. Then, holding up the carved wooden head of a beautiful young girl, Wakako smiles mischievously and pulls down on a cord hanging underneath; the eyes roll up and become devilish and bloodshot and horns sprout out of her head. Another small puppet seems to be a kindly old man's face, but again with the pull of a string his eyes bug out insanely and his mouth drops open to reveal pointy white fangs.

Each of the puppets, she tells me, has a name and a history going back hundreds of years, and life stories that the audience would be closely familiar with. "In painting you are letting parts of yourself show, but in making puppets you're not trying to do that at all." Then she adds, with a laugh, "though it comes out anyway." After a pause she says, raising her eyebrows, "And that itself is interesting."

"But," she continues, "I don't just carve faces in the formal Bunraku puppet style. I sometimes think, 'Huh,

"A person, and a circle . . ." Calligraphy by Wakako Oe, poem by Nanao Sakaki.

Wakako Oe • 211

this is an interesting face, I'll make something like it.'" Indeed, around the house are some intriguing carved wooden faces in a modern style, one smoothly polished with almost Brazilian features, a wry smile, and heavy lids; and another a rough-cut block face with sad drooping eyes.

I think hers is a good model: to have one's feet firmly planted in a tradition, but at the same time enjoy improvising within the forms that our ancestors have given.

Now I look around again, and see that this house is so full: faces of clay and wood on shelves and walls, paintings of blue and gold bubbles on plywood stacked in the entryway, thickets of calligraphy on brown rumpled paper hanging from doors, and bundles of drying grains and herbs hanging from the ceiling. Surrounded on all sides by these things, I can feel the "dance" of the life-world as Masanori calls it. It is such a soothing respite from so many other parts of this land bruised by too much cement, neon, loudspeakers, and engine noise.

I pick up one piece of calligraphy, a poem by Nanao Sakaki, on a soft piece of handmade paper, and carry it with me out to the veranda, the little temple of found nature with the permeable boundary to the outside world. Looking down on me again is the terra-cotta face with the kind gaze, *Thankful*, with his body made of a thick bundle of yellow millet. I think again too of the peace constitution, of what Wakako is thankful for: "the fact that we now have such a precious thing is extraordinary, and we should cherish it and never allow it to be taken away."

I think she has found such an elegant answer to the question of philosophy that she asked as a young woman, "In what way should I live?" And then I piece together the words of the poem:

A person
and a circle
just two meters round
if you have it
you can sit
you can pray
you can sing

Gufu Watanabe

In a world that provides us with more choices than ever before, how do so many people get trapped in lives they don't want to be living? Even though most of us know the problems with chasing after money, we still seem to gravitate to its glittering promises. How did we get into this contradiction? Is there a way out? When I first met the potter, gardener, inveterate collector, and self-trained botanist Gufu Watanabe, I had some unformed ideas that the problem was with the way we use our time, and with the unending river of material things our culture produces. But although I might speak out against this machine-made glut, I too have enjoyed the beautiful and many objects of this world. It seemed to me that Gufu had found a more authentic kind of satisfaction amidst all the relentless plenty.

I've never seen a flower like this one before: it is milky white, huge, and translucent, glowing like a moon in the last of the day's light. And the fragrance! A kind of beguiling, sumptuous smell; but fleeting. "A relative of the morning glory," Gufu Watanabe says to me as he holds it away from the bamboo trellis, "but it only blooms at dusk. It's quite rare outside of Japan."

The paper-thin blossom is almost the size of a person's head, and you can tell it's the kind that won't last more than a few hours. "And this one's also interesting," he continues, bending down, "it's called *torikabuto* in Japanese, and 'monkshood' in English. It is quite poisonous, and in the past was used on the tips of arrows. There was an incident several years ago," he laughs nervously, "when a woman killed her husband by feeding him some monkshood in order to get his life insurance money. It's known now as the 'Torikabuto Murder Incident.' If you use regular poison, it's easy to detect, but a green plant . . . well . . . "

I ask him if we have time before dinner to take a look at what he has growing currently. Happily, he says yes, and we walk down through the thickly planted gardens that he and his partner, Atsuko, put in when they came to this valley more than a decade ago. My contemplative friend with the graying goatee and the almost preternaturally thin frame offers his commentary like offhand embellishments on the flowers and plants we pass.

"This one's called 'goosefoot' or wild spinach—it used to be common in Japan before Western spinach came in." We pass the Cherokee Trail of Tears, the Korean chili pepper, and the sugar potato-root, "You can boil it with soy sauce." We walk one level down and come upon a bush bean that produces a bizarrely square-shaped pod, from the island of Okinawa.

I've walked through Gufu's gardens dozens of times but I am almost never introduced to the same plant twice. As we pick our way through the weeds that are so insistent in this rain-drenched valley, we pass heirloom varieties of Indian turmeric, aromatic bushes of lemon verbena, and long, thick sponge gourds hanging pendulously from bamboo poles. Next to one of the old terraced rice-paddy walls, Gufu points out a strawberry guava tree. I shake my head and think, "He's growing guava in the cold mountains of Japan!"

As the light changes in the sky we walk back up toward the house on the ridge. On the way, he picks some cucumbers (Thai cucumbers, he says) and some fresh lettuce for tonight's dinner with the family. When he goes inside to finish getting ready, I sit down outside to gaze across the narrow valley at the wall of blue-green cedar trees and breathe the sharp, early autumn air. To the right, all the way up to the top of the valley, I see stonework terraces rising step by step until they finally give way to a crisp evening sky. To the left, toward the river hundreds of feet below, the deeply folded valleys recede into the distance in fading hues of rolling gray-green. It feels good to be alive. What is it, I wonder, that Gufu understands that has allowed him to create this kind of life?

When I'm called in for dinner, I slide open the opaque glass door with a metallic *krisshh* sound, slip off my shoes, and pull back the cloth curtain over the doorway to one of my favorite rooms in the world, to me the epitome of country living. There's a solid wooden table in the center of the room, and a small Finnish-made woodstove. On the dark, wood-paneled walls are some prints from tribal minorities of the Orissa state of India, some small, framed illustrations of moths and dragonflies in summer by their friend the children's book illustrator Akira Ito, and above the door a softly ticking Meiji-period wooden clock.

Gufu and Atsuko's two daughters set the table, placing hand-carved chopsticks on little painted ceramic chopstick holders, and then the plates of food come out. As with the garden's unending variety, I've never had two identical meals here. Everything is served on the Watanabe's pottery. Tonight it's a sauté of square Okinawan beans with deep-fried tofu skins, a rich miso soup, tenderly cooked whole rice with a black-sesame sprinkle, and a salad with freshly picked lettuce and silvery pieces of seaweed on top. From a jar I'm served some sweetly marinated and pickled shallots. Gufu brings out a small bowl of dried chili peppers, which I am accustomed to watching him chew on through dinner, his face wrinkling up into virtual Himalayas of pain.

When everyone is seated, Gufu says grace and we begin. During dinner Gufu and Atsuko's two daughters discuss the recent episodes of their currently favorite comic book, not surprisingly food themed—"Deliciosity-

© Junko Motoyama

Glutton." From there the conversation somehow finds its way over to the differences between Gnostic and Coptic Christianity, and suddenly Gufu is asking me what I know about Buddhist statuary in third-century-B.C. Afghanistan. He seems surprised that I didn't know that the Buddha was not depicted in sculpture until at least two centuries after his death. "After the invasion of Alexander the Great, Greek sculpture spread through south Asia. Have you ever noticed the curls on the head of the

Maybe his vast knowledge has to do with the way he spends his time, and that, I've started to understand, has to do with his relationship to money.

Gufu Watanabe • 215

The time he took illustrating his journals keeps giving back to him again and again.

Buddha? They're derived from those of Apollo."

How does he know so much? Maybe his vast knowledge has to do with the way he spends his time, and that, I've started to understand, has to do with his relationship to money. Some inner mettle allows him to withstand all the blandishments to chase after it. Although he lives on almost nothing, he is surrounded by abundance.

When I ask him about this, he says, "I always had the idea in my mind that I could survive without money, but it wasn't until I lived in India and walked with the sadhus, sleeping with them at night on the temple floors, that I understood that such a life was actually possible." It's now after dinner, and the two of us are sitting at the table drinking Himalayan Assam tea.

In any pilgrimage site in India you can see large numbers of sadhus, a kind of ascetic wanderer. They don't work, and they have almost no possessions. They are often dressed in orange and sometimes smear themselves with ash or colored face paints. They spend much of their time chanting or walking from one place to another.

Gufu continues, "If you are in Japan, or if you look to the Japanese Buddhist priests, you can't know that it is possible to live without money. But if you look at the sadhus you think, well, *somehow* I could survive."

I have to ask him, however, "But, in your life today, you do use money, right?"

"That is a problem. When I came back from India, I had the intention to live without money, but it's difficult to do in Japan, really difficult. I live in a house, and have kids, and Atsuko is here as well. That's why I had to change my way of living. If you live like a regular person, no matter what, it's a lifestyle of needing money. If you really want to live without money, you have to live like the sadhus. There's no other way to do it. But I try to live my life with that *feeling*, using just a little money. And I can do it, somewhat." Then he adds, laughing, "I'm like a seventy-percent sadhu. I do feel, though, that the sadhus are giving me their support just by their existence, by their living that way. My feelings are easy because *if* the money ran out, I can just tell myself, 'Ahh, think about the sadhus.' And it will be OK."

But what does that mean practically, I wonder. Gufu once showed me an article that a Japanese journalist wrote about him and his way of life, and one line in it reads, when translated literally, "the everyday of self-sufficiency." As I think about the phrase, I believe that's correct: there's an everydayness to providing for your own needs. I remember one sunny day when I visited Gufu after more than a week of rain. He and Atsuko were turning over little pieces of firewood that had gotten wet, drying them in the sun. Gufu and Atsuko use these mill ends from the local sawmill (what we would call kindling) to warm the house, heat the water for their bath, and do almost all of their cooking. The scraps of wood are delivered to their driveway by the workers at the mill down in the valley, who perhaps consider that the Watanabes are accepting their trash.

As Gufu was patiently turning over each little block of wood spread out on the sunlit ground all around his house, exposing the damp side of each one to the sun's rays, my first thought was, "tedious and repetitive." But then I considered that neither he nor Atsuko has to drive into the nearest city to make money and saddle themselves up with the reins and stirrups of Japan's (very) cash-driven economy.

～

Gufu Watanabe was born in the late forties in a small fishing town in Ehime Prefecture on the other side of the island of Shikoku from where he lives now. Not only was this a time of severe economic hardship in Japan, Ehime was an isolated area, cut off by the Inland Sea from the main island of Japan and from the cultural and economic centers of Tokyo and Osaka.

Gufu collected bugs and stamps as a boy, as many boys in Japan did (and still do), but soon he, like most children, was being pressured by his parents into round-the-clock studying for entrance exams.

"When I was young," he says to me as we sit at the dining table, "it was *the* most important thing to get into a good university. Whatever you wanted to do in life, first you had to get into a prestigious university, and then, after that, you could think about whether it was doctor or lawyer—but it should be a job which will bring money in.

"During high school there wasn't any time to think. I didn't know about anything except studying. There *wasn't* anything else! That's why I went to university as far away from home as I could. I wanted to be free and I wanted to think."

"Huh? Isn't studying about thinking?"

"Not in Japan! 'Study' is for memorizing characters and mathematical formulas for the taking of entrance exams."

In the end, Gufu got in to one of the top universities in Japan, in the industrial town of Nagoya. He attended four years but did not graduate. By his final year he had decided that he wanted to be a potter and didn't attend many classes.

"Well, what did you do every day?" I ask him.

"I'd go mountain climbing or go to the university library."

"So were you doing research in the library?"

"No, just getting books I wanted to read. Like I said: time to think."

The college years are an unusual period in Japan when very little is demanded of a person. For most university students the time is spent in endless rounds of parties and drinking that only stops when they get hit by the realities of the postgraduation work world, that locomotive heading right at them. But this was when Gufu first discovered how much you can do when no one else is controlling how you use your time. This was how he first became exposed to ceramics.

"I didn't really know anything about pottery before. I had seen mass-produced plates and bowls, but I hadn't had the chance to look at real ceramics, artistic pottery, and I had never met a real potter, a *togeika*," he says, using a term that indicates a master or artist of pottery. "And at one exhibition, I met someone who was quite good. He was a guy from the town of Seto, not too far away: Kawamoto Goro. After I visited him I decided it was pottery for me. Before then I had no interest in newer things. Somehow Kawamoto's pottery had a different sense than other contemporary stuff."

Through Kawamoto, Gufu got a job in a nearby pottery company, learning to throw pots by hand. "There were two parts of that company: one was a group of young people making work by hand, and another was guys in their forties and fifties, using machines, and they were just doing it as a job. Most of the young guys stayed for about three years, saved some money, and went independent, with their own kiln and pottery studio. I stayed until I was twenty-eight because I was just playing around and not really saving money . . . going to antique stores and reading. That was my life then: Buddhist books, pottery, and mountain climbing."

After six years of working at the pottery company he decided he couldn't go on forever doing the same thing again and again. "I could have gone anywhere, but I decided on India. I wanted to look at the Indian Buddhist stone statuary, but mostly it seemed like India would be a place with a lot of stimulation."

And so, at twenty-eight years old, Gufu Watanabe set off for India, a place that would influence his life deeply for decades to come.

~

"Have you ever seen my travel journals?" Gufu asks me one evening when I am again visiting their house on the ridge. The weather is decidedly cold now, and the warm room at the center of the old house is toasty with the tiny woodstove burning. The wood grain of the table is illuminated by a single lightbulb hanging from the ceiling with its green, pool-table type lampshade. Gufu slides open the glass door to the tatami room behind the dining room and brings back a small stack of Indian-schoolboy-type notebooks, the pages crisp but each volume in fine condition, the only weathering from Indian humidity and the intensive work that Gufu put into them.

Opening the first page, I have a sense that I am being granted access to a private and little-known archive. It takes my mind some time to adjust to what I am seeing. As I enter into these richly illustrated gateways to another time, I fall off into far views of mountain ranges in the Himalaya seen over ragged rooftops and prayer flags. Then I'm on some steps in front of a steep-roofed, wooden Hindu temple deep in the forest. And now I'm looking out over panoramas of Indian village life with oxen-powered farm machinery and peasants at work in the fields.

As I look through one journal after another, Gufu removes himself to the kitchen to take care of the dishes.

Sometimes, turning the page, I laugh out loud: here are three gape-mouthed stone animals, bulging-eyed and painted bright yellow, who yelp half comically, half grotesquely, pleading at the sky. Surrounding each illustration are packed pages of writing in Japanese, Hindi, and Roman lettering. Here I find a small, sketched catalog of different butter-churning jars shaded in with colored pencil. In the corners of some pages, or scrunched between thick blocks of handwriting there are illustrations of tiny things such as padlocks, the interior of a sliced piece of fruit, and the front and side profiles of a cricket.

It's not only illustrations: Gufu has also hand-drawn maps of villages he visited. And on another page is a diagram of different body parts labeled in Hindi (the face exaggeratedly distorted). I open a new volume and come upon a chart of different kinds of Indian sweets. One column has short descriptions of the taste and texture of each, including the sound the cracker or cookie makes when crunched in the mouth.

He's made careful studies of temple statuary: on one page a severe-faced winged creature: part human, part demon, part bird. On another page a stone lion has detail so fine one could even call it embroidery—each lock of the pleated stone mane with its own interlocking curl, the huge glowing round eyes under the flame-shaped eyebrows, the swept back, wing-shaped ears, and full, thick lips.

In the journals I can also feel Gufu's fascination with the particular ways of Indian rural life. A small hut nestles in a valley by the just-harvested rice fields. A team of oxen circles around a post, powering a wheel that scoops water up from a well using a series of gourds attached to ropes.

He's written down everything! Sketches of milking pots and ceramic bowls are annotated by measurements for their tops, bottoms, and sides. How much were onions per kilo? 5 rupees. Potatoes, 4.5.

In between the pages he has glued thin pieces of printed paper. Looking closer I discover they are bills from restaurants, receipts from ashram-hotels, local bus tickets, and an "admit one" for passage on a ferry across the Ganges. Here, crowded amidst a mass of text, is a tiny illustration of a smiling goddess holding the heads of her decapitated foes. These journals are artifacts of his capacity to be interested in almost everything.

Gufu now comes in and pours me a cup of tea into one of his golden brown cups and sits down to talk.

I ask him about the page I'm looking at.

"This is how much I paid for two hundred grams of apples. Hmm . . . what's this? It would have been better if I had written this in Japanese! I've forgotten what kind of fruit this was: I wrote it in Nepali."

"You know Nepali?"

"Yes, some, but Hindi's more difficult . . . Here we have coriander and some kind of green-leafed herb. These are grains . . . Huh? Is this written Newari or Nepali? I've forgotten my Newari." (Newari, I've just recently learned, is a language spoken by the indigenous people of the Kathmandu Valley. This world of the sub-continent that he is documenting is so full of languages and cultures I've never heard of and, I think with amazement, the one other language that I do know, Japanese, seems to be limitless.)

"Sooo . . . " I begin to ask him, a bit trepidatious, not wanting to be insulting, " . . . Gufu-san, why write *all* this stuff down?"

Unperturbed, he replies simply, "To make a record. If you don't record things, you start to lose your sense of the place. It's also interesting when you talk to other people, or when I want to look up something later. But it's mostly just to make a record, even if I don't use the information."

"Yes, but how do you decide which things to write down?"

"Whatever is possible to write down, I write. How much the bus cost. How much the movie was, or how much the hotel was."

"But *why?*" I ask.

"I didn't have any purpose in doing it."

No purpose! Perhaps I've been too attached to all my own actions being done for a reason. Although I know utilitarianism didn't start with me, it is so deep in my culture I don't even notice it. Listening to Gufu it occurs to me that it may not be so good to be always reaching ahead in time. Sitting here with my friend in a farmhouse in the mountains of Japan, I find my way of seeing the world start to deepen and change. All these little, unlooked-at details create the fabric of memory. By writing them down, we are refusing to let the experiences of our lives get subsumed in the tsunami of time, the onrush of the next, and the next, and the next. I think of so many travelers (myself included) zipping from one location to the next, taking photos of scenery or a building. Have I been missing the beautiful in the obvious?

Gufu is showing me—not that he's trying to show me anything—that the whole world can come alive with these tiny details, ephemera you might call them. But not just a generalized "world," but a specific world, an India of a particular time, and, as it happens, an India that is disappearing every day.

~

Gufu first journeyed to India in 1978, and he stayed for more than a year and a half, continuing on through Pakistan, Burma, Sri Lanka, and Nepal. There's a term in Japanese, *binbo ryoko,* which is essentially traveling on a shoestring, but a more literal translation would be "poverty travel," in which one of the main points is to use hardly any money at all. From some conversations I have overheard between Gufu and his friends, I imagine they might even have been competing with each other to see how little they could live on. Gufu stayed in the dingiest hotels, bed-bug infested or not, and took the cheapest Indian public buses, which I know from experience are authentic adventures in overcrowding, noise, and continuous jolts to the body as the roaring diesel-powered box of welded steel plates hits pothole after pothole at whatever speed a young Indian driver can get away with.

"I got into the habit of not having much . . . and not needing much," Gufu says. "I didn't have an ideology of not spending money in India, I just wanted to be there a

Mornings, Gufu and the other residents of the lodge would walk through the streets of Kathmandu to the local tea stall for morning spiced chai and rice doughnuts.

Gufu Watanabe • 221

A Hindu temple amid giant cedar trees in the Himalayan foothills. From the travel journals, early 1980s.

long time, and I didn't have much money."

Whether *binbo ryoko* was a way of traveling that Gufu and other young Japanese travelers then did out of necessity or choice, one thing is certain: it allowed them to have a lot of *time*. When people say, "time is money" they are usually admonishing you not to waste your time, because then you would be losing money. But of course the inverse is true: Gufu had a lot of time there because he didn't waste money. Time is what we have in this life, and how we use it determines what our life *is*. Why is it that so many people start to value money so much that they trade in most of the hours and years of their life in order to get it?

Traveling cheap means giving up a lot of comfort. But when we make calculations about discomfort we have to remember not to ignore the many discomforts of striving to produce income: the hurry, stress, and humiliations in the workplace that happen when we turn the hours of our lives into cash.

Gufu says that before one of his long journeys, he earned money in Japan by working in the sugar cane fields of Okinawa, surely one of the most grueling ways of earning money that the cash-for-time system has ever devised. I imagine he was extremely disinterested in wasting it.

He traveled entirely without a guidebook. "Guidebooks are not interesting—with a guidebook, there are no 'happenings.'" Instead he gathered almost all of his information from other travelers. And then once, in the Himalayan kingdom of Ladakh, a young Japanese woman told him of a makeshift guesthouse for travelers in the old quarter of Kathmandu that was run by a Japanese student of Nepali Buddhism, Shucho Takaoka. The next time I visit, I find out how this conversation and the guesthouse in Kathmandu ended up changing the direction of Gufu's life.

≈

One warm, rainy mid-July day I stop by the Watanabes' very early, and everyone is out. Clouds cling in patches to the cedar forest steep on the mountain across the valley. I enter the empty house and look up at the clock: still before 8 A.M.

On the dining table, Gufu's handwritten illustrated

journals from Pakistan, India, and Nepal sit in a neat stack. The silence, the tiny bush warbler outside in a tree, the precise, soft ticking of the antique wooden clock, and the scent—soothing, subtle and empty, of seasoned cedar wood, straw, and the passing of time—all of it is deeply welcoming and puts me at ease. While I wait for my friends' return, I make a cup of Himalayan tea using one of Gufu's excellent heavy brass tea strainers from India. With the aroma of this tea from the highest mountains in the world rising from the cup, I sit down and open one of the journals. I have never seen this one before.

There's such intimacy to the journals. A father and son stand together on a statue of a reclining stone goddess surrounded by water. A boy with a ceramic jar balanced on his head walks through the country. An old woman with large-framed glasses makes chai squatting next to a wood-fired cookstove in the cold mountain morning. It occurs to me that Gufu is a curator of everyday life.

He's collected items he came upon into categories, showing me aspects that viewing them alone cannot match. There's a chart of Himalayan wildflowers, carefully illustrated and colored in with pencils that fills an entire page. And here is a mini study of the colorful seals of Tibetan Buddhist iconographic symbology used on documents—shells, fish, brocades, flowers, interlocking angular designs. And in this next journal there's a full page of black-and-white line drawings of bas-relief sadhus with brocaded dreadlocks and smirking faces, a catalog of types of holy men, carved into stone. In these journals I am being taught how to look at India. I am being shown how to notice.

I imagine Gufu in the tumble and crash and noise and dirt of India sitting down on some broken piece of mortar on the street, hunched over, with his bad posture and too-thin body spending hours making precise drawings of a brass pitcher used for water at a café. And I smile. His journals, like his store of knowledge, are uselessly ornate. The feeling is good.

I hear a car pull up. Perhaps my friends have returned from the market. I sit, sipping tea, and in they walk with two out-of-town visitors, all of them with their hands full of pumpkins and squash.

The Watanabes' guests are Takaragi-san, the school teacher, and his new bride. The young couple is embarking on their own life of living in the countryside, and they've come to talk to the Watanabes about establishing their new life of self-reliance. They greet me warmly, and we all sit down at the table to talk.

The Indian government only allows visitors to stay for six months at a time, so when Gufu had to renew his visa he made his way to Nepal. Upon arriving in Kathmandu he remembered the conversation with the young woman in Ladakh, and found the Japanese monk with the lodging house. It occupied several rooms on the second floor of a building above a small store.

Takaoka, the son of a priest who was the abbot of a temple in Japan, had originally rejected Buddhism, objecting to the hidebound nature of many of the rituals, and the money orientation of mainstream temples in modern Japan. However he found in the Kathmandu valley a very vibrant form of Buddhism, and had set up a cultural research and documentation center to help the Nepalis archive and protect their sacred artwork.

At Takaoka's lodge, Shanti-kuti ("House of Peace"), Gufu met some of the people who would become friends for the rest of his life. One of these was his future wife Atsuko, who laughs out loud relating the story, "If you had told me I would have married a guy like him when I first met him, I would never have believed you!"

These travelers, when they were not taking part in Nepali festivals in different parts of the country or researching Nepali temple art, spent most of the day sitting on the floor, drinking tea, laughing, talking, and sharing traveler's tales.

As Gufu tells us this, Takaragi comes upon a passage in a journal that makes him laugh, which he then reads to us, "Stayed up until 3 A.M. with everyone doing a dictionary marathon: nine dictionaries, Hindi-English, Hindi-Nepali, English-Japanese, Hindi-Japanese, nailing down the correct name of every single spice . . . firmly distinguishing anise from star anise." Alongside is a quick sketch of smiling people around a low table on the floor, pots and plates everywhere, the drawing's border a chain of eggplants, peas, garlic, and tomatoes.

Gufu often did the shopping for the group, asking the market sellers for the names of all the unusual foods he came upon and looking them up when he got back. Indeed, in the journals nothing is as prominent as cooking and food. All the fantastic variety of implements Indians use for cooking are accurately rendered: sifting boxes, brass spoons, round winnowing baskets, bamboo scoops and ladles. One of the great things I remember about travel in India is that you can see so much of everyday life right out on the street. Gufu has captured this as well: a busy vendor squatting by two big steel tea urns; a man sifting corn into a large wok over a fire by the side of the road.

Gufu has also illustrated the many specific curry and thali meals just as they were set before him. Each small dish is labeled with notes on recipes and ratios of ingredients, often in Hindi or Nepali. "Sometimes before I finished drawing and coloring the pictures, the plates of food would have gotten completely cold," he says. "But that was OK with me, because I could always make them again later once I had written them down." And indeed, even though he hasn't been in India or Nepal for more than two decades he's able to make a huge variety of sub-continental dishes. The time he took then keeps giving to him again and again.

As he traveled, the journals grew organically, evolving as he did. The early ones, when he was still figuring out how to move around in this foreign place, were more like collections of notes, he tells me. As he became better at the tactics of traveling, "more space opened up in my heart and my mind," and the journals began to have fuller and more complete sketches. At some point the journals began to change him: he was still the same person traveling in the same places, but his way of relating to the journey was different. The journal-keeping was a way not just to preserve the experience but to intensify it as it was happening, a means for a fuller interaction with the life he lived. And then when he got home the journal could be a connection with that fuller, more intensified world.

Eventually, Gufu tells me, the journals themselves became the primary reason for staying on in India: the recording of experience became one with the experience itself.

I think of him making his way almost unnoticed through Indian society, living virtually without money, on his own, a slight person keeping to himself, sketching all day and sleeping on the floor of temples, but having, if anything, a *more* profound experience than many other travelers, one that continues to feed him even to this day.

And, he tells me, that life set the tone, and was the proving ground, for the life he lives now. "I didn't have much stuff traveling. I didn't have any books with me; they were too heavy. One or two books was fine. And I had just a few materials for drawing, some colored pencils. I didn't listen to the radio or read the newspaper since I was in a foreign country and I can't read English much, and yet I was able to survive.

"If you start to accumulate things, you can't travel, so I lived without for a year and half more. So I figured I could live a whole life without anything, and then I wouldn't really have to work when I got back. I figured I could do the same in Japan, and that I could live in the mountains in the very same style."

～

On Gufu's second trip to the subcontinent in 1982, he met Atsuko again at Takaoka's lodge in Kathmandu. They became a couple, and found that they both wanted to live simple lives in the mountains.

Meanwhile, in Japan, rural was out and industrial was in; young people had already been leaving the hardscrabble life of rice farming for jobs in the cities for three decades or more. Gufu and Atsuko returned together to Japan and began their search for a suitable abandoned house in the country to live in. In order to buy a kiln, Gufu worked at his old job at the pottery studio and they moved to a small house in the countryside outside of Nagoya. When their first daughter was born, they began to look for a larger house, but after three years of being unable to find a suitable one in the area, they began to search in Tokushima Prefecture, where Atsuko had grown up. After inquiries at dozens of local village offices, they finally made an agreement to lease two sturdily built old farm buildings and seven very overgrown terraced rice fields for fifty dollars a month. Gufu had his kiln and wheel shipped out and they started to cut back the eight-foot weeds that had grown in the paddies that had been abandoned these last ten years.

Now, as we sit in front of his house in the thin early April sunlight, he says "What I really am is a collector." He is transplanting seedlings into small black plastic pots, more than fifty of which he has lined up in front of him on the veranda.

As he patiently and carefully pinches the soil around each seedling, he says, "When I was a child collecting was all about insects and I had a huge number of them, but now I focus mostly on fragrant plants: flowers, herbs, and spices. But I'm fascinated by all plants—each kind has its own personality: height, taste, shape, color of flowers, the way it bears fruit and changes through the seasons. Human beings can never create variety like that."

Although Gufu spends time in the pottery studio when one of his annual exhibitions is approaching, and cooks a good proportion of the family meals (still extremely uncommon for men in Japan), and though he makes large batches of jams and preserves, filling big glass jars with his signature Indian *achar*, a spicy citrus pickle, and though he'll read Heidegger hours after everyone else has gone to bed, during the daylight hours, he gives over most of his time to gardening: to the ceaseless tasks of planting, transplanting, staking, mulching, weeding, and harvesting the spectacular variety of plants that he's collected over the years.

Conditions are not perfect by any stretch. Weeds crowd the sopping wet soil. (The valley where they live receives more rainfall than any other place on the island of Shikoku. I've seen it rain in torrents for days at a time.) They grow so fast in the summer that even with Gufu and Atsuko devoting a good part of each day to pulling them they can hardly keep ahead of their voracious growth. Typhoons come several times a year and tear up staked vegetables and knock down trees. Wild boar come down from higher up in the mountains, usually at night, and not only dig up their crops, but if they find a wild lily growing out of the old stone walls that hold up the terraces, they'll wedge in their powerful snouts until they dig out the roots. It can cause a collapse of a wall that has been maintained by villagers for hundreds of years. Deer strip trees, moles eat root vegetables, and crows steal the fruit.

Once, however, when I suggest that I would help him if he wanted to fence in the garden, his response is the same as when I asked, "Why not use a wheelbarrow?"

"Naah. I don't think it's necessary, and it'd be a lot of work." And, I smile to myself: another blow against ends-means rationality.

Gufu's love for the odd is nowhere more evident than here in the garden. He grows knobbed and wart-covered bitter gourds that he somehow manages to sauté up deliciously for lunch. There are purple potatoes, bright purple ("an Andean variety" he says), and some bizarre, hard-husked green fruits with milky-sweet, black-seeded flesh. It looks like a vegetable and tastes like a tropical fruit. There are *a lot* of seeds; it wouldn't do well commercially. But once you spit them out, the rest is quite delicious.

He's always involved in some quixotic attempt to

grow something in the wrong climate or place. "Yes, I do wish it was just *slightly* warmer here. Most of the guava trees don't fruit, and some of them wither and die." I think of how bitter cold it was here in February and I know he is mad. "I like regular plants also, but growing only normal plants is not interesting. Sometimes Atsuko gets angry at me because I grow vegetables that we don't eat. But I want to grow the most *interesting* vegetables, especially ones that have some use, either something medicinal or something with a great aroma. To me a beautiful

Gufu's love for the odd is nowhere more evident than here in the garden. He's always involved in some quixotic attempt to grow something in the wrong climate or place.

flower with no fragrance . . . well, you've lost more than half the value of that flower."

The utilitarianism of scent! I could sign up for that. He is collecting the ineffable: a museum of fragrance, of flowers in bloom.

When he seems finished with this round of repotting, I ask if he could show me what's currently in bloom. He agrees.

I look forward to my visits to Gufu's gardens tremendously. There's always something new, and the sheer quantity of different plants reminds me constantly of the ecstatic profusion of the natural world. We take the path next to the old rice paddy boundary and curve around and down to the terrace just below the house. "This here is a plantain lily, and these are Chinese dates; have you ever tried them?" He picks off several of the red, wrinkled pods and hands me a few. They are not technically dates, he says, but have been used in Chinese traditional medicine for centuries, or in tea as a beverage. They're interesting—crunchy, mildly sweet, with lots of small seeds. "And here is the German iris, which is a little different from the Dutch iris."

Bending down, he says, "This flower has an interesting name in Japanese. We call it a 'firefly bag.'" He shows me an orange-red, bell-shaped flower. "The paper lantern shape made someone think that it could be a 'red lantern' if you put a firefly inside.

"I have six kinds of tulips, even though I don't particularly like all these hybridized varieties. Humans always want to make the flower bigger, 'improve' plants, or increase the number of petals. That's why I am not a 'horticulturist.' I prefer weeds."

"Why don't you like hybrids?"

"Well, for example, with a camellia, the heirloom variety is the most simple; it has five petals. But from that people have bred them to have ten petals, twenty petals, and the flower gets much, much bigger. Although it's pretty, it's weak. The original has a feeling of primitivity. Things that are made by people are just somehow . . . weak."

We move down one level, me trying to avoid spider webs and getting my shoes wet from the fresh dew on the low shrubs. "Here are some herbs—this one you call in English 'the marsh marigold.'" I can't believe he knows the folk names for these plants in English, which he doesn't really even speak. "The Latin name for this means 'little frog tadpole.' This one translates as 'white-powder-face flower' in Japanese, or, in English 'Four o'clock' or 'Marvel-of-Peru,' and *stokeshia* in Latin." Then he points to a yellow-flowered bush that he admits he only knows the name of in Hindi, not in Japanese.

And dotted throughout are the trees: quinces and almonds, peaches and mulberries, loquats and apricots, and walnuts, figs, cherries, and persimmons. The gardens are extensive, but they're not *that* big. I don't know how he fits all these trees here.

As we walk inside I ask him why, of all the things that he has collected in his life, he decided to focus on plants.

"Well," he smiles, "animals don't stay put! And you have to constantly feed them, change their water, and if you have dogs, if you had a lot of them they'd get mixed up with each other, and, you know—chaos!" We both laugh. "But plants, they stay where they are . . .

"And though I do like animals and insects, I don't like pets as much. They are too close to humans. I like wild things . . . " then he adds, after some consideration, "except insects that do harm to people. Or monkeys. They come and steal fruit. So I'm not much in favor of them . . . "

I just love the deadpan delivery he gives to this line. But it's also true—wild monkeys do come down from the mountains and steal produce in the area. The problems some of us don't have that we never even dream of!

"And actually I'd like to have more collections, but there are restrictions: place, energy, money, time. Even just restricting myself to plants," he says, laughing at himself, "I've put in so much. Any more fruit trees and my vegetable garden would disappear entirely. So I de-cided on the theme of fragrance, and that kind of limits things."

Gufu then adds a cultural note, as he often does, reminding me that plants are not just botanical items in a field guide, but have been woven into human society for millennia. "Historically, Japanese people haven't had that much familiarity with strong scents. We didn't have flowers like roses, or Western-style spices. The native plum flower has a relatively weak scent, as does our cherry blossom. So that preference hasn't been developed that much in the culture. We do have 'The Way of Incense,' but that's a kind of game for the nobility, going back to feudal times. And that's a rarefied world, even more minor than the 'Way of Tea' world."

But the main thing for Gufu, he says, is to simply have *lots*. "The more abundance you have, the more you enjoy. For example, take chilies—there are a lot of varieties and they have so many different flavors: very sweet ones, or ones with a fantastic smell, or ones with an interesting shape or form. It's like God has gone through all the trouble to make so many different kinds, I feel that to not know them would be a total waste, would be squandering that abundance.

"Atsuko says I should grow plants that are native to Japan and just travel to see unusual or strange ones where they are. 'You don't have to have them in your own

And there, on a table, are three alien-looking ceramic creations. Each of them is about two feet high and seems frozen in some dazed ritual.

garden!' she says. 'It's not fitting to bring them to some place where they are not originally from.'

"But even though that way of thinking is, in itself, good, I want to look at unusual plants regularly, and have them close by. I don't have the free time to go to foreign countries." He lets out a small chortle to himself, because I know (and he knows that I know) that he's got all the freedom he wants, or that anybody could want. "I want to look at that plant all the time and see how it flowers in spring, how it drops its petals, begins to fruit, and then how that fruit grows and how it dies. You can see all that if it's at your own place."

Then I notice a yellow, spiral-bound notebook lying on the corner of the table. Curious, I ask Gufu what it is. He opens the well-worn pages, and I see that he has filled every line with lists of words, with a date next to each one. He explains that the list is of flowers, and he has been keeping a yearly record of the bloom dates for more than two hundred kinds that he has planted.

"It's strange," he says, looking at the list, "they all bloomed on the exact same day, year in and year out for more than eight years, and then, this year, it was a particularly cold winter and they all bloomed exactly ten days late in the same perfect order all spring, until summer came, when they suddenly returned to their formerly established bloom dates. It really is curious. . . ."

I'm really impressed. By means of his garden and this cheap spiral notebook, Gufu has soaked in the complexity of the world for almost a decade without spending hardly anything on the project. It's an abundance that most of us have forgotten to notice. He has tuned his attention to the actual rhythms of nature rather than to some conceptual idea of them.

As I think of the insurrection of plants in Gufu's garden from all over the planet, each fighting the other for photosynthesis, I realize it's a kind of mimesis in living beings of his inexhaustible curiosity, his years of abiding interest in and attention to the world.

~

Gufu and I are talking again about money. This is primarily due to the fact that I'm having a hard time understanding his highly unusual perspective. "These days in Japan," he says, "people really prioritize their work—that's number one. Someone might say, 'I'd like to do this thing, but first, I have to take care of my work.' But for me, I have my work, flowers, reading books, food . . . lots of things, and all of them are at the same level. So I never force myself to work for money. If I am in a situation where I'm running out . . . most people would be really troubled, right? If they don't have money for gasoline, or are unable to repair their house? But for me, I know somehow I'll be able to survive. I always have that kind feeling. That's what I learned from being with the sadhus. Until I die, it'll be all right. I say to myself, 'Ah well, the window glass is cracked, no problem.'

"But I do work a bit. So I'm kind of a mix of a sadhu

and an ordinary person. And . . . " he says, after consideration, "that is actually Christian teaching: 'The amount you need to live, you must work for that. But even as you are working, don't think too much about money.' That level is good, I think. A real sadhu does not work at all. But in Christian teaching, they all worked, Paul, Peter. As Saint Paul taught, 'There is no need to accumulate a lot of money or think about tomorrow. Even if you don't, God will arrange things so that you can live.' He taught, 'This only is enough.'"

I love the bird's-eye view Gufu has: freely comparing the bearded, dreadlocked, chanting, ash-smeared, orange-robed sadhus with Saint Peter and Saint Paul, the early church fathers. To him, it's all just "a person" here or there, working out what seems to be the right way to live.

"Atsuko often says to me, 'Come on, prioritize your work just a bit more,'" he laughs. Then he adds, with a bit of a grammatically unusual turn of phrase, "I work when the circumstances become such that working is what happens."

I ask him what he means.

"Waking up, I may say to myself, 'Today I might do some pottery,' or 'Hmmm, today, I might split some wood,' or 'Today, maybe I'll do a little in the garden, with the flowers.' But if an order comes in, or if something is urgent in the garden and I won't be able to grow vegetables if I don't tend to it, then I'll do that. Without some special circumstances occurring, I don't have much priority either way."

There's a thin, reedlike certainty to his voice when he says this, like flattened metal wire. It's a strength that, I speculate, is one of the key reasons he's been able to create the life that he has. Yet it would be a mistake to interpret Gufu's attitude as ambivalence toward making pottery. Walking into his showroom you are immediately surrounded by such a diversity and quantity of work that you'd think it was an exhibition by five different people. There are yellow mugs painted with rearing Indian elephants that seem to be dancing, glossy turquoise serving bowls with cut patterns around the borders, large white platters with Balinese or Chinese floral designs (Atsuko's painting), perfectly executed. On a high shelf there are delicate, porcelain-looking teapots and big tapered drinking cups painted with large blue palm trees. Inside a cabinet is a collection of yellow-brown teapots made from a granular clay that is soft to the touch. It is like a temple of effusion that has come out of his mind.

And there, on a table in the corner of the showroom, are three alien-looking ceramic creations gazing sentinel-like out on the room. Each of them is about two feet high and seems frozen in some dazed ritual. One, an orange creaturey thing, has turrets of hands for holding candles, an eyeless, ovoid face, and an armless body. Next to it stands an elephant-faced figure made from black clay with circular, almost piglike eyes on either side of a shortened, exclamatory kind of trunk-nose: half mesmerized professor, half petrified celebrant. The third has a bell-shaped body and almost no head at all. Where you might expect hands, bird shapes nest on stumps of arms. The two beings on either side of the professor sprout aberrant and asymmetrical horns, nubs and tabs from their egg-shaped heads. All three of their cylindrical torsos have these incongruous horizontal *slots*, and seem to be asking a question.

"I mixed a number of things for these," Gufu explains to me when I ask him. "It was originally for some gathering; a concert for UNICEF, I think it was. A friend had asked me to make donation jars for it. But I thought just some clay container would be boring, so I put all kinds of strange things on them, and added a few candle stands too. I thought, 'Would people donate more if the container was weird?'"

~

"This one is a Tibetan monk, though he's in Bali here."

It's a late afternoon in September, and I haven't

visited Gufu in quite some time. We are sitting on the yellow tatami-mat floor in the small pottery showroom looking at his most recent creations. He is pointing to a little statuette of matte-black clay. "He's offering tea." Indeed, in the little man's hand is a miniature cup. "I call it *kissako*." When I ask what this means, he replies, 'Drink tea, *then* go.' It's a Zen proverb, from a long time ago."

On the floor in front of us, arrayed around the little man, is a whole phantasmagorical statuary of vaguely smirking, blank-faced animals with wide circular eyes—all made from black clay—a tiger, a hedgehog, a long triangular fish, a chameleon, a lizard, a bull, a turtle. They are gathered as if in some hypnotized tropical consortium, and each animal statue has a little removable lid on its top.

"Over them are some palm fronds," he says, gesturing with his fingers in the air above the animals. "Of course they aren't 'there,' here, but they're there. You know, because it's the tropics," he adds, as if stating a fact. And then he says, after some consideration, "Kind of strange that he's a Tibetan in Bali," as though he had chanced upon this scene in a forest instead of having made it up from his deeply mulched imagination.

"Few Japanese today would understand the term *kissako*," he says. "It has two meanings. One, 'Don't be in such a rush—yes, you can go on your way, but first, drink tea. And *then* you can go.' It also means, 'Whoever you are, high or low caste, you may drink some tea here with us, together.' In ancient Japan, this was, of course, not common."

Looking at this scene of a man offering tea to animals, I get a second layer of meaning: "We don't look down on you animals. Let us spend time together," or, as the Japanese idiom has it, "drink some tea."

Gufu has explained all this to me because of my interested questions, yet I rather doubt many other people know the story. But like the palm fronds around this potlatch of creatures, the story is definitely all there. He's not unwilling to tell someone if they ask, but doing so clearly isn't that important to him. He enjoys his own mind and imagination completely, and he doesn't seem to need even a sliver of recognition from others.

In fact you'd have to work hard to make a pottery showroom any less publicized, or any more difficult to get to. There are prices on most items here, but this small tatami-matted room up a steep and narrow flight of stairs in the outbuilding of a farmhouse more than an hour and a half drive from even a small provincial city is certainly not located to maximize sales.

He's not against selling his work; it's just that he doesn't want to bend his life around in order to do it. If you think about it, it's a pretty healthy attitude. For Gufu, commercialism not only distorts the nature of the artist, but also the art itself. This, I find out, is one of the reasons he is drawn to the work of Indian tribal minorities, from which he draws much of his inspiration for this totemic menagerie in front of us now.

"The art of tribal peoples doesn't reek of human interpretation," he says. (His actual term is *ningen-kusai*, which translated literally means "stinking of people.") "Somehow aboriginal art is distanced from the human character, impersonal. Their figures are almost expressionless, but not quite. It's really fascinating."

One of the reasons that tribal people's work is so different from that of modern people, Gufu speculates, is the accumulation of techniques. "People in Japan seven to eight hundred years ago used to make quality things too because the artisans didn't have that many skills," he says.

"They made quality things *because* they didn't have skills?" I ask, confused.

"Yes. There was power in it. But then they learned all kinds of techniques and the energy and force disappeared. People became pros, and the feeling disappeared. Now only the technique remains.

"When someone creates a work of art for the very first time, it is . . . " he pauses, his voice compacted in his throat, almost as if he were rendering the intense twisting effort of the artist, "a difficult, strange thing. Then he makes—or someone makes—the same thing again, and again. Over hundreds of years all kinds of people make it, and lots of personalities and individualities get put into that one item. Along the way people start saying to each other, 'We don't need this part, and that part, it's too much trouble, let's cut it out.'

"In Japan this is said to be the virtue of folk arts —all the 'unneeded' parts have been taken out. They make the exact same bowl for two hundred years, and gradually that single person's individuality completely disappears. It gets standardized, it becomes . . . " he pauses and then uses the English word, "it becomes 'simple.'"

"But," I ask him, "I thought you *like* simple things?"

"Yaaa . . . That's a difficult question! Some things that are simple are good, but some also are not so interesting. 'Simple' is difficult isn't it?" We both laugh. "Scandinavian furniture is 'simple,' but that Scandinavian stuff is boring to me. I like bent and twisted stuff, that's all gnarled," he says making a twisting movement with his hands.

To Gufu, perhaps, it is *simplification* that is the problem. He prefers rough, unsophisticated, and unexpected work. He's constantly searching for that power.

"Some things can be made for even thousands of

years and stay unrefined and interesting, but if Japanese people do it, within a couple of hundred years, it gets over-defined, and a technique gets solidified, like a mass. From the time the craftspeople are children they get trained in doing just that one thing, and they consider themselves 'professionals.' They stop thinking completely. That's why I'm different from the folk arts crowd," he says laughing at himself.

"What do you mean?" I ask.

"In Japan, there are a lot of decorative things, right? All those little wooden dolls, horse decorations, souvenirs. They're like those cute furry stuffed animals that children collect. Everything in Japan's like that. It has no character."

Then he opens a cabinet and takes out a small bronze statue of a tiger, about five inches high. It is, he says, made by a small tribal group in the state of Orissa, and something he "pulled a hint from" for one of his pieces. It's thinner, rougher, more raw than the black clay pieces he makes.

"This kind of thing," he says, "even if it's made for thousands of years by tribal people, it doesn't get that way. Mysterious . . . "

"And how do you think they do it?"

"I think it's partly because of the lack of publicity of their work. They keep making things with the original aesthetic. It remains in India, and in Mexico too: all those skeletons. Not so much in other parts of Asia, perhaps because there's been so much 'development' and economic growth."

Then he says, after some more consideration, "Maybe it's also because tribal people live the way they always have. Their way of surviving is what you call in English, 'primitive.' Thus their way of thinking stays primitive. Each person's way of life influences their tastes, so if you live at a certain level, you like things that are at that level. Or so it seems to me."

He continues, "In Japan—it's the cultural history I'm talking about—there was an increase in complexity. Everything was 'getting better.' And as the way of life has changed, the way of making art became adapted to the way of living. It happened almost automatically. People became estranged from the primitive. The work of Japanese craftsmen has become incredible, in one sense, but

"I call it 'Drink tea, then go.' It's a Zen proverb."

Gufu Watanabe • 235

boring. It's a kind of industrial craftwork. China has gotten that way too.

"Their pottery has an incredible level of technique; the things they can make are so amazing to the point where you'd think that a human being couldn't have made them, that they had to have been made by a machine, or a god!" he says laughing. "But it just doesn't interest me.

"But when the Persians make a copy of Chinese art, or illustrations on pottery, *that's* interesting. Persians used to make copies of the old Chinese blue-and-white china, seven hundred, a thousand years ago, when all that pottery was coming in to Persia from China, right?"

I shrug my shoulders. He thinks I would know this?

He continues unfazed. "Persian art from that period is also primitive in a way. The lines, they're very good, not like the lines you see Japanese people drawing, so clean and perfect. For the Persians then, the forms they're drawing are 'off.' It's like they weren't concerned about it being correct. They were probably able do it a *little* bit more skillfully, but they somehow did it poorly anyway. And that's why I'm practicing being talentless. But I find it almost impossible to do. If I could actually get bad at it . . . but to imitate being bad at it, that just won't work." We both start laughing.

And then Gufu says something that brings a lot of things about his life together for me, "I myself am trying to live close to that way, to see if I could get that same kind of feel.

"Those pictures from a thousand years ago in Persia came out of the life of poor people then. So if I lived a similar way, then maybe I could draw such pictures, but I . . . I live in Japan. I grew up poor, actually, but all around me, the culture was at a sophisticated level. That's why no matter how I try, I can't draw a picture like they did. My goal is to draw a line with some 'flavor' to it. But somehow, I just end up drawing a clean and pretty line, that is to say, a boring line. I have to destroy that habit."

A flavorful line. Such a small thing, but such a big thing if you are trying to make good art. And, for Gufu, drawing that kind of line depends not just on what is going on inside of you but on having an energized life.

"So then are you trying to make your life like that of aboriginal people?"

"Honestly, I think it is impossible for me to make a real primitive piece of work because my way of life is not primitive, and neither is my head. I have studied—and live in—a Japanese person's culture. And there are many good parts of Japanese culture, even if they are not primitive—even in the midst of so many material objects that have been over-publicized. So I think the things that I make are really a combination of the two. In any case,

I don't want to make an exact copy of something that a tribal person has done. But I try to pull out the essence from the primitive places in their work, and then I just relax about it and let that mixing occur."

I look down at these creatures in front of us again: the smirking fish, the squat and self-possessed hedgehog, spikes all over his back, and I lift up their lids. Lids! I ask him about them. "The pieces from the Indian tribal minorities," says Gufu, "were essentially for ornamentation, to put somewhere, or for ceremonies, but I made them into something that can be used. In Japan, there are a lot of decorative things, aren't there? I don't really like them. Things that can be used are better."

"Used?" I ask.

"Yes, I know," he adds laughing, "you can't *really* use them. But . . . just a little, somehow . . . say, open one of them up and put something in it, even a few peanuts, some chili paste. And then when you lift up the top, take a quick look, something comes out of your imagination. That way there's some relationship between it and yourself. And if you have this piece around, just every once in a while you might say to yourself, 'I might take this out for a party, or when people are coming together.'

"But if you just put it there and it doesn't move, that's not interesting. So I only make things that can be used."

Just as Gufu wants to make artwork that is not just decorative, he also wants to avoid making pieces that try too hard, as he puts it, to ingratiate themselves with our own human tendency toward sentimentality.

"You know that kind of art that is always trying to attach itself to you, that's always saying 'Please buy me,' or 'I sure am cute!'" he says with some distaste. "The way it behaves is unpleasant. But I like the ones that say 'I am me! I am different than you!' They act like a lion, 'Hey punk, I'm going to kill you!' It doesn't try to cling to you. It says, 'I may be a container, but I'm not going with you; I reject you!'

"A cat doesn't have that quality. It wants to get fed, so it slinks up to you, rubs itself against you. There's a lot of pottery and folk arts that have become like that. Japanese artists, they tend to make stuff like that . . . though they shouldn't.

"People are like that too. They meet someone else and they make all kinds of faces to get the other person to like them. Some people walk around hoping to get others to take care of them. It's the world of romantic karaoke ballads. You know, 'Don't throw me away!'" He adds a little warble to his voice to help me get the idea, and I laugh.

He continues, "If the artist has that feeling, it just shows up in their paintings. If they think, 'I'm going to

it, a strangeness; it's as if the art itself doesn't give a damn for you. You've seen primitive art, right? Whether they are drawing people or animals, it's the same kind of face. It's a person, though not a person. It's mysterious how they do it. But if we modern people make something, it just gets unpleasant. The human weakness . . . it just comes out. Now, if you take Rubens, he paints the portrait of that person intact, just as that person is. Ruben's portraits are good because his personality isn't in them."

After a pause, Gufu adds, "What I am talking about we call *kiritto* in Japanese. It means sharp, strong of spirit, not mushy or sentimental, like the wife of a samurai. Atsuko is a bit like that, she'll say, '*That* is mistaken!' The wife of a samurai doesn't sob that her husband got killed in the war. She just says, 'There's nothing I can do about it.' Even if your household runs out of money, you always show the same strong face. You don't go around groveling for money. You say, 'Even though I am poor, through my own power, I'll do it.' That is *kiritto*. The samurai survives by means of the will and spirit only. There's something elevated in the feeling there. They want to eat, but they don't say, 'I want to eat.' As it is said, 'The samurai glories even in poverty.' They chew on a stick."

All of a sudden it strikes me that Gufu and Atsuko and many people living as they do in Japan may be more like samurai than I had thought. There is, after all, a real

"And then when you lift up the top, take a quick look, and from your imagination something comes out."

sell this thing,' something gets weird, and wrong, in the work. When most artists draw people, they let all those unfinished things in their heart run through to the surface and come out in the painting. It happens to me too. When I make something with a face it still ends up looking too friendly, too gentle. I have to make it more animalistic. My own pictures still just reek of the human.

"But in primitive paintings," he says, with real awe in his voice, "there's *none* of that! And there's a humor to dignity to surviving by your own power. They have prioritized a solidness of heart and a richness of the spirit.

Then Gufu adds, "While there are good parts to *kiritto*, it can a little bit too cold or inhuman if you overdo it. Nonetheless a certain amount—the correct amount—of pushing yourself, for us human beings is in fact good. You shouldn't quickly bow your head, and ask for help."

I think back to what Gufu said to me long ago, in its literal translation: *"The thing that is for you, do it yourself."*

~

The Watanabe's woodstove is radiating heat and the February cold has just broken. It will soon be spring. I've brought Gufu a catalog of heirloom seeds from a West Coast seed-saving group, and we've been enjoying looking up words in our corresponding dictionaries and telling each other about the peculiarities of different kinds of plants. The house is quiet: the two girls are in town visiting their grandmother, and Atsuko is in her study working on a newsletter for her anti-nuclear group. I ask Gufu about his theory of collecting.

"Well, there's a psychology to collectors, isn't there?" he says. "The way I feel about it, if you don't collect things,

they just disappear, don't they? They get thrown away and just become garbage. With some things, of course, it's good that they're thrown away, but others—someone has gone through all the trouble to design something, like a stamp or a label, some interesting thing. That object is a memorial of that particular time, that whole era, say something that best expresses the feeling of the 1970s. If that thing ceases to exist, the whole feeling of that time gets extinguished. It's a shame, and a waste.

"If a museum does the collecting for us, that's fine, but there are certain things that museums don't collect and won't collect. A strange bottle, or something like that. Of course museums collect expensive and important things. That's why I don't collect expensive things . . . well, it's also because I have no money!" he laughs. "I just collect things I like, especially if no one else is collecting them. People throw away a lot of good things."

"In order to show to people?"

"Not at all. I just go upstairs to the storage area sometimes to look at things in a box, and think 'Hmm, that's interesting.'"

"But how do you decide what you'll collect?"

"Everything is interesting, anything."

I smile: still the unrepentant maximalist.

"But I can't collect everything, so I only collect what I can. As a boy, I used to collect postage stamps. Now I only collect stamps of flowers. Labels are interesting too. Indian things, of course . . . *interesting* Indian things. I like brass and bronze and small wooden things. But I don't like souvenirs. I only want things that are actually used in daily life, especially in the kitchen.

"Of course one might say that I should just use Japanese kitchen utensils to make my food, but when I use what they use in another country, in India for example, when making *puri* or *chapati* with an Indian kind of rolling pin, it makes the food taste much more real. For me, just looking at things, real things, from India, I feel their energy flow into me, and something wells up in me, and I think, 'Yes! I want to make something like it.' I feel the atmosphere of India and I become connected with the person who made it. If you are somebody who is making things, it's important to have old things, real things to work from. When the physical object is lost, the entire power and energy is lost. If I tried to make something just from the image inside my own head, or used a copy or a fake, I would be totally unable to make it. A physical thing, an antique, or even a bottle of chili sauce, is like an intermediary between us and another time, between now here in Japan and back then in India.

"We modern-day people just somehow end up making modern things that give the feeling of our modern age. But by the same principle, if you have old things around you when you are creating something, you get connected to that older world."

Later, going up to take photographs of the ceramics in Gufu's pottery showroom, I notice that there's another room next to it that I had never noticed. The door is open, and I peek inside. Here is Gufu's room of collections. I call down to him—he's working on his kick wheel in his pottery studio below—Is it OK to look in the next room? Indifferent as always to my interest in him and his life, he calls up his answer, "That's fine."

I duck under the low frame and walk in.

Each cabinet has its own mini-classification. On just this one set of shelves—toys from mid-century Japan—there are wind-up cars and dump trucks and fire trucks on one shelf, and on the next a line of toy race cars with helmeted heads visible through the windows and painted numbers on the side. The shelf below has wind up putt-putt boats in the original boxes, white ambulances, and several motorcycles, all facing in the same direction as if to some purpose—headed into the future but arrested in time. It's a whole 1950s world of cheaply made tin and plastic toys, many in their original plastic bags that together form an entity that individually they could not. Just looking at these few things together, I can feel a time I did not live through, a world now long gone: a poor

Japan, a hopeful Japan. You can see it on the tiny faces of the drivers through the car windows.

Across the room, on a small set of shelves that he has built especially for them, sit a set of nine carved wooden doorstops with iconic-faced farm animals perching on their sloping tops. In yet another cabinet are wooden tops in a box, four miniature red postboxes, and a rusty gyroscope next to an old red horseshoe magnet.

Gufu's passion for superabundance—not unlike the Hindu aesthetic, I think with a smile—is everywhere in this room. Then suddenly I get it: there's an *interior* world to these collections. They are not only "an intermediary between us and another time" as he says, but also an intermediary between us and our imaginations. He's fashioned a way to be with the infinitude of objects in the exterior world and yet not lose that interior world that is so nourishing as well. And, I think, it is the same interior world out of which emerges the Tibetan monk serving tea to a lizard in Bali: a lizard with a black clay lid which you can lift up and "take a quick look and, from your imagination, something comes out."

Yet I wonder if this is the way Gufu himself sees his project here. The next time I visit, however, my hypothesis is confirmed. In the middle of some other conversation, I idly ask him what he had been thinking about.

His answer is, "Dreams."

"Dreams?"

"Yes, but not the ones you have at night; the kind of dreams when you imagine your future, what you hope to come true."

"And?"

"It's been occurring to me that they are very important . . . but I'm not talking about trying to make them into reality: just having them."

I tilt my head.

"Once you make your dream into actuality, the dream itself ceases to exist. But if you stay in the world of your dream, your imagination can expand and expand. That's a characteristic of the dream. If you are always stuck in reality, your thinking doesn't spread out and grow in the same way." Then he adds, somewhat poetically, "Because, as for reality, there is but one.

"On the other hand, though," he says, "if you stay in your imagination *all* the time, soon your dream doesn't work anymore because dreams need reality as nutrients. Without nutrients, animals and plants die, and if the nourishment for your dreams runs out, the world of the dream gets smaller and smaller and eventually dies. So you need both: dream and reality, imagination and actuality. Thus you have to talk to all kinds of people, look at many kinds of plants, eat all kinds of things to make your imagination new, to keep that interior world fresh. Then your own world can expand and can grow."

~

For all this thinking about imagination and dreams, however, there's another side of the equation of his life that has remained a question for me, and I've avoided it out of politeness for a long time. When I finally decide to ask, I find out that, for him, maybe it isn't separate at all. "In India, Gufu-san, most people are not poor because they want to be. You are able to make money because you live in Japan, but besides the sadhus, a lot of Indians live that way because they *cannot* make money. They're forced into poverty by circumstances. Isn't that a big difference?"

He answers, not ruffled at all, "There is a small difference, but in many ways it is the same. A lot of people in India are impoverished and it's true that many are suffering. But not all people who are poor are that way out of lack of choice; there are plenty who are consciously choosing a life of little money. They put more emphasis on having a lot of time, or being in nature, or pursuing their spirituality. They want to have an enjoyable life more than they want money. Yet . . ." he says after some con-

sideration, "some also think 'I want money too!' They believe that if they just had money they could enjoy their lives *more*.

"But I have grown up here in Japan, right? And I have seen the life of having money—though I haven't had it myself. I've witnessed it here for years. It's obvious that it doesn't necessarily lead to more enjoyment."

Hearing this, I remember that Gufu didn't grow up middle-class and then reject the comfortable life as an adult. The postwar Japan he was born into was a very poor place. Perhaps he simply chose to never step on the train of Japanese economic progress that was roaring out of the station as he was growing up.

"So why," I ask him, "do you think those Indians believe that they would definitely enjoy life more if they only had money?"

"Having money and having a lot of material things is not always bad," he responds philosophically, "but when that becomes everything, when it becomes more important than human feelings, than the heart, then it is a mistake."

"But you said a lot of people in India these days are thinking, 'I want to be rich,' right?"

"Yes, Japan has become like that too. Recently in the news there was an incident where some brothers and sisters got together to kill their father. Such things have been increasing here. It's obviously not because they are poor; it's because relations between the hearts of the children and the parents are so bad."

"But . . . " I persist, "why does this happen, do you think?"

"When we speak of human beings, they are just weak in that way. Rather than relating to others, people just keep trying to increase the number of things they have, and going further inside of the world of relating to those things, or relating to the Internet, even though the relations with your family or other people around you, or relating to our own hearts and emotions is much more important." He pauses, reflecting . . . "Humans may just have that tendency. And it's easy for it to come out: that is why money and material things are so dangerous."

"Dangerous?"

"If people don't have money, that bad tendency stays hidden, even though almost all people have it. It would be better to be a person without that tendency, to be able to have money and not have that weakness come out. But this is really difficult. People with a spiritual or religious quality to themselves, even if they have a lot of things they'll be OK. Or for the few people who don't have that bad part, they can get rich and it's not a problem. But average people get ruined by having things. They become less and less able to think about

© Junko Motoyama

anything besides themselves, or their things, or money. This tendency is quite close to our essential nature as human beings."

Listening to him, I think that maybe I've finally understood where Gufu gets his inner fiber. He doesn't go out to eat or entertain himself with movies, or even take vacations. (He returned from his most recent travels abroad more than two decades ago.) It's not that he's

There are prices on most items here, but this small room up a steep flight of stairs in the outbuilding of a farmhouse is certainly not located to maximize sales.

Gufu Watanabe • 243

© David Laidler

"*I got into the habit of not having much, and not needing much.*"

stoic, he's just relating more deeply, more powerfully, with something else.

~

It's winter and Gufu and I are again out in front of his house. We're both looking at the sharp blueness of the sky, watching the gusts of wind blow powdered sheets of snow off the boughs of the cedar trees on the other side of the valley.

"It's important to me to be someone who has time," he says. "There's a term we have in Japanese, *furyu*: the characters are 'wind' and 'flow.' Someone with *furyu* has time to write haiku, or can appreciate flowers, and they have space in their emotions to look at the moon or the stars. They're not too busy working or making money. Those people who don't have *furyu* are not full people.

"That's why I don't want to work in a city. I'm not interested in competing with other people or giving up my own way of thinking and way of doing things. If I chased after money, I wouldn't have my freedom anymore. For me, it wouldn't be worth it. I enjoy my life too much just as it is."

We both watch the dramatic curtains of white powder take flight back up into the air for a minute or two, and then he adds, "I think all people want freedom, but they've got this idea inserted into their head about money. So they take jobs that compromise their freedom, because they are afraid that they can't live without money."

I ask him, "But if your life got to a real crisis, you wouldn't join some company?"

He answers unambiguously, "No, I wouldn't sign up with a company."

"But," he says after a pause, "I might do some other job. If it really came down to it, I might do something like clean up a bathhouse. There's no responsibility in that." He's laughing. "Or cleaning up garbage; no boss comes and says stupid things to you. I'd clean up garbage to pay the electricity bill. Garbage itself is interesting. Most people would hate that, but I don't. Clean it up and it becomes beautiful! But as for *making* things, well . . . that's like making garbage. Working in some plastic factory, or making anything—somewhere in your heart you've got the feeling that junk is being made. But helping with someone's garden, or cutting tree branches, it might be fun. And if you do maintenance, your heart doesn't become strange or unclean."

I smile. He's worried less about running out of money than about his mind and heart getting "off" or unclean.

"But you have chosen a job that is making things . . ."

"Yes, that's why, as much as possible, I try to make things that are not garbage. That's also why I don't make too many things. If you make too many things, even if they are good things, they become garbage. The world already has too many things. And the things that I make are very difficult to turn into garbage. Pottery will return to the earth, and become soil again."

Now we've moved inside and I'm sitting with him in his studio. He's back at work, kicking the wooden potter's wheel. The tiny woodstove here in this outbuilding is keeping the cold somewhat at bay. A little kettle boils on top of the stove and the voices of a couple of announcers come out of a small transistor radio.

"So," I say to him, "you'd rather *not* have money?"

But he surprises me. "No. It would be better to have it."

"Really? So if I were to give you one hundred thousand dollars . . ."

"I'd be overjoyed."

"You'd take it?"

"Uh hmm!" He grunts his assent, nodding his head down once, decisively. But then he adds, "But I probably wouldn't use it much." And we both laugh.

"Then why would you be overjoyed?"

"Because I could do what I wanted, be more free, including in my work. Without money, there are things that I cannot do, right?" Then he pauses, thinking, and adds, "But even if I can't do those things, that's fine with me."

"But if you had it, what would you want to do?"

"I don't know . . . perhaps . . . just a little something . . . like . . . umm . . . I could do a few more of the things I want to do. Well, actually there isn't much . . ."

I shake my head and smile.

"Well maybe if the car was broken I could fix it sooner. But if I didn't have money, I'd think to myself, 'Ach, nothing I can do about this!' I'd just hunker down and struggle through it."

"So why would you want it then?"

"I don't know; I just have the sense that it would be better, somehow, to have it. For something."

I smile and once again shake my head. We listen to the radio for some time in silence and then I ask him, "Gufu-san, remember when you said to me, 'It takes time to be poor'?"

"Yes, it's true. You have to get your own firewood,

or grow your own plants. But there's a lot of pleasure in that for me."

"But I'm just wondering, all that time you take doing so many small tasks, isn't that frustrating for you?"

"No, not really."

Remembering something from a previous visit, I ask, "For example, turning over the tiny little blocks of damp firewood, isn't it tedious?"

"No. I think, 'That's just what this life is.'" He says this with absolute firmness.

"But most people would rather be reading a book or something, not turning over firewood to dry it."

"There's nothing to do about that," he answers. "I've given up on that kind of thinking."

"So you simply think, 'There's nothing to do about it,' and that solves the issue, just like that?"

"Sometimes it doesn't, but I try to think that way. It might be better if I didn't have to turn over the firewood. But to me there is no question of 'Which one is more important?' I think, 'It's all equally important.'"

"Do you still read Heidegger a lot?"

"Yes, quite a bit."

"But isn't reading Heidegger more interesting?"

"Yah . . . there is that . . . " his voice trails off slightly. "But it's just what I said, that's what this kind of life is." As he's speaking I think I detect just the smallest note of sadness, his voice lowered, like perhaps my asking this line of questions is making him a bit disappointed. I have a moment of regret for having pushed him. But then he repeats himself, his resolve returning, "This way of living is a human being's way to live. That's what it is."

~

"So, Gufu-san," I ask, "what will you do with your life next?"

"I'm not sure what will happen. Almost everyone wants their lives to change, and they're making a lot of effort toward that goal. But me, I don't do much of that. Because even if you push things to change, they might not. And if you don't do anything, they might change anyway. So I don't try to force the impossible. If a change doesn't come, there's probably no need for it. And if there is a need, the impulse, 'Do it this way,' will come from my surroundings without any effort or thinking on my part.

"To think about it one way, I'm deciding, but in another sense, . . . " there's a very long pause, as if he's not quite sure whether to speak it out loud, "it isn't me deciding. In reality, behind me there is some kind of 'power' acting, like a guardian spirit. I feel that. Somebody, something like a spirit says, 'Work!' Then—Go!—I work. It creates a feeling inside of me that says '*No matter what*, I just have to do it.'

"But just now, I don't feel that very much. And in times like this if I don't have the feeling, I can't produce very good work. I'd be just like some employee of a company—I hate the company and I hate what I'm doing, but I'm told to do it by the boss and I do it for the sake of the money. So until the energy comes and flows into me, I don't do it. In fact, to say it better, I can't do it.

"And there are a lot of things I want to do in life. I am not sure which is my main road. But even though I may not find it before I die, that doesn't bother me. So these days, I am just setting everything in place, waiting to get pushed from behind, or pulled from above. That's why the most important aspect of my life is freedom.

That's always what I wanted. And that's why I chose this life in the mountains, to be around nature and to be free.

"Whatever it is that is your purpose in life, you can't push yourself into it. Otherwise it's something you are doing just in order to have a job. Doing things 'in order to' or 'for the purpose of' is no good. I want to do what I really, really want to do. Then—*Yes!*—I'll do it, right now.

"Atsuko has a lot of things she wants to do—working on the environmental problem, Amnesty International and human rights, fighting the dam on the river, social problems—a lot of things. I think that will appear for me too, naturally, but you can't force it. For me, pottery, flowers, vegetables, country life—from these, I trust the next thing will appear."

Koichi Yamashita

Even though so many wisdom teachings talk about humility, our daily habit is to admire people with advanced degrees or important positions. And if we ourselves have accomplished things that society recognizes as superior, we may fall prey to the all-too-human tendency to get proud. We may try to use our accomplishments as a kind of psychic safety blanket, to blunt the edge of our own worries by saying, "I'm established in my profession." Yet, is avoiding this anxiety the best way to make the biggest choices in our lives? One phenomenon that often goes along with our admiration of intellectual achievement is that we tend to look down on doing work with our hands. Is it possible, however, that we are losing something nourishing without even knowing it? Koichi Yamashita has gone from being a university professor to what he calls "an artist of farming." He has found a living philosophy and a feeling of sympathy with the entire life-world in that most basic act, growing his food.

The zapping racket of cicadas rising and falling, undulating in and out of sync, wakes me up soon after sunrise. Although it's only six thirty, the thick heat of day is already upon us. It pours in through the open window in waves, and seems fused into one substance with the clatter and yazz of the insects. After gazing out the window at the hundreds of different greens in the valley and listening to the river below chortling intermittently, I head down the steep staircase to join my hosts Koichi Yamashita and family for breakfast.

I am a guest at their small house at the end of a mountain road in remote southern Shikoku. Quite naturally, there is no air conditioner, and, as all our ancestors did for centuries, we adapt to the heat, and do not map out any particularly ambitious activities for the day. It occurs to me that perhaps environmentalism is partly a matter of not trying to accomplish too much.

After breakfast Yamashita takes me across the valley to the rice fields where he shows me how to use a hand-powered rice-cultivating machine, a device like a push plow attached to two tiny metal boats, each of which floats in the watery mud and has a rotating metal paddle in the middle. You push the boats through the water, one boat on each side of the row of rice plants, and the paddles dislodge any weeds that are growing in between. It's quite an elegant machine.

"It's almost impossible to find such a hand-powered machine anymore," Yamashita tells me. "Everyone's using tractors."

While I bungle my way along trying not to run the paddles over the young rice plants, the sinewy Yamashita patrols the outskirts of the field, looking for holes in the bank left by moles, which can drain the whole paddy of water. Twelve-year-old Shanti, Yamashita's second daughter, works alongside us in the hot sun pulling weeds. After a few hours, we head back to the house for lunch, where I learn that before he was a rice farmer, Yamashita was a university professor in India with a Ph.D. in Hindu philosophy.

Although he and his family came back to Japan and settled in this valley five years ago, before that they spent more than a decade living in India. There Yamashita taught Japanese language and literature at Shantiniketan University (founded by the Indian poet and 1913 Nobel Prize–winner Rabindranath Tagore) in the northeastern state of Bengal.

In his first years of teaching, Yamashita would commute between the rural campus of Shantiniketan and Calcutta University, where he completed his Ph.D. His dissertation, he tells me, was based on Sanskrit documents from the second through fourth centuries, and he later published it as a book comparing the writings of yoga philosopher Patanjali with Buddhist philosophy.

But now, Yamashita says, he finds most of his wisdom in the rice fields. "I would like to be an artist of farming, to achieve the same level of artistry and creation of beauty as does a novelist or a painter."

After lunch, we spend the hot afternoon sitting and

talking in the deeply shaded house. The floorboards are stained a rich saddle brown and are shiny from years of people sitting and talking, living life on them. The afternoon light pours in from the open *shoji* doors and silhouettes the wafting, lazy smoke from the mosquito coil and from the tiny conical bidi cigarette that Yamashita holds between thumb and forefinger. The house is open to the world.

He answers my questions in any easy and frank way, but seems mostly the type of person to keep quiet and observe. His air is bemused. Around his head he wears a sweat-soaked strip of cotton cloth, his eyebrows arching over sad and contemplative eyes. His face is meditative and weathered, his voice is tenor and slightly raspy, and he laughs often in a self-deprecating way. Overall his aspect suggests a life spent listening for the sounds of vaguely sensed notions.

At about 2:30 P.M., when the heat is just reaching its peak, a large stinging fly zooms into the house. Several people in the room cringe instinctively, but in a hardly-perceptible instant, Yamashita's hand darts out, snags the madly careening bug, snaps it hard onto the wooden floor and then picks up and tosses the stunned insect out the open window. His face remains impassive.

I ask him about the book he published on Hindu philosophy and he explains some of the fundamental dif-ferences between Hindu and Buddhist ways of liberation. "In Hindu thinking, there's the concept of *Atman*, which is the self . . . but not the individual self, the transcendent self. It makes one a human, and it's very important. It is thought to be identical to the all-pervading spirit of God, or *Brahman*. But in Buddhism, such a 'self' is not only false, even thinking about this self is what gives birth to suffering."

I ask him if he is still continuing his research, and by way of an answer, he just laughs. "Nah! In the end, I couldn't understand all that stuff! I threw up my hands. 'I give up!'"

Then, pausing, he adds, "It's all logical, of course, and I understand what those guys were saying, but as far as 'satori' and 'emancipation'. . . *yah!*"

And then he adds, more quietly, "Yet when I'm by myself, out in the rice fields, working with the plants, I am simply glad. I understand that I myself am living, that I am in possession of a living spirit. In the rice paddy with the plants you just naturally develop a feeling of compassion, of sympathy . . . " he pauses for a second, and decides to add, "of love.

"The plants are giving me a gift. They cause me to really think deeply. It's not just a 'natural farming' technique; it's a way to think about what it is to grow your food right in the midst of nature.

"You see," Yamashita says, deciding to take it further, "the ordinary way of thinking is that the human body and the rice plant are totally different, separate. But something I realized recently is that the human body and the rice plant are not separate entities. If you make a thorough investigation of the question, you will see that there are not many lives, there is only one Life. Both rice plants and humans are made up of the same substances, the same atoms and molecules. A rice plant starts small, grows larger, produces its seeds, dies. It is in possession of a life, just like a human. Humans aren't higher up. But this is not something I think; it is something I directly feel."

In order to explain a bit more of his thinking, Yamashita now hands me a recent newspaper article he has written about his way of farming:

Attempting Food Self-sufficiency

We lived in India for more than ten years, and there were many good things about it, especially how people took things slowly and how preparing and eating food took a long time. That was such a good feeling for us. But one of the reasons why we came back to Japan is that we wanted to eat in a more principled way. To nurture our lives, we felt that it would be correct to cultivate the land ourselves. While surrounded on all sides by the inconvenience of countryside living, you can get a rich enjoyment of the flavor of your own humanness.

We have lost much in the pursuit of convenience, but we can find these things again in old ways and objects, those that are genuine and valid, and learn by taking a page from the past. My partner and I believe this is very important for the growth of our children's minds and bodies.

In September of 1995 we started to actualize our idea of attempting food self-sufficiency. Since we started farming, we have never used any synthetic or chemical fertilizers or any pesticides. In the second year of being here, we were allowed to rent about half an acre of rice paddies by a neighbor who owned them. They hadn't been used for more than a decade

"When you are a farmer, the other party is a living being."

Koichi Yamashita • 251

rules of self-sufficiency: (1) Don't buy things. If you want to eat noodles, sow your field with wheat. (2) Don't throw things away. Use all your crops in their entirety. Return all inedible parts, and human manure, to the field. (3) Reuse. Devise ways to utilize things considered useless by others.

In addition to these principles we added four objectives for farming: (1) Be lazy. Save labor by cutting corners and not doing unnecessary work. (2) Be stingy. Don't spend any money. Forget about the economic system. (3) Be safe. Don't use poisons on your food. (4) Don't be greedy with the soil. Determine its actual fertility and don't try to get a bigger harvest than you ought to by using too much fertilizer. If you understand what your soil can really produce, you will have a stable harvest from year to year.

In addition to rice and wheat, we mainly grow potatoes, millet, beans, and peas, all of which can be stored for a long time. As for vegetables, we only have a small kitchen garden. At first glance it seems that nothing but weeds are growing because we use the method of simply cutting them back and not pulling them out.

"To be in the rice fields, or in your vegetable gardens surrounded by plants: it's a great thing for your mind."

and the neighbors worried on our behalf as to whether they could even hold water. With these paddies we were able to grow enough of our staple food. The next year we were allowed to use another half acre, where we have grown millet. The secret to success is to know the particularity of each piece of land.

Though we are just renting this land, and have none of our own, we made these three

One of the men who owned some of the land we rented at first had the ideology that people should not allow any weeds at all. He just could not bear the sight of our garden. As a result, he asked us to stop using that half acre. It was very disappointing because our organic farming had been going so well. In fact, the weeds were protecting our crops.

I work in the rice fields and I work as a school teacher for a salary at the same time. You could call me a Sunday farmer. I think there should be an increase in the number of weekend farmers among people who work for salaries. To support this, I think it would be good if local governments or the agricultural cooperatives collected information about rice paddies and fields that are abandoned and available for people who wish to do farming.

To be in the rice fields, or in your vegetable gardens surrounded by plants: it's a great thing for your mind. Furthermore, you and your family can get food that you know is safe. Farming is thus a benefit for your body and your mind.

[TRANS. ATSUKO WATANABE WITH ANDY COUTURIER]

After I've finished the article, Yamashita says, "It's just like teaching kids."

"What is?" I say.

"Farming. If you put seeds in good soil, they will grow. If you put the kids in a good environment for learning, they will learn. So for me as a teacher, my job is to make good soil. But most teachers and parents focus just on harvesting the crops. We talk about humans raising vegetables, but that way of speaking is mistaken. Vegetables raise themselves. We simply lend them a hand. Similarly, we have to shift the emphasis in teaching away from what we do and go back to the child. In farming, we tend to say, '*I* did something. *I* put in this much fertilizer; *I* put on this much pesticide.' In education, most teachers try to cram the children with facts. If we think about the student as a rice plant, then for such teachers the chemical fertilizer is the classes, and the pesticide is the test. And then, just like plants that rely on too much intervention, the children become weaker, and they get all kinds of 'sicknesses.' Then, when even a tiny wind comes along, they just fall over.

"The Ministry of Agriculture in Japan provides guidelines on how to grow things to the farmers, and they follow them, just as they are told. It's the same with the Ministry of Education and the teachers. They trust the government-sanctioned curriculum without any shred of doubt. And then they are proud of their big harvest: they get the students into a good university."

~

Now it is later in the afternoon, and the sun begins to cast shadows over the valley. The heat relents, though only slightly, and Yamashita and I decide to take a walk in the valley in front of his house. Although the mountains are steep around us, and very high, the valley itself is quite small. He takes me by a beautiful waterwheel-powered rice threshing mill house that he helped to build a few years back, working with others in the village. As we talk, I'm impressed with how much Yamashita involves himself with the local community. Even though he has lectured at international symposiums on topics such as "The Epistemology of Intercultural Language Usage," "Buddhism and the Structure of Understanding," and "The Yogic Critique of Buddhism," he also gives informal talks at community centers in nearby towns and villages on Indian cooking, the haiku poet Basho, and Carlos Castaneda, as well as on the Lepcha tribal minority of North-East India. He and his partner Asha Amemiya have held joint exhibitions locally as well, she showing her work in batik, and he showing his photographs. Every month he puts out a handwritten newsletter about his family, their life, his farming, and various philosophical thoughts he has about education or about living in nature.

As we talk more—and I feel like I have to pry the information out of him—I find out that he studied the Upanishads in Sanskrit, can read classical Chinese, and published the first book on Japanese grammar in English in India. With Amemiya, he published a book on the culture of Darjeeling and the ancient Buddhist kingdom of Sikkim to the north. It contains much of his research on festivals and folk religions and is also a walking guide to many of the temples and monasteries there.

But I can tell that Yamashita doesn't have one shred of attachment to these accomplishments, or any feeling of entitlement about the respect he should get for having these letters after his name. His voice is exactly the same answering my questions about his scholarly work as it is when he tells me about raising chickens or the paperwork he has to do at the elementary school where he teaches.

~

In the morning, Yamashita goes off to work at the elementary school and I spend the morning interviewing

Amemiya. I also spend some time looking through the many vignettes in his monthly newsletter:

We have an insect here that drives me crazy. It eats the roots of the plants, and they die. It really gets my goat. But if I set up the proper environment those insects don't thrive. I don't have to intervene too much and the plants are strong. Growing food naturally, we give them water, soil, and sun, and they'll do all right. It's the same with raising children: if we tell them what to do too much, or if we exert our will too much and meddle, we destroy their originality and their personality.

* * *

I can't help but say that the school uniform they make middle school students wear reminds me of the army. Its purpose is to create this group consciousness in order keep out those who aren't in the group. The rules for these uniforms are that they must be black or dark navy, and there can't be any designs or patterns on them. They look like clothes you wear to a funeral. That's not the feeling that a junior high school student has! It's unlikely that their hearts will feel free and lively if they're forced to dress this way.

* * *

If we teachers just input facts into the students' heads, they're not going to be able to judge things well. It's not the kind of study that will get them to know themselves. It constricts their hearts.

* * *

In Sikkim, in India, there is an aboriginal tribe of people called the Lepcha. One time, leaving the university for some time off, we spent about three weeks with a family in one of their villages. They had no electricity, and the only things they bought were sugar and salt. They pressed their own oil, they grew their own rice, they had cows and pigs and goats, and they knew how to keep silk worms. Their way of life was the real thing.

I'd like to get my life back to just the simple things: a picture, a plate and a pot, a flute, some vegetables, cooking a meal, reading a story.

What do I need to buy? I have to buy fish, and also I can't make gasoline. Maybe I could make my own booze from rice. But, then, on second thought, I might use up all the rice we've grown to eat, and Amemiya-san would get mad!

* * *

When there's flooding and your rice doesn't do well, it's not that there's too much rain. You can't put the blame there. It's more that you don't know how to handle the situation when there's too much rain. The rice seedling doesn't have any plan. It just takes what is put upon it and tries to accomplish its own life with the things that it is given.

* * *

The Earth, as everyone knows, has aged for 3,600,000,000 or 4,000,000,000 years. From this fact, we see, we who are living now are the result of the Earth being that old. One soul of one person, and one seed of rice or wheat is the fruit or crystallization of that many years of this Earth. When I understood, or rather felt, this fact I was so delighted that I had no words at all to explain it.

[TRANS. ASSISTANCE NAOKO SAKANE]

When Yamashita comes back from the elementary school, he sits in the small corner of this small house he has set aside for his studies and looks through some of his papers. Later he plays his small Indian bamboo flute quietly to himself. As the afternoon turns to evening, I notice that Yamashita seems to have a lot of time to talk with his three daughters, something relatively uncommon in the Japanese social-economic system where most children may not see that much of their fathers. He really listens to them too. When he asks them questions he is truly curious about their answers.

Although Yamashita and Amemiya grow and prepare their own food—both of which definitely take a lot of time—they seem to be suffused in timelessness, in an endless present. I ask Yamashita about this and, after thinking quietly for a bit, he offers a concise parable. "Two hundred years ago, it took a week to travel from Osaka to Tokyo. People would walk. There wasn't any other way.

"What that means is that people back then *had* that much time, that they could afford that time. Now, on the bullet train, it takes three hours. Everything is quicker. But we don't have that week anymore.

"Think about eating a meal," he adds. "We might consider that if you include all the time it takes to till the soil, pull the weeds, harvest the vegetables, cut the vegetables, cook them and serve them to a table, the process of eating may take four hours. Nowadays, it's possible to simply pop something in a microwave oven, and *Ching!* it's done in a minute.

"What do you do with all that time that it took, those four hours? The answer is that you are busy, busy, busy all the way up to that one minute before you throw that package into the microwave.

"But what about the hours you might have taken to grow the vegetables, harvest, and cook them? That process is *connected*. You feel a sense of time. The process itself *is* life. Just popping something in the microwave, *Ching!* It doesn't give you a sense of life."

~

It is some years later. I've just arrived by train back to this town in southern Shikoku, and, after being picked up at the station by the wiry Yamashita, we pull into a tiny fish market by the side of the road. "The fish here is very, very cheap," my old friend says as he hops out of the car.

I'd forgotten how really far away this place is. Even taking fast trains, in a land of fast trains, it took a good part of a day to reach this remote train station. From the central hub station in Osaka it is several hours until one crosses the big bridge across the Inland Sea, then several more hours to get to the central mountain range of Shikoku Island, through the dramatic Oboke Gorge with its clear roiling river, then down into the nearest medium-sized city, and then a couple more hours south from there to this small town. Living here is very different from being three hours outside of Tokyo and connected with all the culture and art that spills over from there.

When Yamashita gets back into the car grinning,

"We have lost much in the pursuit of convenience, but we can find these things again in old ways and objects."

Koichi Yamashita • 257

He looks over at me and says, "Five years have passed, but it's like we just met for the first time a second ago . . . like the sound from Murata's bamboo flute . . . gone!"

He continues, "Eric Dolphy, the jazz saxophonist, said, 'When the music's over, it's gone in the air, and you can never capture it again.'" And then, after a few minutes of contemplation, he says, "But actually the music is still going on. We met yesterday, and today we meet again. The music is still going on. During these intervening five years, that music has been going . . . going . . . going on. And thus, we met yesterday. The music is not yet over." He smiles.

He then tells me that we have to make a stop before we get back to the house to clean up his *juku*, where he teaches. I admit, I'm a little surprised. *Juku*, at least as I know them, are cram schools where kids are sent by parents eager to have them do better on college entrance exams. But if Yamashita has decided to start one, I'm sure something else is going on.

While we straighten up the small room on the second floor above some shops along the main road, he tells me that he is no longer teaching at the elementary school. When I ask him why, he says to me that he got quite sick a few years back and was unable to work. When the new school year came around, the school district decided not to hire him back.

> "While surrounded on all sides by the inconvenience of countryside living, you can get a rich enjoyment of the flavor of your own humanness."

holding some fresh silvery fish, I remember also that the ocean is much cleaner here away from masses of factories, and that this part of Shikoku has always been a fishing region. The common phrase for this area is "facing away from Japan, and out toward the sea."

As he drives, I look at his weathered face and I notice again his contemplative eyes. In some ways, he is like a jazz musician, "cool," at ease, "hip" in the 1950s sense of that word: in an authentic way, not posing at all.

"I had too much experience," he says, seemingly without a shred of rancor, which I am sure I would feel toward a system that would rather have a teacher without such a long résumé (much less a Ph.D.) simply so that they could pay them less. So he now teaches kids after school here.

"My life changed a few years back," he says. "Now I teach at this *juku*. But I think with the way things are now in the schools, this is better."

Thinking he might be trying to look at an unfortunate situation in the best way possible, I ask, "But if the school district asked you, would you go back to teaching in the schools?"

"No, I wouldn't go."

"Why is that?"

"These days the learning that children do outside of school is more important, I think. And there's not much good scholarship happening in the schools anymore. But at home, the parents aren't able to help either. Even if the children ask them a question, the parents don't know how to answer it because they haven't gotten a good education themselves. So if the schools don't do it, and the parents can't do it, and mostly they're too busy anyway, the best place to do it is in a *juku*. So even if I don't make much money at it here, I think it's more important."

"But you only see them a few hours a week."

"That's true, but I teach them *how* to study. And after that, they can teach themselves. That's the natural way to do it anyway."

≈

On the way back up the valley, he tells me that in the intervening years he has also led two campaigns to block the siting of two nuclear waste dumps in this region. Both, I find out, were successful. He states this without much emotion, but from my knowledge of recent Japanese politics, I know that it's almost impossible to stop the central government in Japan once they've made a plan to do something. I don't know how he did it, but then again, I remember, he's very, very smart.

I ask about his daughters and he says that his oldest, Himalie, is finishing her major in foreign languages in Osaka and that Shanti will be going off to study to be a school teacher at a university in Okinawa next year.

We pass by his rice fields that I worked in several years back, and once we arrive at the house, say hello to Amemiya and their youngest daughter, Kanchen, I ask him how the rice farming is going.

"This year's pretty good," he says, "but a couple of

years ago there was an illness that the rice plants got, and a lot of them died . . . in fact, most of them died."

"Did you find out why?" I ask.

"I can't say that there was one cause. All kinds of factors were overlapping. With farming, it's complex; you can never say '*this* is the cause of the failure.' But also I didn't take care of the rice paddies as much that year because I was so busy fighting the nuclear waste dump."

"Do you think that you're getting better at farming over the years?"

"Not at all. And all farmers will tell you the same thing."

When he sees my confused face, he adds, "The reason for this is that when you are a farmer, the other party is a living being. If you are a carpenter, and you build a house, and then another house, and keep doing it, even if you are unskillful at first you get better at it. But with rice, there are some parts of it that there's just nothing you can do about. If it's not a good seed, even though it sprouts, and you take care of it well, it won't turn into a good strong plant. Or if you have good seed, and they all turn into great young plants, but then you have a typhoon tear through that blows it all out, then what? No matter how hard you struggle, in farming there's a part of it that's uncontrollable."

"For example, we had a typhoon come through here two weeks ago. That's twenty-four hours, or forty-eight hours of wind and rain. The flower on a rice plant only opens for three hours. Then it closes. That's it. And one year the forty-eight hours of wind and rain overlapped that period exactly. So the rice wasn't pollinated. It didn't matter how much time and energy and work I had put into that rice field. I thought, 'I worked *so* hard, and . . . '" He lets his sentence trail off without an ending.

"So don't you get discouraged, or lose heart?"

"Sure I do."

"And you don't think, 'I'll just get a job and go out and *buy* my food?'"

"No." He answers, with his usual conviction, and detachment.

"Why not?"

"Every year you think about this in advance and put away some extra in reserve for the next year. That's what we did that year. The barley did well, and we had a lot of that, and some corn."

"So you didn't eat much rice that year?"

"It's not the thing that I *want* to eat, but the thing that I have available to eat. What I have now: that's what's for dinner."

I think, hearing this, how utterly addicted I have gotten to choice. Ever since I was little, supermarkets have always had peaches or pineapples at any time of year. I say to him as we sit together in this humble dwelling, drinking delicious tea, that city dwellers might look down on rural folks.

He answers, "That's true, but no matter how much money they have, they don't make food, do they? They depend on farmers."

"Do you want anything from them?"

"No, not really. I just want them to understand about us farmers, to understand that because there are people who are growing their food, there are vegetables in the supermarket. Maybe people look to see whether they're grown in Japan or in China, but nobody thinks, 'Where in China? Who is growing it?'"

Feeling a little feisty, I ask, "What if they were to say, 'It doesn't matter whether I know who grows it.'?"

He looks surprised for a second, and then he smiles and says, "Then I'll tell them that I won't sell it . . . to *you*."

～

It feels good to be back here. The kids have grown up, and there are a few more cats. Life goes on as before. The mountains are still green, and the insects in the valley keep up their cyclical cheering, jeering cries, reverberating off the walls of the mountains. I can feel the southerly clime in the intensity of their siren shrieking that crests in and out of consciousness as we talk. I can feel the fertility of Japan.

In the evening, after a delicious dinner—Yamashita cooked the fish over a little clay hibachi, and Amemiya prepared the rest—and after a wood-fired bath, Yamashita tells me that in addition to teaching children after school, he brings in a little income by tending an organic green tea plantation.

"Is it manual labor then, that you are doing?"

"It is," he answers, with a bit of a chuckle.

"Can I come along with you tomorrow?"

"And why not?"

We start out the door early, just after seven, and Yamashita loads his pruning and digging tools in the back of the mini-truck. We drive out to the end of his valley then continue on the main two-lane road for about ten minutes through several tunnels in this very mountainous area, take a right, and start heading up.

As we follow switchback after switchback I see another part of this area, not visible from down by the river: the endless rows of dark green and deeply folded mountains under the gray-clouded sky.

The plantation is much, much larger than I expected,

"If you don't pull this weed, it gets mixed in with the tea leaves and tastes terrible."

continuing for a long time as we drive from the bottom section to the top. Yamashita tells me that it is a side venture for a man who made a lot of money in construction and has a recent interest in growing things organically.

Yamashita parks the truck and we walk into the rows of low bushes. He shows me a viney weed that grows around them. "If you don't pull this weed," he says, "it gets mixed in with the tea leaves and tastes *terrible*. So I have to get it all out. And," he adds, "if I just pull the vine from the top part of the plant, it snaps halfway down and grows right back. So I have to pull it out from down at the roots." He squats down, and reaches *under* the tea bush and yanks out the weed. I grimace. It looks like really hard work.

"I imagine that if the tea is not organic, they deal with this weed with herbicides?" I ask.

"Exactly right," he answers.

"So if I'm out in the world enjoying organic green tea from Japan, somewhere here there's somebody doing the squat labor of pulling this weed?"

He smiles an ambiguous smile, and nods. I notice the incredible drama of the sky and mountains behind him. Then he says, laughing, "You are drinking my sweat and my tears! It's *The Grapes of Wrath*, exactly."

Trying to put it delicately, I mention that it's a long distance from teaching Meiji-period Japanese literature at a university.

"It's OK," he says. "I don't mind too much. And it won't last forever. It's a kind of yoga practice. Or to say it in a Buddhist way, a type of *kugyo*." When I look up the word, the dictionary equivalent in English is "asceticism," or "penance." The *ku* is the same character for painful, or bitter.

Yamashita continues, "It takes about four hours to do one row, and one week to get the whole section. There are twelve sections bottom to top. By the time I finish all the sections, the weeds have grown back at the bottom!" he laughs.

Somehow, I feel, it's not quite fair. But then I consider that if we in the world want to drink organic tea, someone has to do this work, and it's pure classism on my part to think that people with a lot of education should somehow be above it.

Then Yamashita adds after a period of some silence,

"But no one's watching over me," he says. "And it's good to be outside."

At lunch time, Yamashita takes out a bento box that Amemiya has prepared for him, and I ask him a question that has been on my mind for a while, seeing him work two jobs and growing all his own food as well.

"Do you feel like you are too busy?"

By way of answer, he says, "I don't make much money at all."

"Oh, I'm not talking about money; I'm talking about how much *time* you spend working."

"Well, I *do* feel that I don't have enough time to read and write for myself. But that's not going to go on forever. Perhaps for the next three or four years, until my youngest daughter goes off to university."

"But what I'm asking you is, well, if I write about you in my book, 'He has the luxury of time,' do you feel like that's accurate?"

"Well, I can have time. If I want to go to the tea plantation at seven I can go, or if I want to go at twelve, or if I want to leave at any time, I can leave. It's up to me."

"But," I say, trying to get at the core of things here, "a lot of people in the U.S. are working and are busy doing things from the moment they wake up until the moment they go to sleep. It's 'Work, work, work; do, do,

do.' And not everyone is getting rich doing this. Being busy isn't all about money."

He smiles knowingly, and says, "But usually, they are busy for money."

~

Later, back at the house, it's another hot afternoon, and I look over at the corner next to the window where Yamashita sits and does his intellectual and writing work. I think about the train ride, and how very far he is from the cultural life of the big cities.

"When I come out here," I say, "and we talk about Patanjali and *Atman* and *Brahman*, and Dogen the Zen priest . . . you and I can talk about it. But way out in the country here, do you have people to talk about this with?"

"There aren't such people around here, not really."

"Do you miss having people like that around?"

He answers softly, "Yeah, I do." He pauses, thinking. "There are a few people. Anyway, there's no real need to discuss such things."

"Do you understand the reason I am asking this?"

"Yes, I think so . . . " Another long pause.

I begin, somewhat hesitantly. "Some of the people

who want to live in the country, well, they may not have a particularly active intellectual life or at least they don't read complicated books; it's not their taste. Maybe they listen to music, or they do something else . . . "

"Uhh huh . . . "

"But you have a Ph.D. in philosophy and now you're teaching junior high school mathematics at a *juku* and pulling weeds out from under tea plants. And you don't seem to feel any dissonance or conflict in yourself about this . . . " The cicada sound out the window ratchets up to a higher pitch, almost like a steel drum in its intensity and insistence, then fades. "And that's particularly curious to me," I continue, "because a lot of people who have an intellectual life want to live where they can *feed* that intellectual life, so they would never move out to this village in far Kochi Prefecture because it's 'in the middle of nowhere.'"

He laughs his tenor laugh, but doesn't say anything.

"But you don't feel that way, and so I want to know a bit more about that feeling you have . . . "

"You do?"

"Do you understand what I'm asking?"

"I understand," he says plainly, and there's a long, long pause. His heavy-lidded eyes are blinking.

"So *why* don't you feel that, do you think?"

"Why indeed, I wonder . . . ," he says, as if for the first time considering such a question, which is interesting to me because I would assume that to be the *first* question to come to mind of someone like him before contemplating such a move to the country.

Then very placidly, he says, "One possible way to answer that . . . and this is only one, if I were to use an example . . . "

There's another pause. I wait.

"A book . . . when we speak about a *book* . . . a book is not a thing to read, *it's a thing to write*."

"Huh? I love reading books."

"The reason I say this is that what I'm talking about, this study of philosophy, is not a *discussion*, it is thinking. How should I say this? It is *innnnn*-sight, sight into something. It is not to debate this and that and the other thing, but rather deeply thinking about one thing, for a long, long time. You go much deeper writing a book than when you are reading it.

"If you are buying a lot of books, you think, '*Ahh, hmm*, this book says this thing,' and '*Ohh, huh*, this other book says the other thing.' And now maybe I'll buy this one and that one. And you think about a lot of mixed-up things. But to *write* a book, it's something that happens inside your own head: you think and think and think, for a long, long time. And at the end you bring out a book.

When you write a book, it is a 'self-to-self' discussion. Isn't it? It is! So in that meaning, you don't *need* another person to discuss it with."

I nod my head, considering all this, and his choices in life.

Then, feeling playful, I ask, "So when you are doing your yogic training in the tea plantation are you having a discussion with yourself?"

He laughs at me with his whispery soft voice. "Naah, I don't do that!"

Then, after we pour another cup of tea from the pot, he says, "There is a Zen story about a master who made his student give up on the meditating and the koans, and had him just clean up the garden, every day, cutting weeds, sweeping, raking. And the student had no aversion or hatred for this. He just did it every day. And then, one day . . . Enlightenment!" I look over and see a big wrinkled grin on Yamashita's face, as if to say, "You see what I mean?"

~

It's the end of my visit and Yamashita is driving me back to the train station. I remember that there is one last thing I have forgotten to ask him.

"So, how did you first get interested in Hindu philosophy anyway?"

"At first I wanted to study Buddhism, but then I realized that Hindu philosophy includes, or envelops Buddhism, and I wanted to understand what was at the *root* of Buddhism."

"Well then, how did you get interested in Buddhism in the first place?"

"I came across a book of D. T. Suzuki's in a bookstore.

"It's the same with raising children: if we tell them what to do too much, or if we exert our will too much, we destroy their originality and personality."

Koichi Yamashita • 265

Perhaps that was it, and I had a very good teacher in social studies in high school; he taught ethics, politics, economics, everything, and he talked to us about Buddhism."

"But he spoke to all the other students too. Why did *you* get so hooked?"

He laughs again, "That, I don't know!"

"OK, but what about Buddhism got you so interested at first?"

"In Zen, of course there is a theory and a logic, but you could say that further back, behind the logic, or you could say *above* the logic, there is something else, something that cannot be contained or explained by logic, and *that* was what had interested me: that which cannot be expressed by words."

"So you went to study philosophy at the university in Kyoto?"

"Yes, but my parents were against this course of study. They said, 'What will come of that?'"

"And you got your Masters in Hindu philosophy there as well?"

"Right. And then I got my Ph.D. in India."

"That's a lot of reading and writing to get to something that's beyond words!"

"Yes! Can you believe it?"

"But then you eventually gave it up?"

He nods as he drives, saying nothing for a while. And then, "What I *can* say is this: you cannot understand it from a book."

"Do you mean that after all those years studying words, you realized that it can't be put into words?'"

He laughs with me, "That's right."

"And all along this road, you didn't yet know that?"

"Nope."

"Do you feel you understand it now?"

"Well, I have the *feeling* that I understand it." But then he adds, "In fact, it is not 'understanding,' and it is not 'knowledge.' It is a direct awareness, or intuition. It's not the kind of thing you 'understand.' It's like I said before to you: one grain of rice, and the whole earth, they are the same. "You can't learn that from a book."

10 Jinko Kaneko

At one time or another, almost everyone has felt a mysterious power in nature. That instant of mystery can be so compelling that the memory of it can stay in our minds for years afterward. The odd thing about it is that as soon as we try to capture that energy, it seems to slip fleetingly away. Powerful art too, when it works and moves us deeply, can give us that feeling that we've seen beyond what is actually visible. Fine artist Jinko Kaneko is one of those rare people who has not only been able to contact the mystic energy in nature but can also communicate what it feels like in the paintings and fabric work she makes. Although she says she has no "answers" when I ask her how she manages to capture that spirit, simply by being in her presence, in her home and surrounded by her works, I get a whiff of the incense of that nonmaterial world.

The morning light is pink on the highest peaks of the Japan Alps as I arrive by train for my meeting with painter and textile artist Jinko Kaneko. A few minutes later, when we crest a hill in her car, I can see the milky silhouette of Mt. Fuji in the far distance through the hazy mist beyond the massive ridge of mountains that surrounds the broad valley.

"Yes, it's beautiful to live here," Jinko tells me in reply to my words of awe, "but it's a very difficult place to make a living."

Still, when we arrive at her small studio and gallery, I immediately sense a lush abundance that conveys a wealth of a more intangible kind. She puts some water on for tea and shows me around her wood-paneled atelier. Skeins of silvery-hued yarns hang from oak racks, and a tall wooden frame displays one of her creations: a rendering in felt of a multiarmed and many-headed Hindu deity, lithe and androgynous, with skin of mustard yellow against a background of deep evening blue. Upstairs I am shown an array of one-of-a-kind garments: a chemise of white silk with patterns in hand-dyed indigo, a variegated burgundy felt overcoat spangled with glowing white half moons, and, most stunningly, a long felt wizard's gown of slate blues, star clusters, and cloudy galactic nebulae.

For the second time in one hour I find myself expressing an admiration bordering on astonishment. Jinko, however, seems almost indifferent to my praises, as if she were far away. Like her art, she emanates a seriousness and a love of beauty, as though moved by a lyric inaudible to others.

The tea water is boiling and we enter into the other part of the building, where she runs a Himalayan curry restaurant. Handmade chairs surround a table constructed from thick slabs of light blond wood, and Zairian *makosa* music plays from speakers hidden inside mottled brown gourds suspended from the high ceiling. On the wall behind the table hangs a long woven tapestry and in a high corner an inlaid Hindu altar houses the elephant god Ganesh, who looks down on us from above. Sitting with Jinko here in this evocative and unique building that she helped to design and build, I feel welcome, and at home.

As we talk, I notice that there's both contemplation and humorous detachment in the manner in which she answers my questions. Her relatively deep voice often has overtones of laughter at the seeming joke of being human. The Japanese she uses also is somewhat elevated, even at times archaic, lending an air of poetry to our discussion. Friends are "compatriots"; her own high-school-aged son is referred to as "the one of few years." Yet her manner is simultaneously intimate, as she uses the personal pronoun *boku* for "I," which is usually employed only by men, and only with people one knows well.

She tells me that she is currently preparing for a show of new paintings opening in a few days. She has been exhibiting paintings again recently, although she worked mainly in fabrics for many years. The style of painting she works in, though richly colored like oils, is actually a much more ancient technique in Japan that uses ground-up stones to produce the colors, and was used for the paintings in palaces and temples.

Although she trained to do this work, and though

she is clearly extraordinarily talented, Jinko stopped painting after college and moved to mostly working in fabrics. Partially, she says, this had to do with having kids: "It's hard to hold a brush to your canvas in the middle of a pile of toys." But there were other forces pushing her away from pursuing a career in painting in Kyoto where she studied.

"The art world there is extremely old-fashioned. Even if you have a lot of talent, you must maintain a delicate balance of relationships with your teachers. If they suddenly decide they don't like you, it's almost impossible to get into a show.

"One of my compatriots at school was studying with a master and his work was very beautiful. There was an important exhibition coming up in which everyone naturally expected that he would show his work. But the teacher said to him, 'Boy, you go get me one million yen [$10,000], and then you can be in this show.' My friend was so naïve; he was shocked, destroyed. He was so damaged that in the end, he committed suicide. So I knew what that painting world was all about. I also knew that as a woman it would be especially difficult. I just didn't see a place for me there."

Soon afterward, she set out to travel in India and Nepal with her college roommate, Atsuko. She would end up staying abroad for several years.

"What made you decide to leave Japan?" I ask.

"Well, as for going to India," she says simply, "there really was no incongruity in doing so. I was brought up in a temple, and my father was a priest in an esoteric sect of Buddhism, so we had a lot of Indian people coming to the temple and staying. I was quite used to it."

"But," I ask, "why did you stay there for so long? Most people travel for only a few weeks after they graduate."

"There was nothing to prevent me from leaving Japan in the first place, and I really didn't have anything to come back to," she says. "When I left, I had basically discarded Japan, and I didn't want to return. I had no idea what I would do if I came back. I had thrown away everything when I left. I had no job, and no place to live here, so I just stayed in India. I had become discouraged painting pictures, and as I said the art world didn't seem like a place that I could survive in, especially as a woman."

I notice that there is both contemplation and humorous detachment in her manner.

Jinko answers in a similar vein when I ask why she chose to live in the mountains when she did eventually come back to Japan. "My father worshipped a mountain deity, so again there was nothing unusual in my choosing a mountain life."

I am surprised by her offhand and almost indifferent tone, as if she has simply been subject to the inexplicable movements of fate. Then, when I ask about her art, the way she speaks is also as though she herself were surprised by its presence in her life, as if it were only com-

ing through her and not as a result of a concerted, intentional act. Everything simply seemed to happen that way, or "there wasn't any contradiction to it turning out the way that it has." To me, "no reason not to" is an unusual way to go through life; but when I see what she has created, either in this restaurant, in her work in fabrics, or in her paintings, I have the feeling that she understands something that I, as yet, do not.

Of the stories Jinko tells about her years in India and Nepal, certain scenes seem emblematic of her finding the inexplicable beyond what is visible on the surface of the real. "One evening in Nepal," she says, "I came upon a festival of lights, with hundreds of people holding candles in the night. Amongst these candles I could feel a gathering of thousands of fairies. It was one of those moments when I knew that this world is not only made from things that you can see." She also tells me of climbing a mountain inhabited by wild green monkeys and owls hiding up in high branches, and about walking across rivers barefoot to get to a cave where the Buddha trained. Then, in response to my question asking what she felt she was looking for in Nepal, she uses a term that I have to look up, and I find that, in Japanese, the way sunlight appears when it shines through the leaves of trees is expressed with a single discrete word. "There's a sparkling river," she says, "that flows inside of that light, and that was what I was trying to find in Nepal . . . and at the same time I was trying to see into the scenery that was inside of myself."

~

In Nepal she studied weaving and dying methods for fabric, and ways of preparing different kinds of curries. "The way of using spices was different from tribe to tribe and place to place, and it was wonderful to be surrounded by mountains such as the Himalayas," she says.

Jinko tells me that her restaurant, Bontenya, is named after an incarnation of the Indian deity Brahma who appeared to Buddha to tell him to spread his learning and enlightenment to others. I thus imagine that she may do some spiritual practices. But when I ask her, she surprises me again.

"I don't do anything in particular."

"But," I ask, sensing something about her that I cannot quite pinpoint, "how do you find ways to keep the sacred as part of your life when most of the world around you, and most people in it, seem to be completely occupied with mundane reality?"

She corrects me right there, "I think it's a mistake to think that so-called 'ordinary people' are not on a spiritual path. You have no idea what is happening inside of them."

And then, after a moment, she adds, "The life that we live in this world is, I think, about polishing, cleansing our beings, our inner spirit. It's a world of meeting other humans, of coming into contact with the chaos of the world. We meet so many completely different kinds of people in life. There are those that we feel are wonderful, and others not so; there are people you admire, and people you despise. I don't want to use the word 'level' for people, because that implies that the self is grandiose. And how can we know what is higher and what is lower? It implies some sort of ranking. But maybe there's no other word. The important thing for me is to intently observe how I react inside when meeting someone new. When I direct my consciousness to the other person and examine how I feel and respond inside I . . . well, I can only say that I enjoy doing this, it's what I like to do. Perhaps that's how I keep the sacred as a part of my life."

~

Jinko tells me that she has to start getting ready for her lunch and dinner guests at the restaurant, but encourages me to take a walk around the neighborhood. It's August and the rice fields are at the peak of their green brilliance. Electric blue dragonflies zoom above the gently waving tips of the millions of individual rice plants, and bright white egrets fish for frogs at the rice field's muddy edges. When I cross a bridge I glimpse two great blue herons, stately and huge, flying upstream over the small river with slow powerful beats of their wings, their yellow eyes looking forward as if they were meditating.

When I return to Jinko's restaurant, I am again effusive about the beauty here, but she wants to remind me again that despite the scenery, it's far from easy living in a rural area with long-standing conservative ways of doing things, especially as someone from a different part of Japan.

"The people in this area gather together for a lot of different traditional reasons and also to make decisions about such things as the water pipes and community weed cutting. I think a lot of those meetings aren't really necessary, and as a woman and an outsider, I am at the bottom of the ranking: first there are all the men, and the oldest ones are higher than the younger ones, and then there are all the women, and I am at the bottom of that ranking, because I don't even come from here. It's tiring. The village mindset is narrow, and there are all kinds of tasks to do that take me away from my painting. I feel drained."

The phone rings, and it seems to be people making a reservation for dinner tonight. I signal to ask if it's OK to look around the restaurant and studio some more, and she waves me on.

I walk down the stairs and through the large room with the woodstove where her customers eat their curries, pass underneath a huge carved and brightly painted Balinese bird that looks down from the rafter with wild, demonically grinning eyes, go through a door, and come upon another room, disorganized, with stored paintings and stacks of colored fabrics piled up on shelves. I stop in front of a dyed fabric hanging on a large wooden display rack: in a field of dark blue night a pheasant rests among the tall grasses, its yellow eyes alert in an umber red mask. Behind it a waterfall of stars spills into the dangling roots of a banyan tree. The whole tapestry glows with an aura on the linen cloth as the light passes through, hinting at a transparency to the phenomenal world.

Then I notice a painting not put up to be viewed, leaning against a wall in the back of the cluttered room as if it were forgotten. Under the outline of a white bird perching on a branch, transparent like a ghost, the leaves of a winter lotus wilt into a pond. Under the surface, I can see their transformation into decay at the bottom of the pool. She has reproduced the quality of looking through water exactly; the hairline-precise details of each leaf edge and grass blade seem as if they were etched on glass, all of it together suggesting, hinting, once again, the ungraspable.

As I return to the main room, Jinko is off the phone

and she puts on another CD, this time lilting flute music from the Andes of Peru. As I sit at the counter talking with her, she caramelizes onions on the stove, a huge batch of them for salad dressings and to put into the Nepali sauces.

During our conversation, people come by to ask questions or drop things off, and I can see that Bontenya is a gathering place for the local community of craftspeople, musicians, and activists. I meet a broad-faced and smiling man, affectionately called "Uncle" (in English) who comes to install the metal chimney for the woodstove, as well as Ms. Akamatsu, just back from studying the baking of whole-grain bread in Germany, who delivers some *naan*, or Indian flatbread, for the weekend's restaurant customers, and Mr. Mitsui, who, Jinko tells me, has climbed many of the peaks of the Himalayas but is one of the few in this extended community of alternative people who is actually from this area. He has been so successful with the "no-cultivation" farming method that apprentices come every year to learn from him.

When we are again alone, I remember that Jinko was raised in a temple, and that her father was a priest in an esoteric sect of Buddhism. Hoping to find out something about the mystique in her paintings, I ask about her childhood.

"Well, it was different than growing up in an apartment building," she starts, but then pulls back, saying, "but it wasn't anything special."

"But," I say, "I do get the impression that you learned something that most people didn't . . . "

"It's true I was raised to accept the power of the sacred. And I liked to play around in the forest and hide in the mountains. I saw all kinds of things . . . " and then she stops, stirring the onions, saying nothing.

"What kind of things?"

"Well, it was more a sense of *presences* than seeing . . . They weren't things you could actually see. Probably it was just a series of associations in the imagination . . . and I had a lot of those."

"Are you speaking about spirits?"

"It could have been. It also could have been the presence of an animal, a snake, a flying squirrel. Anyway, something mysterious. Or maybe it was just a cat or a

The flowers glow as if they were lit up from within.

dog. It was more of just an atmosphere. . . . " She stops, and stirs the onions again, and adds, "Anyway, I'm not good at words."

She walks over and puts on another CD, this time some modern Japanese folk music, with sweetly uplifting vocals, lilting melodies, and hammer dulcimer. The first song is about making offerings to the mountain gods.

"Tell me more about the temple in the mountains where you grew up," I prompt, hoping that this might be an easier way to draw her out.

"When I go back I feel like I am being welcomed by all the things there, by the trees, or the objects in the house, or the rocks, or the stones statues of the Buddhas there. Or maybe it was just myself of the past."

"Hmm. Then do you think then that your own past self is still there?"

"That's oversimplifying it."

"Well, I'm just trying to understand . . . "

"Even with other Japanese people, this kind of thing is difficult to talk about. Not many people can understand it. So I don't speak indiscriminately to people who can't comprehend it. It's meaningless to them. Anyway, we can't know with certainty things that are not actually visible to our eyes. That's why this kind of talk is a problem. For me, I just think of it as a kind of play inside of myself."

After a moment she adds, "But it is not possible that *everything* is a coincidence. I think that there is a reason I came here, probably, or that I've made connections with the friends that I have, or that I have met you, Andy. But that's only a maybe, and I don't get attached to it. I just enjoy thinking, 'Well I wonder if that's true . . . '"

Now it's time for dinner, and among the guests are Wakako and Masanori Oe, and we share a meal together. Afterward they speak with Jinko, and we decide I will spend the next couple of days at their house at the other end of the valley while Jinko finishes up her work for the exhibition.

~

After I've spent a few days with the Oes, Jinko comes by late one morning to pick me up and take me to the gallery. On our way, we stop by a vegetable stand at the train station. As I watch her, I see that even when she chooses which vegetables to buy, she seems far off, listening for sounds that I cannot hear.

After driving through the wooded back roads for some time, we arrive at the gallery where her work is on display. The avant-garde rustic design of the building is arresting. Natural light pours in from the skylights, and there's a quiet café attached, and a large wooden deck in the back. While Jinko greets the occasional visitor I take a close look at the paintings.

There's a delicacy to the coloration, but intense at the same time. Except for the deep nighttime blues, none of the colors are highly saturated, yet they seem somehow to pulse. The flowers glow and the leaf edges shimmer, as if they were lit up from within. I look more closely.

While I know that the flowers cannot be lighting themselves, some part of me is sure that they are, just as the moon fills the night. Looking into these paintings is in some way like looking at the stars: there's a distance, but as I pour my attention into them, more and more depth is revealed. It is as though within the sphere of the plainly visible there are many different layers. Those leaves: I didn't notice that they were blue, dark blue. There's a gold dusting; is it pollen or . . . what *is* that? And these white roses with their red stamens dancing . . . the thorns are orange. Every single flower petal is flawlessly drawn—the folds, the layering, the shadows and gradients, the ridges and creases. The whites glisten. Yet to even notice these details I have to point my mind at each element, focus on it alone, and try to articulate what it is, because even though these colors are odd, this fact isn't shouted at you. The force of the unusual simply suffuses.

I move down to another painting. A foaming river at night passes under the huge moon, and the mountain seems to be crusted with a molten blackness overlaying a glowing brown underneath. At the bottom, back behind the sedges by the river, the burnt-orange ferns. Above them, the Japanese pampas grass with pollen beads that shimmer yellow in the night. Even the black of the night is radiant like velvet. How can night shine like this? And what is it back there, behind these flowers, behind this sky?

No matter how I want them to, Jinko's paintings simply won't give up their secrets. There are halos around the blossoms. How was she able to paint a halo that my eyes perceive as real? It occurs to me that the question which the invention of photography posed for realistic paintings has somehow been answered in her paintings. Don't forsake the realistic; infuse it with spirit.

Later, outside on the broad deck with the woods surrounding us on all sides, I ask her about how she does it.

"Technically, it's very difficult," she says. "The colors are made from ground stones, and mica, pearls, silver, and even gold." Then she explains how the whites are made from the shells of oysters ground into a powder, and the adhesive is made partly from the marrow of bones (she mentions that the marrow of cow bones and deer bones have different strengths). As she explains the techniques to me, I am sent to my dictionary again and again: how does one make emulsions; different techniques for blotting or blurring; preparing a fixing solution from paste or starch. "If you do watercolors or oils, you can just get the paints from a tube," she says.

Then a family comes by whom she knows and they join us at the outdoor table. The man and woman are musicians who studied sitar and Indian singing on the subcontinent for years—Jinko mentions that we listened to their CD a few days ago at the restaurant. Their son is in his late teens and is dressed in the red, yellow, black, and green of a Rasta. We all talk about how we love Jinko's paintings, and the man says something I feel myself, "If I had money, I'd definitely buy them." Jinko is unimpressed. She pretends to clean out her ear with a stick and looks off and away saying, "The number of times I've heard *that*, I cannot even begin to count."

Then Jinko gets up to greet some new gallery visitors and I fall into a conversation with Ms. Shingo, perhaps an art patron type of person, whose husband is an architect down in Tokyo, and who has a second house, a refurbished fine old building, here in the mountains. "Jinko can do anything," she says fiercely, "and I just tell her that she should only paint, and give up on the restaurant. She's spreading herself too thin. She can find those things in nature that are invisible, and paint them. You can actually feel the wind in her paintings, the power and energy of life itself."

"Yes," I say, "it seems to me that with that kind of talent, she would be a quite famous painter."

"I know! I think so too," Ms. Shingo agrees. But then she adds, after some consideration, "But you know, there's something a little bit spooky to her paintings too, and Japanese people get afraid so easily. They like manga, and comic-book kinds of drawings. Their kind of art is 'light' and 'fun.' But for me, Jinko's art is very compelling. I think she should stick with it obstinately! I tell her, 'Go, go!' I tell her she should have the attitude of 'I will do this only!'"

Later, when I'm back with Jinko, I bring up Ms. Shingo's words, and she sighs, "If I had a sponsor who'd pay all my expenses, I tell you, I would."

As we drive back to the restaurant, taking rights and lefts on ever smaller streets, I notice occasional tiny little signs pointing toward Bontenya. Some of them are fading, others covered by the branches of trees. It must be hard for people who've never been there to find it. We talk a little about her finances, me trying to be helpful, and she says, laughing, "I just don't have any idea what to do to make money come my way."

When we get back and sit down again at the wood-slab table, she tells me that she also picks up some work doing drawings for reports on archeological digs and cooking for a summer camp nearby. "I actually want more quiet time," she says, "more painting and art-making time. I may not sell many paintings, but whether I sell them or not, time passes, and having regular exhibitions causes me to make more pieces." Then she adds, laughing, "This restaurant is my Buddhist training in patience, my burden to bear."

After a pause, she adds, "Before he died my father came by here to look in on me. He wanted to know how I was planning to make a living. I told him that I would go on as before, painting, making art, running the restaurant. I could tell he was disappointed, but I told him that I would be fine. I told him that this was the way I wanted to live, . . . " she pauses, and then says in a slightly different way, "I told him that this was the way I was going to live."

Tonight is one of the nights that the restaurant is not open, so the two of us have a relaxed dinner together. Afterward, as she's straightening up I look through some of the books she has out next to the table: *Celtic Fairy Tales, Plants and Trees of Nepal, Romanesque Art, A Pilgrimage of Sound, Paul Klee on Art*. With what these titles suggest, I start to get a sense of what she is perhaps chasing after. She puts some classical music on the stereo this time and since I've quieted down with the questions, she seems somewhat more open and willing to talk.

She brings a book to the table and says that this might help me understand her art. It is by the French symbolist painter from the nineteenth century, Odilon Redon. When I admit to not having heard of him, she doesn't hide her surprise at my lack of culture, but then she adds, "It's the world of the mysterious, the world of

It is as though within the sphere of the plainly visible there are many different layers.

Jinko Kaneko • 277

illusion." Looking through the images, I see pensive faces emerging from the shadows. Here an aging jester's head grows on a single stem of a plant in an infinite ocean at night; a weeping Asian face looks up at the sky as it moves on eight hairy spider legs. The black-and-white lithographs capture the bizarreness of our interior world, though not without a meditative, quiet quality at times. It's an Edgar Allen Poe world, but less ominous, and with a little more light.

"So is this the kind of thing you are aiming for in your paintings?" I ask.

"What art *should* do, I think, is advance the generation into the next era. It should be one step ahead of the ordinary, ahead of what is already known. Art is what pulls on the next age. I'm not saying that my art *is* that, but that it would be good if it could be."

We both finish our tea, and with these words of hers and Redon's images playing in my mind, I go off to bed.

~

Waking up in the very early light of this mountain valley, I go downstairs and sit in the back studio with the summertime light pouring through the tall windows. There's a grace to the morning air. Everywhere are stacks and piles of beautiful things, many covered with soft accumulations of dust: a box of incense, an almost mischievously smiling, female-featured Buddha painted on a card, glass bricks, two light-blue glass vases forgotten on a window ledge next to an exquisite, jade-colored ceramic frog. On a table I see last year's gathered bunched herbs. Images and tiny sculptures of deities of many kinds are scattered around on shelves. I think of the phrase "in the dust of this world," but now in a different way.

A number of unfinished paintings are out around the room as if Jinko left mid-stream, distracted by some overheard melody. Through the window I see the flapping wings of a butterfly among the hundreds of pink rose blossoms on the overgrown bush that arches over the door, its leaves trembling in the wind. On top of an oil heater, there are stacks of plates and trays with dried paint, the backstage workings of the transcendent paintings.

It is not in a polished world that this kind of richness is found, but only in the middle of music, good food, dirty dishes, coffee cups and ashtrays. I get the image of a child following a trail of spilt petals and bread crumbs, a woman wandering absently, zigzagging, the things gathered yesterday spilling from her fingers as she blithely seeks after new ones, one after another. This hodgepodge is like a teaching discovered amidst a world too busy chasing after new beauty to clean itself up. She will get to the dishes eventually. But before that she'll probably find herself making something new, or planting flowers or mint and lemon balm in her garden, or talking to a close friend, or mixing pearl or mica or silver with deer bone marrow for a painting of a waterfall.

There's a maidenhead fern sprout on a table, curling in on itself. I'm not sure whether she will paint it or cook it. Next to that a jar of honey. I hear a piano line coming from the other room. She must be awake.

~

When we finish our light breakfast of bread and yogurt and jam, I ask her whether she thinks she will still be here in her small house in the Japan Alps in ten or twenty years, running this restaurant and making her art.

"Well, I never thought I would be here this long, so I'll probably go . . . somewhere." She pours me some more tea, brings over the cream and sugar, and then, tentatively, adds, "Some place with a wider view than this one. I want to make my own garden, a garden of the ancients."

"A garden of the ancients? Do you mean old plants?"

"No, not in that meaning. I have an image in my mind of a garden from a long-ago era, of antiquity."

I wait again. She is silent. Then, eventually, I ask, "Won't you explain it just a *little* more?"

"But this is just my dream . . . " she says as if dismissing it, but then she relents a bit, adding, "I know that the air is clear, very clear, and there is a lot of space. And the colors are also very clear and sharp." She takes a sip of tea, thinking. "There is some good water, flowing water."

"And?"

"And there are symbolic trees, perhaps a tree with white blossoms. It would be a place where I could meet a higher level of my own self, a place where she and I could meet. But now it's just in my mind, 'an ancient garden in my mind.'"

Then she looks at me, and says, "You probably still cannot understand, right?"

"Well, not perfectly yet, but a little bit."

Then, looking out the open door at her flower beds growing tall in all directions, she adds, laughing, "And while thinking such things I've made *that,* that overgrown mess!"

"So how would you make an ancient garden?"

"I have *no idea!*" she says. And then she adds, "I just want to stand on the land . . . and make *something.* It's just an image, and to put an image into words, that's almost impossible. Words are so fixed, so set, and then to put *that* into English words, you won't get anything, Andy!"

Maybe she's right, I think. But then it occurs to me that if she manages to capture in her paintings something that goes beyond the visible, then it is at least theoretically possible for me to express something in writing beyond what can be said.

"Anyway," she says, "it's childish of me, thinking of all these grand things. I'm just saying that I enjoy playing in the world of imagination. It's a kind of game, like 'If I think that, what will happen?' But everyone does that kind of thing; it's not special to me.

"On the other hand," she adds after another sip of tea, "thought is energy. And when I consider this restaurant, I've heard from a fair number of people that they can relax here, that they enjoy being in it. Before I built it, that was the image I had. I thought I should make a place to bring light down into this world. All things that become realities start in that place of someone imagining them."

Masanori Oe

People try to work out the riddle of their own consciousness, and as far as we know they have been doing so for millennia. In the 1960s, for so much of the world, this question became urgent, and an entire generation—faced with war and at the same instant a plethora of new ways to expand or open consciousness—pursued it with everything they had. The fruits of this exploration were many, but what answers have we found to the original riddle? Having survived a brush with death as a young child, the writer, filmmaker, and philosopher Masanori Oe set out on a journey to understand this fundamental question. The answers he has found, and the implications of them, have guided his thousands of readers on a path of sustainability and to a deeper understanding of what life is really about.

"This is the same fire that burned with the blast from Hiroshima," Masanori Oe says to me, pointing to a small brass lantern on a table in front of us with a tiny flame burning inside.

"This very flame?" I ask, taken aback somewhat.

"Yes. It has been kept burning, passed on from person to person to help us each remember what happened that day, and how it must not happen again."

He explains that in August of 1945, a woman who lost her son in the bombing went to the city while it was still burning and, believing that the spirit of her son was inside that flame, captured a bit of fire and brought it to her home a hundred miles away. She kept it burning for more than twenty years, and then passed it on to a Buddhist priest, who decided to make it a symbol of peace, and took the flame on a walking pilgrimage across Japan, burning in a lantern, and passed it on to others, lighting new lanterns for those who would take the flame. "We have it here for some time before we pass it on," Masanori says.

The presence of the flame as we speak is both sobering and intensely powerful. I soon learn that Masanori's awareness of the presence of death has shaped the course of his entire life. Since the days of his experimental film documentaries on the psychedelic movement and the fierce antiwar protests in New York and Washington DC in the late 1960s, and his translation of *The Tibetan Book of the Dead* into Japanese, he has explored in a very fundamental way what this thing called "life" really is.

When I arrived for this, my first meeting with him, the first place he took me was a natural spring high up on the sloping sides of this broad alpine valley. The clear water upwelling from the pool, he said, has been trickling underground for more than thirty years.

After we both drank full draughts of the incredibly fresh-tasting water, he said, "Being here, in the mountains, I feel that there is nothing missing at all. When I lived in Tokyo in the '70s, all around me there was culture and civilization. In one sense, that is one form of 'illusion': that is to say, something that exists in our minds. People tend to think that without those things, they couldn't even live. We think, living in society, that we are lacking all kinds of things. That's why we make movies and books and all kinds of material objects, creating more 'civilization.' The whole time we are chasing desperately after some nourishment elsewhere. I too was living inside of that illusion. For humans, creating all these objects and culture gives a sense of abundance.

"But just being here, there's nothing that I lack. I look around and I see the meadows full of grasses and wildflowers, the earth, the stars, just as they are, existing, and I know I too am existing. Just knowing that I *am*, I can feel perfectly satisfied."

One of the things that is so interesting about this statement is that for almost forty years, Masanori Oe has created many of these cultural objects himself. But perhaps these have come directly out of that sense "there is nothing that I lack," like this spring coming out of the ground.

As I learn about his truly prodigious output, I am

amazed at how many things a single person with a sense of vision can accomplish. Besides being a movie director and an author of more than ten books, Masanori is a sculptor and a woodblock print artist, an interpreter of Native American and Australian aboriginal spirituality for Japanese audiences, a photographer, an ecological educator, an antiwar activist, and a translator of the work of Hindu and Buddhist sages. In the early 1970s he helped to found one of the first health-food stores in Japan, and helped to write the first Japanese version of the Whole Earth Catalog. The films Masanori made in the U.S. in the late '60s are still shown today in universities and film studies programs, and he has organized massive festivals of alternative culture attended by thousands of people.

Back at the house, as we sit down to talk and Wakako brings us some aromatic tea made from freshly picked herbs, I ask Masanori, "Were you always interested in such alternative things? How early did it start for you?"

"Well, one place to begin," the clear-voiced man with the meditative features says, "is something that happened to me when I was three years old. I was born just one month after Pearl Harbor and I remember a little bit of the war. One night right before the end of the war, the city next to our town was firebombed and the entire

city, *all of it*, was burned . . . totally black. And then the airplanes started coming toward our town just to the north. I was with my mother in a crowd of people running away, panicking, screaming, heading toward the mountains. As I ran along we crossed a bridge and my foot got stuck between two stones in the bridge and I couldn't pull it out. The more I panicked and struggled, the more stuck it got. And I had somehow lost hold of my mother's hand. She had my baby sister in her arms, and somehow in the chaos, she didn't notice that I wasn't still with her.

"All of a sudden all the other people were far ahead of me, and I was by myself and a B-29 bomber was coming upon me from behind. Everyone in the crowd was far away, and the reality of death was thrust right at me. The machine guns from the plane were strafing the ground, *rat-ta-tatta-tatta*.

"Until that moment, I had always been with my

"We are being asked if we might be able to see the life inside of our food."

Masanori Oe • 283

"Humanity is trying to create new myths, a new cosmology, a new way of understanding what this world is and who we are." Woodblock illustration of the tale Jumping Mouse.

thrown into the world. There was me, the world, darkness and fear, and the question of "life and death."

—from *The Dreams the Universe Is Seeing* by Masanori Oe
[TRANS. MATTHEW STEVENS]

"For most people, this happens gradually—they become aware of an 'ego' and they separate from their parents. But for me, it was sudden: the city was charred jet black, and the airplane was firing at me. This question of death overwhelmed me, and from that time I had a real terror of it. Whenever someone around me died and I was forced to think about it, I had this incredible dread.

"When I look back at this now, I see that this was the starting point on my journey. To the very degree that I couldn't get clear about this issue of death, I would be unable to see what for me was Life. Since then, I was pursuing the question 'Where from, where to?'"

Japanese sentences often leave the subject implied, so I ask him whether he means where he as an *individual* came from and is going, or whether he meant the question in terms of humanity or the cosmos as a whole.

His answer shifts everything.

"In the Eastern conception of things," he says, "the large external universe and the universe inside each person are not separate: they are the same. Thus the dreams that

mother—it was just one world. I hadn't woken up to the idea of a 'self.' I suddenly understood that I was *alone.* In fact, that was when I understood that 'I' existed. So the very instant that I realized 'I am,' that I existed separately from others, was the same instant that I realized that 'death is.' I realized that I could die."

The fear of death separated me from the world. At that time my mother was the world itself, and when I got separated from her "I" was humans see are actually also the dreams of the universe. I don't feel that an individual human's origin and destiny are different from that of the universe as a whole."

~

Masanori Oe grew up in the house of a woodcarver for the traditional dramatic art of Bunraku puppet theater: his father. But it was a time, just after World War Two, when traditional arts were being abandoned by almost everyone. His father (whose biography Masanori wrote years later in a popular volume) knew that there was no way that Masanori, the eldest son, would be able to feed himself by following in his father's career, something that would have been expected before the war.

"We were in a period in Japan when, in the space of one minute, everything that we had before crumbled: the values, the social order, all the old thinking, everything. The U.S. Occupation authorities reinforced this—all of our culture was a big myth, a superstition. We were told that our old value system and traditions had created the war, and *look* what happened. It was all a big mistake.

"My uncle came back from the war sick, and he died young, and so did my cousin, and of course there were so many people who died in the war. All everyone could think about was how to get some food. The teachers didn't know what to teach; they were confused themselves, and the textbooks had a lot of parts that were inked out. But there weren't any new textbooks yet either."

Wakako joins us at the table and adds, "And only a few years before that they had been teaching that the emperor was great and the teachers were shouting at the children to 'Memorize all of it, now!'"

Masanori continues, "That was the psychological scenery then: everything had fallen apart. Even the folk festivals disappeared. There was no money for that kind of thing, and no interest.

"At the same time, the experience I had at the end of the war led me to have no confidence that my mother or father could protect me. There was *nothing* I could rely upon, nothing I could trust. Later, when Japan started to get richer and a lot of American culture came in, even though on the surface things were getting better, underneath, unconsciously all of this was locked up inside of me. I began to resist everything. I couldn't believe in these things that had crumbled before my eyes."

When Masanori says this, I look up at the light in the small lamp on the table and think of all the echoings of past events that reverberate through our lives.

"Is that why you turned away from following in your father's profession?"

"In that period it was impossible. He couldn't even feed us doing it. People were watching movies, not going out to Bunraku. You could put on a show, but nobody would come. The more you put on shows, the more you would go into the red. So he recommended that I get a salaried job."

"But did you *want* to go into carving puppets? Were you interested?"

"Not at all. Even as a child I wanted to separate myself from traditional culture, and do something that involved the imagination more. That whole traditional world felt like a lot of pressure. I wanted to get out of there and be independent.

"Also I felt at the time—I feel differently now, I should say—that it seemed lacking in imagination: just doing the exact same puppet show again and again. There was no possibility for creativity, just an endless repeating of one pattern or form. I wanted to seek my own expression in the outside world.

"I got interested in making movies after I was exposed to underground film, Bergman and French New Wave cinema."

I shake my head. What a distance to go: growing up in a house where his parents meticulously carved puppets according to formulae that were three hundred years old—for use in plays equally ancient—to wanting to make avant-garde movies.

~

As soon as he got old enough, Masanori left his small Shikoku town to go to art school in Kyoto, majoring in sculpture. After he graduated he wanted to begin his study of independent filmmaking, but he says it was impossible. "We didn't have 16mm cameras in Japan then." So he took a job for a year to save up money to go to the U.S., where it was possible for individuals not associated with big studios to make movies on their own.

"Until after the Tokyo Olympics in 1964, you actually couldn't leave the country."

"What do you mean, you 'couldn't'?"

"The government wouldn't give you a passport."

"You mean you were in effect prevented from leaving?" I ask, somewhat shocked.

"That's right. Unless you were with the government or a big company, or got invited by someone who would sponsor you, ordinary people couldn't get a passport. And you couldn't get dollars: no one would exchange them for yen."

"Wow. So for twenty years after the war, most people could not leave?"

Masanori just raises his eyebrows at me, as if to say, "You see how it was."

In 1965 he took a boat across the Pacific to San Francisco and then made his way to the East Coast, where he managed to get introduced to a professor of film studies at Columbia University in New York.

"I went to the U.S. to study filmmaking, but it happened to be the exact moment when both the antiwar movement and the psychedelic movement were happening. People in the U.S. were saying, 'We have to go beyond the values that we've had up until now.'

"In fact, the first night I got to New York," he lets out a slight laugh, remembering, "a woman I had just met said, 'There's a psychedelic party tonight; everyone's going.' And they invited me along. That was my first night in New York! At that party I met Timothy Leary—although I didn't know who he was at the time—who was doing his experimentation with LSD and psychedelics. That was the same time that this movement was getting started. Our teacher, Bob Lowe, had started a film collective on the Lower East Side, and I learned filmmaking there in a place just off Bowery, in a really tough neighborhood. Later on we at the studio helped to put on liquid light shows at the Fillmore East."

What a very different America, I think, from the one that had sent a bomber at him when he was three years old.

Then, Masanori adds, "You should talk to my friend who I made movies with, Marvin Fishman. He lives in Vermont. I have his contact information . . . "

Next time I am back in the U.S., I give him a call.

～

"*Absolutely* I remember Masa! In his time in the U.S., I was perhaps his closest contact. We made a number of movies together.

"Our teacher Bob Lowe started a studio downtown because he couldn't teach the way he wanted to at Columbia. We called it 'The Third World Film Studio'; it was on the Lower East Side in a decrepit building off Bowery with a bar on the first floor. We called it that because we had so many different kinds of people there: me as a white Jewish kid, two people from Venezuela and one from Chile, a woman who was from an aristocratic family in the southern U.S., a man from India, and a Puerto Rican street kid named Angel who we took in.

"I still remember clearly the first day I met Masa. One day we heard a knock on the door. It was a big metal door. I opened it and there was this skinny Japanese kid with black frame glasses, and he had a cardboard suitcase. Not a cardboard box, but a cardboard suitcase. All he said was—his English wasn't very good—'I come here, I learn to make film. I sent here.' What could we do? We said 'Come in.'

"He was a very focused person. We all studied together with Bob Lowe, who taught us everything—lighting, how to build sets, how to rebuild a camera if it broke when you were on location. As I remember, Masa was very adept at it. We all had 8mm cameras, and Bob had us make a film every single day. We had to shoot it, edit it, and project it that night in front of everyone else, and get critiqued. And I did a lot, like forty or so, but Masa was a real protean producer. He did sixty or eighty films. He was completely focused.

"Masa was the most unorthodox filmmaker of our bunch. His films were very abstract. He'd take the ordinary object out of context. It was a very creative and unusual view. We did it all ourselves then: hand-processing, hand-splicing, everything. He did more editing than I did, especially sound editing. He had a highly unusual way of editing.

"Masa had a little corner where he slept. The rest of us had our families, some of us had jobs. But he was always 'right here, right now.' He couldn't have been more focused. We'd be going out, and he'd just stay there all night editing films.

"We all became what we called a tribe; we socialized together, smoked dope, all that. Masa wasn't that much into the drugs, though. There were all kinds of groups at that time. We were called a 'work tribe'—we had stuff to do. Another tribe would be about feeding people. There were perfectly fine crates of lettuces or carrots being discarded at the produce market on the West Side, and our tribe would load them into our truck—we were the only ones who had one—and then bring them over to the tribe who was cooking for everyone, and at night they would feed sixty or more people. I think this influenced Masa too, how people cooperated together. It was great, a real anarchistic form of cooperation.

"But there were more political tribes. They were rougher, very grungy and very straightforward. They were *not* drug takers and not at all into psychedelic things. They were doing very gritty political work in Newark. And on the other side there were Hare Krishnas and people going to listen to talks by Indian gurus. Sometimes we'd go over and listen to Allen Ginsberg chanting. Myself and Masa were on the more colorful, hippier end of it, at least at first, before the war started reaching its intensity. It was a whole conglomeration of alternative culture on the Lower East Side: we were all trying to find our way.

"We were also part of producing events for Timothy Leary called the 'Psychedelic Celebrations,' and lots of other liquid light shows. We had many surfaces to project the images on, and sometimes we had fifty or seventy different projectors going. The light shows were designed as sensory overloads to engage the senses: so many images, multi-surfaces, the fluidity, the rich, heavy colors, and *motion, motion, motion*. The idea was that disorientation, that sensory overload, can lead to a breakthrough.

"We evolved as well. At first we were just making films, and then as the alternative movement gained force and as the war progressed and things got heavier, some of us went a more political direction, and others of us did not.

"So at the same time that we were making experimental films, we were exploring how you deal with wars. My impression at the time was that Masa was a sponge, just absorbing everything. When Masa first came, the war wasn't as predominant in our minds.

"We filmed The Great Be In in Central Park in the spring of 1967. We titled the film *Head Games* to indicate that even though the event had the idea of protest of the Vietnam war to it, this kind of thing, a Be In, was not the answer to the war. Everyone was in costume.

"Over the summer, our studio had started a project called *The Psychedelic Cowboy*, which was up at the ranch of the Hitchcock estate that Timothy Leary was using. There were all kinds of people, rock-and roll-bands and people living in teepees. Although I love Timothy Leary, we couldn't get him to get things together or get to the set. Filmwise it was a disaster, behind schedule and over budget. It was chaos, and we were there to try to make a film. We had raised money, and had equipment, with deadlines. So Masa and I decided we were not happy and went back to New York City. Masa was not a druggie, and he was a very organized person.

"By then the old studio had started to collapse and had run out of money, so Masa and I went independent to do our own thing. At that time my involvement in antiwar groups was increasing. Masa was not an integral part of a lot of those group meetings, which were interminably ideological, and I suppose that he didn't follow a lot of it.

"By the time we went to film the march on the Pentagon in October of that year, 1967, things had changed

"Whatever medium I used, I was pursuing the theme: 'Where from, where to?'"

Masanori Oe • 289

a lot. You could see how much the focus changed in the difference between the films. We called that *No Game*, to say that this was not a game anymore: this was violent. It went on to became a major film. The demonstration was a mind-shattering experience for all of us.

"The film shows how a nonviolent demonstration became violent. The question was how do you take care of each other, and how do you film violence and not get hurt?

"Masa and I had a lot of experiences doing that. I remember one time we were in Grand Central Station, and I was filming a policeman beating up on a pregnant woman, right there in the middle of Grand Central Station, at which point the cops grabbed me. I took my camera and flipped it maybe fifteen feet in the air to Masa, who caught it and ran away. I was arrested, and jailed.

"There had been a change in the mood of the country. I don't know what we expected, but just in those five or six months between the spring and October, the police became less tolerant; there was a lot of talk of 'lawlessness' and here we were invading the Pentagon, the center of U.S. military might. They brought in a lot of U.S. Marshals: you've seen those images—redneck thugs with pot bellies, crew cuts, and truncheons.

"That movie we made was a real shocker. We were trying to make a statement that this government was becoming repressive of free speech, and we were trying to make it in as stark and shocking a manner as possible. The black and white gave us a grainy look, and then we made it more high contrast. We wanted to say, 'Here is your government.'

"I remember one thing Masa said to me at that time, that I never, ever forgot. He said, 'Violence changes consciousness.' That's a direct quote, and those three words, they never left me. I think he was saying that you could see that in two ways. Because he was from Japan, he saw that Hiroshima and Nagasaki changed the militaristic view of Japanese people. But he could see that violence could make people get more depraved, which is what happened.

"So at the end of the film there was this rush on the Pentagon itself, and it was ugly. It was at night and the cops insisted that the lights of the television networks be turned off. They knew they were going to be using clubs on us, and they didn't want it filmed. The demonstrators were being beaten in the dark, and in our movie, all the activity was being illuminated by the flashbulbs of the still photographers. You could see the hopeless violence there and the determination of the authorities to clamp down on us.

"You'll notice in *No Game* there's a whole section of jumbled camera, where the violence was happening, where Masa and I were literally in the middle of it. You have to imagine yourself with thousands of people around you. You're hemmed in on all sides, and you have these guys coming at you with clubs swinging like crazy. That is disorienting, and that was very intentional. You feel very trapped, and what you see is a swirl of body parts, an arm, an elbow, a shoulder, a hip, you're off balance, you're knocked back this way, you look up that way because you have no choice, somebody pushes you and you look back that way, then you're pushed further and you see somebody's shoe, like little pieces of craziness.

"And that was the idea for the film; it was edited with that specifically in mind: to bring about that sense of *You are here, now* in the middle of an uncontrollable situation.

Masa and I were very nimbly doing a dance, with a camera in our hands swirling here to avoid being hit by a club. We'd turn, and there'd be a club coming down and we'd swirl around that way, and the camera was running all the time, in wide angle, and then the club would come down, and then you'd flip the camera around, and get a face of some ugly-looking cop with a club in his hand.

"But as filmmakers we had to think one fraction of a second ahead as we were shooting, whereas the other people were in the moment in a more immediate way than we were.

"We inserted stock footage of actual Vietnam war violence into the movie. We wanted people to connect the demonstration to what was going on in Vietnam directly; that was *why* we were protesting.

"What was on Masa's mind daily, and I saw it, was life: how we live it, what are the ways that we live it badly, what are the ways we can live it better. I think he was on a quest then, a learning mission, and what he's doing now is in part an outgrowth of what he went through then, the festivals he leads, and the way he teaches people to talk to each other. He intensely lived it during that time and he could envision how this could be a better world. I feel like he brought the sixties back to Japan."

⁓

Masanori Oe • 291

The next time I journey to visit the Oes' home in the mountains, I tell Masanori about my conversation with Marvin, and I ask if he might have some of those films he made at the time. Happily, he does, and we arrange to see them with some friends later that night.

When we've all gathered, Masanori sets up the screen and projector, turns down the lights, and then all of a sudden I'm plunged back into another world. Even though I'm in this mud-walled house in the mountains of Japan, I am able to witness the immediate and vibrant, chaotic '60s counterculture world in full blossom, "as is."

People parade with signs and painted faces, dispersed on the streets of a late-winter New York, some perhaps high, or angry, or just playing guitar on the grass. It's a slow-motion movement of carnivalesque faces with soap bubbles floating in the air in the war-torn fever dream of the Us-versus-Them, red-scare, Gulf-of-Tonkin, daily-body-count sixties. These are more than documentaries, though. They are art. It's a controlled kind of wild: the hand-held camera shots at cockamamie angles and the syntax of rebellion inherent in the cuts between police batons and street protest, the voices shouting each other down. Yet neither are they gratuitously shocking, or easy, or pat.

The camera movements don't startle, but neither do they settle. *What's next? What's next? Who knows?* Flash-ing lights, throbbing and dreamlike, and absolutely unresolved, like dreams are. It is not bomb-throwing that's at the center of this rebellion; it's an insistence on another way, a turned, or sideways, or maybe upside-down way, but different.

The gyrating hips and the morphing red-glow lights of hallucinogenic nights are thrown into sharp contrast with the jump cut to the suit-wearing, straight-faced, body-tight old white men of the Establishment. I think to myself that even in his twenties, Masanori was presenting audiences with dream versions of their own experience, or rather revealing the dream nature that underlies "real life" all of the time.

Now a woman approaches the camera holding a sign at an antiwar rally in the streets, walking almost as if dead. On her white-painted face there's a blood-red tear. I know this is now forty years ago, but the immediacy and drama of that white face with the grieving tear, a response to the shock of war, brings the folly and the hurt of the whole Vietnam nightmare directly to my consciousness now.

The lights come up just slightly as Masanori prepares another film, this one entitled "Great Society." He says that his studio was asked by the national CBS people to do a major project, an overview of the entire decade, for the annual CBS network convention in New York, with permission to use footage from the CBS archive. He explains that it was made with six different screens going simultaneously in order to show the many-sided nature of the times, how everything was happening all at the same time.

Now we're into fast-cut, jump-at-you images, one after the other. The screen splits into six, strobe lights flashing, soldiers marching, JFK shot, Oswald shot, miniskirts, Vietnamese POWs, space walks, napalm-burnt children, fighter jets dropping bombs, the American flag, LBJ driving home a point forcefully at a lectern. Too much is happening at once for the mind to perceive. The soundtrack is riveting and disturbing: heart beats, guitar distortion, gurus chanting, a woman screaming as someone is shot, a koto twanging as a mushroom cloud fills the sky.

The images jumping from race riots to liquid light shows to atomic blasts are all in present tense here, not an artifact, or shorthand for "the sixties" digested by some future generation. The images are contemporary, and are rendered as such by the hallucinatory film grammar, prompting again the dilation of the psyche.

When the lights come back on, I am transformed. Only sixteen minutes. The film is a masterpiece, and everyone in the room knows it. None of us can speak. He's captured the overlapping movements: a new spiritual consciousness not separate from the very political, antiwar immediacy of the moment.

Masanori says that CBS refused to show it again, and there were threats from affiliates to drop out of the network if this was the kind of thing that CBS wanted to spend their money on. He says that with six different screens "the overwhelm and disorientation break down barriers and open people to the possibility of a change, a change in consciousness."

Talking afterward together, drinking tea, Masanori says, "Today people think the word 'psychedelic' means just taking drugs, but the main meaning is from the Latin roots of the words, *psyche-delos* 'to open the soul.' So if the method for doing this was drugs, that was OK, but it also included yoga, meditation, and the exploration of thought itself."

He tells us about meeting Timothy Leary and Richard Alpert when both had only recently stopped being psychology professors at Harvard. "I talked with Alpert more than with Leary—this was before he went to India and changed his name to Ram Dass. He was still in the 'serious professor' period, wearing a necktie. He and Leary were both looking into how we should interact with psychedelic drugs, especially in relation to the human spirit. But it was all in the context of Western psychology. The question was, How should we understand those experiences? And how does that relate to the universe's message?

"But nobody understood that then, and neither did

More than two feet long, the book is bound together with thick white string.

Leary or Alpert. People were trying to discover what was happening inside of them, and everyone was confused. There were accidents all the time, people overdosing and ending up dead. So people were going to speak with gurus from India or looking to the Yaqui Indians or the Western esoteric spiritual mystery schools. Everyone was exploring and studying and confused at the same time. I was in the middle of that also, and was having that kind of experience at the same time I was making movies."

I find out later, reading one of Masanori's books, that something deeply transformative happened to him during this time.

One night at the Millbrook Center at a psychedelic session, I took a pill that was passed around. After thirty minutes I started seeing visions. It was an incredible and ecstatic experience that transcended every aspect of myself. I was glowing and shining and be-

ing everywhere at the same time. At the end of the night I stepped outside and when the sun rose, that was the dawn of a new world. There I was the newborn self, flooded with light. Life bloomed and sang. My life transcended any life-and-death situation; I felt infinite. When being alive transcends the boundaries of "life-and-death," it blooms like a flower in eternity. If you go beyond the boundaries of individuality, life sparkles within the vast universe, and a world that is beyond life and death emerges.

I realized that I am bigger than I thought I was. This experience was the source of energy of everything that followed in my life. But at that moment I stayed there, and the philosophy and understanding of that experience came later.

—from *The Dreams the Universe Is Seeing*

Later, I ask him about that time, and he says, "A lot of people saw visions and gods, but a lot of them got stuck in that world, and many of them had difficulty understanding the meaning of what they saw." Then, after a pause, he adds, "That, however, is not peculiar to psychedelic experiences. Most people experiencing the 'real world' often don't know the meaning of the events that happen to them either. It's a problem in the exact same way."

~

After returning to Japan from the U.S. in 1969, Masanori began showing his films and speaking around the country, telling young people about the psychedelic movement in the U.S. But, he says, he still hadn't found the answer to the questions raised about death when he was three years old. And he felt that this deepest question of "Where from, where to?" could not be answered by the ideas of the psychedelic movement alone.

So, in 1971, with his new partner Wakako, he left for India. He had the sense from his days in New York, especially in listening to the music of the sitar, that he might be able to find some answers there.

As soon as I arrived, I felt that I had come home. It was the first time I had felt that in my life and it was a very joyous experience.

Everything was all mixed up there. There was goodness and virtue, and there was vice and evil. There was bright light and there was darkness. There was the sacred and the vulgar, there was God and there was hell. The feel and texture of life was there in the wind, the water, and the light: all of it mixed in a great chaotic mess.

It was all right in front of my eyes in India. And from that chaos, I felt the rapture of being alive.

People were going to the Ganges, offering incense and jasmine flowers to the river to begin their day. In their daily life, the gods were alive everywhere. So gods for them were not things that live beyond us but things that live with us. It's not a concept or an abstraction but a living and breathing thing, something that exists here in a very real way, as trees, water, and life itself.

I also understood the power of myths and legends: they lived them right now. Those myths were full of life. I was overwhelmed by the power of myths and by the people who live within the reality of their gods. This presented another question to me then: What is the reality of a "god"?

—from *The Dreams the Universe Is Seeing*

And then, later in his journey, spending some time in Kathmandu, Nepal, Masanori came to the third turning point of his life.

Returning from a trekking expedition in the vicinity of Everest, we stopped in Kathmandu for a while. Living in a single room in the area where many Tibetan refugees were staying, one day, by chance, my eye stopped upon the title of a book in the market. It was *The Tibetan Book of the Dead*. I remembered that this book was something recommended to me some years ago by Timothy Leary, but I never had the chance to read it. I bought it right then.

The journey of the spirit described in *The Tibetan Book of the Dead* was practically identical to the spiritual journey I had on the psychotropic substances I took in the U.S., and it felt to me that this book solved brilliantly the various experiences that my heart went through at the time.

—from *The Dreams the Universe Is Seeing*

Having felt that he had come upon something truly precious in *The Tibetan Book of the Dead*, when he returned to Japan Masanori began the slow process of translating it into Japanese. At first there was little interest from publishers in the volume, so he and Wakako decided to publish it themselves, by hand. Now sitting with him in the morning sunlight in Wakako's veranda of organic sculptures, Masanori takes out the volume, and I'm surprised by its size and format. Tibetan scriptures are traditionally made on long thin sheets of paper, he explains, so

they decided to reproduce the format, but in a larger size. More than two feet long, the handsome volume is bound in bright red cloth and stitched together with thick white string. He says that the two of them spent six months at their place in Tokyo collating pages, making the cloth bindings, and sewing together one thousand copies.

Soon the book became quite sought after, and Masanori was approached by many different publishers, each of them saying, "Why don't you publish with us?" Even today, more than thirty years later, it is still in print.

As Masanori had upon his return from the U.S., he gave lectures and taught classes, now not only on the psychedelic movement in America but also on the wisdom teachings of the Tibetan Buddhist tradition. By this time, in his early thirties, Masanori had already gone through a lot of experiences very unusual for people in Japan. He had things to teach that people felt they needed, and he was a gentle and talented teacher. He started to become well known.

Together with editing the footage they had taken in India—later made into the film *Song in Dedication to the Love of the Void*—Masanori and Wakako began a decade of translating and publishing Asian religious texts. Throughout the '70s they lived in Tokyo and educated young people who were disillusioned with the materialism in Japan about the spiritual traditions of other parts of Asia, and introducing them to more healthy ways of living. Because of many "closed-country" policies of the Japanese government throughout history, most Japanese people had been cut off from the wellsprings of Hindu and Buddhist thought from which many fundamental aspects of Japanese culture had originally developed.

Through the sales of these books and film screenings of his work, and through living modestly, the Oes were able to make enough to live on. They also began work, with a group of seven or eight people, on a Japanese version of the *Whole Earth Catalog*. It was not a translation but an entirely new book of ideas for ecological living: natural foods, organic agriculture, independent education, alternative healthcare, and a more sustainable economy. Although in the end it was not published as a collection of resources and products, a version more focused on ideas was, under the title of *The Gentle Revolution*.

Growing out of this research, the Oes helped to open a resource center in a four-story building in Tokyo. It had a natural grocery store on the first floor, with crafts for sale in back, a whole foods restaurant upstairs, and on another floor a bookstore and teaching space where Masanori and others taught courses on consciousness, yoga, tai chi, environmentalism, and peace activism. The complex was named, playfully, "Hobbit Village," and still exists, although the Oes are no longer active in it. Many

of the people who Masanori taught during those years have since gone on to be innovators in the fields of natural medicine, organic agriculture, or the movement for world peace. Some have opened natural bakeries or become therapists or ecological architects or anthropology teachers at universities.

Listening to all this, I can see that from the beginning both of them have been at the center of the Japanese alternative movement.

While teaching in Tokyo, and later after he and

"There is nothing but eternity, and dreams are a way to enter it."

Wakako and their two young children moved into the mountains, Masanori completed translations of books by Hindu sage Sri Ramana Maharshi, south Indian philosopher J. Krishnamurti, and two books by eleventh-century Tibetan Buddhist and poet Milarepa. Soon he began to publish his own books, including *Gaia for Beginners* (about the scientific hypothesis that the Earth is a single self-regulating organism), *Our Power to See Dreams* (about aboriginal Australian "dreamtime"), *From the Forest of Spirits* (about his current life in the Japan Alps), and *To the Source of the Spirit* (an autobiography and compilation of poems, essays, and interviews).

One book, a version of the Native American parable of Jumping Mouse, was illustrated on every page with Masanori's highly unusual woodblock prints, which he printed and hand-bound himself in a limited boxed edition. In this tale, the mouse rejects the busy life of the other mice around him in order to seek the great medicine lake in the mountains in which all the world is reflected.

Of his books, one that perhaps encompasses the largest overview of Masanori's thought is *The Dreams the Universe Is Seeing*, a theoretical and philosophical book that ranges from his early experience of being confronted with death, through the psychedelic movement and India, and in the end toward a new understanding of Zen Buddhist philosophy.

When Masanori brings them all out for me, I can only shake my head, knowing how much it takes to write a whole book, and I remember what Marvin Fishman said about his protean production. Indeed. Yet I have never once visited Masanori when he seemed rushed or stressed.

I ask him now why he stopped making films and moved to writing. He says, "Movies are visionary, but when I wanted to clearly reveal the experience of meditation I felt that I needed to use logic, and words are very good for that. Also after four years in the U.S. and not speaking Japanese, my own mother tongue felt incredibly fresh to me: I felt that I was able to play.

"But whatever medium I used, I was pursuing the same theme: 'Who am I? Where from, where to?' I simply tried to find the best tool, the easiest-to-use tool at the time to go deeper. So that could be flower arranging, or tea ceremony, or it could be words. Before movies it had been sculpture. The medium doesn't matter so much."

∽

Masanori has not only continued to carve wooden sculptures, and illustrate many of his books with original photography, but he has also been active in the movement against land mines, in helping Tibetan refugees in India, and in opposing the forced relocation of the Dineh (Navajo) peoples from their traditional lands in Arizona in the U.S., even helping to arrange the journeys of Hopi elders to come to Japan and speak on the topic.

For all Japan's economic connections with the other countries of the planet, in many ways it remains a place where most citizens know little about the outside world. I can see that for his whole life Masanori has brought the ideas and cultures of other peoples of the world into view of the Japanese public, particularly the non-European ones, those lesser-known to most Japanese.

In 1988, and again in 2000, he and Wakako helped to organize two massive festivals of sustainable culture. Held in the mountains, they were attended by over six thousand people and emphasized both political action and internal development and spirituality. I can see that for Masanori these realms never came to be seen as separate. These "Festivals of Life" also helped introduce new generations to those values and concepts that remained conspicuously absent from mainstream Japanese society. Workshops and symposiums over these eight-day events included ecological home building, natural childbirth, women's health, alternatives to nuclear energy, human rights, environmental education, and the impact of war on women. There were also art installations, theater spaces for the performance of plays, dance, poems and movies, and a Native American sweat lodge. Masanori tells me now that the overarching theme was about sharing ideas on how to make human interaction with the earth less destructive.

> The mystery and fascination of life is based on creativity, which is the source of the dynamic order in nature. Every human being also has the creativity of his or her own nature. The twentieth century was a century of the destruction of nature. We want this event to be a place where we can find solutions, so that the twenty-first century can be the century of symbiosis, of living together with nature.
>
> —from the festival brochure by Masanori Oe

The true meaning of the festivals, Masanori says, was beyond the dissemination of information or organizing around issues of nuclear power, war, and the environment. He says that the purpose of the festivals was to help find a new mythology, a new cosmology. It takes quite a bit of time asking questions until I understand what he means by that.

Before I get to my larger question about how a big mountain festival can lead to a new mythology I have to

Two twin teenage boys come by for an outdoor tea ceremony. Masanori often mentors them in writing essays as part of their study at a community-run alternative school.

ask him, "So are you saying that mythology and cosmology are the same?"

"I use the words interchangeably in my writing," he says. "Myths are a kind of cosmology in that both words express an outlook on, or a view of, the world. They are not just tales about the gods."

I have to think about this for a second until I understand that to Masanori the word "cosmos" or "universe" doesn't mean something out in the stars but something we are intimately part of every day, that is to say our experience here on Earth. He doesn't build a boundary in his mind between this earth and the skies. The macro forces exist all the time around us; there is no separation.

"And when you say 'myth,'" I ask him, "are you using the term in the Jungian sense, that is a primal story that explains something about being alive?"

"Yes. In Japan, the old myths broke down after the war and people needed a new way to understand our place in the universe. So because it is impossible to go back to the old myths, we will have to make new ones."

Myths and our view of the universe have guided humans throughout history; they are a way to filter the experience of the world, and have answered the question, "Who are we?" And they have told us where we came from and where we are going. However these stories were destroyed after the Second World War in Japan, and that has made us isolated from the natural world. In the Sixties a new movement for exploring myth and spirituality emerged, and the time has come for us to find a new cosmology or understanding of our place in the universe. This will take us beyond myth and into a "greater story." That is what we must build.

—from *The Dreams the Universe Is Seeing*

"So we need to 'open' our myths to solve this problem," Masanori says.

"What does it mean to 'open' a myth?"

"Not all traditions are correct of course; there's all kinds of 'noise' to them. Myths and traditions come from an essential teaching, but all kinds of ethnicities and specific local cultures interpreted this essence, and then people with authority in each country transformed those myths to suit their own purposes. So if you take all that additional stuff, and understand it as the myth itself, that will be a mistake."

Wakako, overhearing us, joins the conversation, making an objection that I was thinking of myself, "But Masanori, it's difficult to say what the 'essence' is, don't you think?"

"That is true," he replies, "but for example if you think about 'Christ,' it is a symbol of God. A regular person can't see God, of course, but through this symbol of 'Christ' it's possible to feel it. But when people are too wrapped up in the particular symbol, if they make it too much into a solid, impermeable material thing and insist on that, it will usually lead to clashes and conflicts. We need to create a new kind of myth, a new story we tell ourselves about why we are here, to make a world that does not create wars."

"So," I ask, "how do we determine what is the essence in a myth, and what is not?"

"A place to start is to ask whether it has boundaries, or not. It isn't tied to all kinds of value systems; it isn't fixed. That's what I mean by opening our myths."

"But how then was the Festival of Life a 'new cosmology' or a new way of understanding our place in the universe?"

"We conceived of it as a place for people to regain their awareness of their own spiritual nature, to find their own creativity or creative force that had been lost. And in fact, I believe that's what the whole earth is actually for."

It takes me some time to absorb the implication of what he has just said.

After a moment, he continues, "People are alive by means of the circulation of the spirit and the movement of the cosmos. Without those we couldn't even be alive. And the systems of our world—academics, science, education, medicine, culture, and civilization—all are manifestations of this spirit but also of the current myths or cosmology that we are living. And these are what we must go beyond."

One of the key words that I find comes up in Masanori's writing and conversation is *koeru*, a word with a number of different senses to it: "to cross over," "to exceed," or "to go beyond." His use of it is linked to his understanding of the boundaries we tend to create, just like the boundary he became aware of as a child when he first saw himself as a discrete individual confronted with death, and to the boundaries he first broke through in his psychedelic experiences in his twenties. He wants to teach us to go beyond these boundaries, to help us reorient from a view of the world as full of hard, impermeable substances to a world that is "a circle without edges," as he says.

"We have to go beyond just thinking about it as one or two festivals," he says to me now. "We want to emphasize having a 'Festival of Life' every day, because we ourselves, every day are alive. It's *all* a festival. Every day is radiant with the life force, the enjoyment of being alive, of making sound, and of that sound meeting the ears and hearts of others, which resonate with it. This is how we can make the life spirit shine.

"That is why we chose the word 'symbiosis' as a key word for the festivals. Since living is about relationships, in fact living *is* relating, wouldn't it be possible to think about ourselves as 'co-living' with each other? We do live by means of each other; I'm supported by the entire life-world all the time. My very existence is only because of relationships. As the multiplicity connects with itself, this world is made.

"People use the phrase 'the spiritual world' as if they were speaking of an incredibly special place, for example, something that happens during meditation, and 'becoming one.' But whatever issue we are discussing we have to connect to all parts of the life force. For example, we may say that because the environmental problem is so serious we need to develop alternative energy, or we ought to be growing organic food, or we might start a new way of healing people and treating illness, but it stops inside the boundaries of medicine, or food, or energy. We discuss each of these category by category, separately. They haven't been connected and tied together with each other well enough yet.

"So whether it's the things we eat, or conceptual thinking, or doing yoga, or developing natural energy, or new industrial technology, doesn't it seem that we could bind all these together to build a society with each other that really caused the life force to shine? We have to admit that right now the world of scientific technology doesn't see things from the perspective of this thing we call 'Life.' So we have to look again at the techniques of science from the perspective of the life force, and the same with education, and with agriculture, and with economics. We have to reexamine all of them in order to find a new system that will make us all shine, and reconstruct our society from there."

Many years after Masanori left the house with the small puppet-carving studio where his father and mother worked, and moved away from the small town where he grew up, he came to a new and very different understanding of the meaning of this world of tradition that his father lived inside. In a very popular book, *The Dream Danced by the Wooden Puppet,* Masanori tells of his journey to a deeper comprehension of his father's life and work.

Bunraku puppet theater in Japan is very different from Western puppetry. Not only does it have a stature in the culture equivalent to that of formal theater in the West, but each individual puppet is manipulated by three people dressed in black who work in intimate unison with each other so that the puppets seem very much alive. The ability to move the puppets in this incredibly lifelike way is considered an "intangible art" in Japan, and the puppeteers train for decades so that they can execute the most minute and delicate movements of a hand or finger to render, for example, the way a living person might move their whole body when cocking their head to hear a sound. Through their skill, and because of the hundreds of years of refinement of the craft, the puppeteers, who remain in full view during the play, slowly disappear to the viewer. You get pulled out of your own grinding world of thought and into the moment of the play.

The puppet in Bunraku is not a living creature; it is basically dead. And it continues to be dead throughout the play. To make it come alive the viewer of the play must breathe life into it moment to moment, and I believe that is the secret of a puppet performance.

The world gains reality only by internalizing it. Capturing something external into ourselves is the only way to make it become real. It's no longer something that's out there.

The Oes seem always ready to make themselves available to all who might come by, modest about their accomplishments and interested in what others might have to offer them.

Masanori Oe • 303

First the hand that controls the puppet disappears; then the person who operates the puppet disappears; and then the person watching disappears. Eventually even the puppet disappears and what remains is a dance of awareness within oneself. The musician creating the music, the operator of the puppet, the audience, and the puppet itself are in a dance of awareness. This is subsumed into the internal dance. The dance happens within your self, within your awareness.

The puppet is in essence like a dancing shaman creating existence moment to moment. It is an eternal world beyond space and time. And by this dance, it creates a rupture in daily life, and can lead people to a transcendence of the world.

During the show, everything else is not real. Because there is only Now, it takes you into eternity. Each moment opens up into the infinite, that which is without boundaries.

—from *The Dream Danced by the Wooden Puppet*
[TRANS. MATTHEW STEVENS]

Thinking about what Masanori has written here, I find myself starting to understand these abstract concepts,

"infinity" and "eternity," which had been so opaque to me before. Of course I've read about such things, but I just couldn't understand their relationship to my own life. Yet it is through Masanori's particular genius that I am able to finally get a glimpse of what they might mean. Perhaps this is the skill of a real philosopher: the ability to take concepts like this and make us feel their actuality.

Masanori explains to me now, "When I was a child, I thought Bunraku was very conservative, that it lacked in imagination and creativity. Now I see that the very most imaginative and creative place in this three-hundred-year-old art has been preserved in it, and that is why it can give people that transcendence. So even if we call it 'traditional,' each time something new is being created, moment to moment. There is *more* than enough creativity inside of puppetry; I understand that now."

Listening to Masanori, I remember what he wrote about what he saw in India: "I understood the power of myths and legends: the Indians lived them right now." And I see that this is what is happening in "the dream danced by the wooden puppet," as he calls it.

∽

We are out in Masanori and Wakako's rice field, the wind

rustling the thousands of swaying stalks. "If you plant one seed of rice," he says, showing me the heads of a few rice plants on the stalk that he holds in his hand, "it produces ten stalks, and on each stalk you get one hundred new grains of rice each. So from that one seed of rice you get one thousand grains of rice." He looks at me smiling, "That's much better than putting money in a bank."

As we talk, Masanori tells me that agriculture, and teaching it to others with Wakako, has been one of the main things he has been focusing on this past decade. He tells me how he arrived here, in these fields, after so many years of exploration. His experience in the U.S. helped him glimpse the nature of the spiritual world, but his questions about it led him to go to India. There he met people who live close to their gods. This caused him to open to the spirit in nature, and he became convinced that he should try to interact as deeply as he could with the natural world. And for him, that meant growing his own food.

When we discuss the method they are using of growing rice and vegetables without digging the soil or even pulling the weeds, I ask him whether this way takes a lot more work. He replies, "It might not be easier or produce the maximum harvests, but I believe it's absolutely necessary for humans now to relearn what we have forgotten about the spirit of life. In the long term, agriculture that

plunders the earth will break down. We have to find a way of growing the food we need to live that will last forever. This is one of our attempts at that.

"With no tractor and no outside fertilizer, this method allows the farmer to learn directly from the wisdom of the plants . . . and at the same time we reduce our own sense of superiority. Everyone has seen the mistakes brought about from humans trying to control nature. What Wakako and I are trying to do here is to see what happens, inside of us, when we let ourselves be *controlled by* nature."

I nod my head considering this. Even organic agriculture as I am familiar with it, with its petroleum inputs of cultivating machines or trucks to haul in manure or bat guano or lime from far away does, as he says, "plunder" the earth. What would it mean for me if I really let myself be controlled by nature?

I believe that we must take a new look at farming and see that it can be the pillar that will support the healing and repair of this world. It will show us how to understand the relationship of the human and the earth. Nature is the reflection of our internal spirit, which is the foundation of our culture and the world.

—from "The Psychedelic, Tibet, and Natural Farming"

"It's absolutely necessary for humans to relearn what we have forgotten about the spirit of life."

In order to establish a new world view based on ecology, we must understand that we only exist in relation to other things. Everything that exists ultimately is not material at all because it is created entirely from relationships. Unless you really understand this point, you can't have a world view that is truly ecological because ecology is fundamentally about relationships.

—from *The Dreams the Universe Is Seeing*

When I ask Masanori about this passage, and what he means by saying that all things are immaterial—which I admit I am having a hard time accepting—he explains that for centuries scientists have explored the world, dissecting it further and further down until they arrived at a fundamental piece or part that was believed to be indivisible, which they called the atom. But now in modern physics, *even that* has been shown to not be solid, but to be composed of relationships, of quantum probabilities.

Yet, he continues, most of humanity thinks that this world is one of discrete individuals with conflicting needs, competing with each other and surrounded by hard material objects. He refers to this system as a myth, or archetypal story: our own industrial myth of market rationality. He explains it using the Japanese term *jyaku-niku-kyo-shoku*, or "the weak become the meat of the strong who eat them," or survival of the fittest. It is, he says, destroying us and even our own ability to survive on this planet. As he wrote in a recent magazine article:

I honestly feel that in the midst of our free market competition society, the world is getting more and more violent. Market principles and market rationality preach that the strong must devour the weak. We are being asked if each of us will be able to resist being at the mercy of marketplace rationality, and whether we might be able to see the life that is inside our food. If we don't we will buy things just because they are cheap. We just say, "It's a low price, I'll buy it." Similarly we farmers will grow corn simply because we are given money to grow it.

I think in this generation we are being

asked to go beyond this kind of thinking, and we have to if we really want this earth to be sustainable.

—from "The Psychedelic, Tibet, and Natural Farming"

~

Later on in the day, Masanori takes me to a lovely shrine far up in the mountains, surrounded by woods, just downstream from a huge and roaring waterfall. As we walk around we come across a stone statue of a fierce-looking deity holding a sword. He mentions that this god is known as the one who cuts away obstacles for people, and that by connecting to that god, people can connect to that primal experience of "cutting away."

I ask him, "So do you think that this statue itself has power?"

"Yes," he says, "but only because it is a conduit between the deity and the person looking at it."

"Hmm. But for Americans they've never even *heard* of this god. Does it have power for them?"

"No," he says, "and that's how it is possible for people to destroy the sacred sites of the Native Americans: because they have no meaning for them."

"But does this statue *actually* have power?"

"It is only in the relationship of the person to this statue that there is any meaning. The god is *in* the relationship. On New Year's Day, as you know, Japanese people go to shrines to speak to the gods. When they feel this relatedness, the god 'exists.' But it's not simply a stone statue; there's a feeling between it and the person, and that *is* its reality."

"What do you mean by that?"

"When I feel or sense that stone statue, I have an awareness of it, and in that conversation, that relatedness, the statue has a reality. We could say that the relationship is an existence in itself. That's what I mean by the liberated mind not creating boundaries. If we deny the relatedness, and focus on solidity and material objects, as is common in Western philosophy, then we are more likely to create clashes or conflicts."

He then offers another example: "Flowers are currently used in flower arrangements, in *ikebana*, or as gifts; but previous to that, they were offerings, a conduit for connecting the living to the souls or spirits of the dead. They were something to go in between. That is why flowers are offered at graves. It is in our relation to those flowers, that feeling, that we are able to relate to the spirits of the dead."

Masanori's being able to explain the meaning of a flower offering, or a stone statue holding a sword, makes me think about the presence of the storyteller in all traditional cultures. Before writing and literacy, carved stone was a way to transmit stories over centuries. But it wasn't just the stone statue by itself. Always accompanying the statue or carving was a priest or a wise person; they were the second part of the set. The object and its story went together to explain something important. And that is the role that Masanori is playing in informing me—and his many readers and the people in his wide network—of the meanings of these messages from previous generations that are scattered among us. By "translating" them, he is helping us re-see these many objects from the past that we might otherwise have written off, explaining to the modern mind the ideas and artifacts of the traditional worldview whose meaning has been obscured over time. His stories show us what they may still have to offer us, and what their purpose might be. For the animist world view has not just been forgotten, but actively erased, and now people are trying to recover it so that we might be able to understand in a new way the great mystery that is this life.

> Humans are the kind of animal that wants to figure out the puzzle of our own existence; that is our instinct. We are all trying to solve the puzzle of our lives, getting one section together here or there; but there are so many other larger

areas. But if we do solve it, we arrive at what our ultimate identity is, and feel the ecstasy of transcending the separation of human and universe.

> —from *The Dream Danced by the Wooden Puppet*

We are back at Masanori and Wakako's house now, talking in the evening, and I ask him something I have been wondering for a long time, "What is the meaning of the title of your book, *The Dreams the Universe Is Seeing?*"

He pauses for just a second, and says, "The dream that the universe is seeing is *this Earth itself.*"

Ohh, I think to myself, nodding my head, finally getting it. My understanding of everything he's been talking about shifts. Other philosophers in the Asian tradition write about this world being "maya" or illusion, with a negative connotation. Masanori takes that negative implication out of it and calls it "dreaming," which changes everything.

He continues, "The dreaming by the universe created this world. Humanity is attempting to reach beyond this dream. But where? We are trying to create new myths, a new cosmology, a new way of understanding what this world is and who we are."

If I understand what Masanori is saying, and I'm slowly piecing it together, he believes that because all the myths of the world have emerged from the dreaming of the entire universe, the way for us to find a new orienting story, the "greater story" or myth for our lives, is to build the power to see our own dreams. By using the word "dreams," he includes inner images that arise from the unconscious, daydreams, night dreams, and visions we see in meditation: anything that goes beyond the ego-self. And these individual dreams, in the Eastern conception of things, are not separate from the dream dreamt by the entire cosmos.

"There is nothing but eternity," he says, "and dreams are a way to enter into it."

We think that we've created a materialistic world, but actually we created this world through the game played by consciousness. Television is a product of consciousness, as is the Internet. The hardware for these is extremely materialistic, yet before these material things were created, first a world was built inside of human consciousness, and we continue to go after our desires within our own consciousness today.

As a result, we have created a culture extremely rich in materials yet at the same time we are losing our physical, bodily awareness. In the process we are harming our own bodies as well as the environment, increasing pollution and illness. Our bodies are facing a danger not seen in the past, and we are at the same time in danger of losing awareness of our hearts and spirits.

On the other hand, people who are drawn to the spiritual world often lean too strongly or overly focus on the spirit and heart. They are drawn to the universal consciousness to such

"I believe that farming can be the pillar that will support the healing and repair of this world."

a degree that they also are losing awareness of their physicality. Their awareness travels to somewhere beyond, and they lose perception of the presentness of their bodies, the quality of being here now.

I believe our essence exists in a place where our bodies are supported by our spirits.

—from *The Dreams the Universe Is Seeing*

～

In the search Masanori has made—in this journey around the world and his exploration of *psyche-delos*, or the opening of the soul—and through his translations and writing and organizing and teaching and also through his own experiences during meditation, Masanori has found a crucial insight into the question he asked as a child, "Where from, where to?"

In one of his books Masanori tells about being at his father's bedside at the moment of his death. Masanori writes that death was but a slight modification of his father's shape, as if his father were melting into the world all around him.

For Masanori, the earth is a place of dance, the kind of dance as of thousands of snowflakes. The snow just kind of floats; it doesn't really drop anywhere. And in the same way, if this whole world *is* life, there is no place for life to drop. It's just life all around. And it is this shining, boundaryless place that we can tap into when we calm down and recognize this vastness within us. Then we can act from that place and avoid the injuries to ourselves and the injuries to others and to the environment, our home.

He says to me now, "We humans are used to saying things about death such as, 'When I die and pass over into the next world . . . ,' thinking that the phenomenal world and the spiritual world are separate. We use the term 'over there.' But they are not separate. There *is* no 'over there.' Over there is right here. There is no other world.

"It is not a transition from living to death, not from one thing to another. You are still connected to everything. We exist in the midst of eternity all the time."

I look again at the flame from the atomic blast at Hiroshima burning quietly now in the lantern and emitting a peaceful light, and I sense intuitively that Masanori Oe has surely gotten hold of one part of the truth.

In Gratitude

My mentor Claude Whitmyer once said to me, "All books are written by groups of people." Sitting in his office that day, as I looked at his shelf of books, all of a sudden my vision changed: all those different groups of people collaborating, right there on the shelf. Since then, my understanding of how true this statement is has grown and grown. So, too, the book you hold in your hands is also a collaboration between many, many people.

And now, as I look over the sheer number of people there are to thank for their help in bringing this book to fruition, I am humbled at how many have cared for it all along the way.

This book would have been impossible without Cynthia Kingsbury, my life partner and source of much practical wisdom, who has traveled this journey of writing this book with me for over fifteen years, and who has believed in it from the beginning. She has labored with me over every edit, word choice, photo selection, and translation decision, and stuck with the process through the interviews, the book proposal, and the many human relations that every book must negotiate. But even more than that, she has been an utterly reliable source of wise counsel over the thousands of decisive moments that it takes to create a book.

The genesis, and the very existence of this book, can be attributed to one of the most spirited and passionate people I have ever met, Atsuko Watanabe. She reached out to Cynthia and I at first to invite me to her homestead in the tiny mountain village of Kamikatsu, and subsequently introduced me to every single person in this book. She also translated many pieces of the original written Japanese into English. This is her book as well.

Each of the eleven people profiled in these pages gave so much of their time, fed me one fabulous meal after another, advised me on political, social, and cultural issues, explained complex words and concepts in Japanese, laid a futon on the floor for me at night, and then helped me find the correct train schedule to get to my next destination. This book would not have been possible without their participation. Although he does not have his own chapter here, the guidance of Abbot Shucho Takaoka of Tokurinji temple runs through these people's lives, and his vision of what is important in this life informs much of what their lives and this work have become.

A great debt is also owed to my mother, Edith Couturier, a historian and a biographer, and someone perennially interested in other people's lives. Also I would never have been able to have any of these conversations at all were it not for my two amazing Japanese teachers, Saiko Toyonaga and Mariko Shimomura. If any of us communicate at all across the gap of cultures, we must give a deep bow of thanks to language teachers. Four other people have given much of their time in many translations: Naoko and Yoshiki Sakane, Matthew Stevens, and Izumi Motai. I was also fortunate enough to be granted a long and fabulous interview with Marvin Fishman, who made films with Masanori Oe in the 1960s.

I also received generous feedback from numerous friends who read early drafts of many of these chapters. They spent hours helping me cleanse the manuscript of much dreck. They are Ginevra House, Amy Rasmussen, Nina Geraghty, Deirdre Bailey (who also contributed the beautiful map of Japan to these pages), Kim Sevcik, Autumn Linn, Catherine Benedict, my sister Anna Lisa Couturier, my cousin Jim Boorstein, Jane Brunette, John Gibler, John Chung, Rachel Levy, Fani Nicheva, and Esti Feller.

In 1999–2000, a series of articles ran in the *Japan Times* profiling each of the eleven people in this book, as well as eleven others. Of these others, I would like to first especially thank two amazing women, indefatigable in their generosity and depth of heart, Eiko Noda and Ruriko Hino, both of whom have supported me in countless other small ways over the years as I have crisscrossed Japan. In addition to these two, I'd like also to thank Miyuki Kobayashi, Keiko Haraguchi, Tama and Yukio Ozaki, Hidenori Takebayashi, Michio Takaragi, Taeko Takezawa, Nako Oizumi, and Taizo Ichikawa. The family members of some of the people in this book also gave generously of their time: Himalie and Shanti Amemiya, Yuriko and Nako Oizumi, and Junko and Michi Tomizaki.

Many books that are planned never reach fruition, and this is often for lack of encouragement and support. The fact that this book is in your hands now is very much due to the moral support given to me by so many people along the way. They include, first, my two mentors and teachers, Susan Mathews-Scott and Claude Whitmyer. They also include family members, including the ones mentioned above, but also Will Boorstein, John Couturier, Joan Poole, Greg and Graham Couturier, Melissa Chaney, Nicholas Palmucci, and many friends as well, including Hank Glassman, Cathy Smith, Chris Twemlow, Adam Kinsey, Akiyo Kawabata, Margaret Stawowy, Hsiao-ti Falcone, Thomas Kirschner, Kai Sawyer, Seico Benner, Jeff Kovar, Bob Von Elgg, David Abel, Robin Bishop, Johnnye Gibson, Osprey Orielle Lake, Kim Tolleson, Rebekah Eppley, Anne McCaw, Sara Bernard, Makoto Imaeda, Ellen Kane, Ted Smith, Lalit Mojundar and family, Keiko Kimura, and Sarasa Weinstein.

I also would like particularly to thank some people who too often go unthanked, those who do the tireless labor of the publishing trade and who accomplish the decisive work in the creation of books and magazines and newspapers. For this book, chief among them is the helmsman at Stone Bridge Press, Peter Goodman, who maintained a belief in the craftsmanship in publishing in the face of strong headwinds, as did Linda Ronan, the book designer who brought true artistry to the physical shape of this book. Also much thanks to Ari Messer and Nina Wegner. I want to especially thank Suzanne Kamata for providing the all-important introduction to Stone Bridge Press, without which this book might never have come into being.

I should say, in addition, that like many human activities in this world, publishing runs on trust. It is thus that introductions to editors and publishers are one of the most important gardens any writer must cultivate. I want to thank all those who helped me to connect with other members of this fine profession, and those who labor in its often obscure editing rooms yet who are responsible for us all being able to read things of real quality. In my case, these include Mason Florence, Robert Hass, Denise Carrigg, and Sean O'Toole. At the *Japan Times*, I wish to thank my editor, Ms. Yamaguchi, who decided to take this project on, as well as my line editors Aleck McKay-Smith and Mark Thompson. At *Kyoto Journal*, a fine literary publication that ran several longer pieces which were to grow into chapters of this book, I would like to thank Ken Rodgers and John Einarsen, and at MIT Press I would like to thank David Rothenberg and Wandee Pryor. For other publishing help and advice, thanks to Gaetano Kazuo Maeda and to Kalle Lassen, publisher of *Adbusters* magazine.

In my travels around rural Japan, so many people helped me I could not possibly thank them all, but to an incomplete list I want to add Kyoko and Hideo Ito, Koyomi and Goro Goto, Kumi Koyama, Reiko Iwamoto, Mr. and

Ms. Koyo Kida, Hiromu Sora, Minoru and Sumie Tamura, Kozo Shishido, Maggie Suzuki, Taka Asai, Manik Man Bajracharya, Ashok K. Aryal, Hatsumi Yano, and Keiko Saita. I want to also offer a special thank you to the good people at the Tokushima City International Association and the Tokushima Prefecture International Association. Living as a foreigner in another country is difficult, and the many volunteers at these groups gave again and again unselfishly of their time so that we strangers could adapt and have a good life in an unfamiliar place. Their decision to offer absolutely free classes in Japanese helped make the conversations that you read in this book possible.

Many of the photos in this book are my own, but I have been graced to be able to use the photos of several other fine photographers; these include Junko Motoyama and David Laidler, Hiromi Hayashi, Yoshihiro Aoyama, and Takanori Mimura.

I should thank, too, the nation of India itself, whose exuberance, spiritual insights, and color have nourished me and nourished many of the people in this book, and continue to do so today.

I'd like to extend a special thanks to Gary Snyder and Alex Kerr, who have not only lent me their personal support but have also, through their writings, inspired me with the possibilities for what can happen in rural Japan. Lastly, I would like to thank all those people most of us tend to forget about, those that help us through all of life's crucial logistical interstices, the bus drivers who drove me out to these small villages, the restaurant workers who fed me so many nourishing meals, and all the people who grow the food without which we could not even make it from one day to the next.

A.C.

About the Author

ANDY COUTURIER is the son of a biographer and a civil rights activist. During his four years of living in Japan, he wrote for the *Japan Times*; worked with local environmentalists fighting large dam projects, rainforest destruction, and huge electric power plants; taught English; and studied the interconnections between Japanese aesthetics and innovative new forms of writing. In California, he and his partner built their own house using only hand tools, developing a piece of raw land into a functioning rural homestead with solar and hydro-electric power, running hot and cold water, and a Japanese-style bath.

Andy has studied Buddhist meditation and many other Asian philosophical systems, and has traveled extensively in Africa, Southeast Asia, and India. He has been a researcher for Greenpeace and has taught writing for more than a decade. He is the author of *Writing Open the Mind: Tapping the Subconscious to Free the Writing and the Writer* and has written for *Adbusters*, the MIT Press, *Kyoto Journal, Creative Nonfiction, The North American Review, The Oakland Tribune,* and *Ikebana International.* He directs his own creative writing center, The Opening, at www.theopening.org.

Andy welcomes your thoughts and comments on this book, either by mail to P.O. Box 881, Santa Cruz, CA 95061 or by email to *andy@theopening.org.*